HISTORY

OF

TENNESSEE

From the Earliest Time to the Present; Together with an Historical and a Biographical Sketch of Henderson, Chester, McNairy, Decatur, and Hardin Counties, Besides a Valuable Fund of Notes, Original Observations, Reminiscences, Etc., Etc.

ILLUSTRATED

Nashville:
THE GOODSPEED PUBLISHING CO.,
1886

This volume was reproduced from
An 1886 edition located in the
Tennessee State Library and Archives,
Nashville, Tennessee

All rights reserved. No part of this publication
may be reproduced, stored in a retrieval system,
transmitted in any form, posted on to the web
in any form or by any means without the
prior written permission of the publisher.

Please direct all correspondence and orders to:

www.southernhistoricalpress.com
or
**SOUTHERN HISTORICAL PRESS, Inc.
PO BOX 1267
375 West Broad Street
Greenville, SC   29601
southernhistoricalpress@gmail.com**

Originally published: Nashville, 1886
Reprinted with New Material by:
Southern Historical Press, Inc.
New Material Copyright 1978 by
The Rev. Silas Emmett Lucas, Jr.
Easley, SC
ISBN #0-89308-097-7
All rights Reserved.
Printed in the United States of America

HENDERSON COUNTY.

THE surface of the county is somewhat diversified. The county occupies the high lands between the Mississippi and the Tennessee Rivers. It attains an elevation of 720 feet above the sea level at Lexington. The highest lands are found in the Highland Ridge, which extends nearly due north and south through the center of the county. From the peculiar surface the streams of the county flow in almost every direction. Beech Creek, a river, rises about ten miles west of Lexington, and flows almost in a direct line east through Decatur County, and empties into the Tennessee near Perryville. Beech is the largest stream in the county, and was so named from the growth of timber on its banks. Its principal tributaries from the north are Big Creek, Brown Creek, Lick Creek and Haley Creek. The first of these was named from its size, the second from a settler, the third from its deer licks, and the last also from a settler. The tributaries from the south are Wolf, Piney and Cane Creeks. The first of these was named from the animal, the second and last from the growth. In the south and west are Doe, Hurricane and Jacks Creeks, which flow into Forked Deer. The principal streams in the west and north are branches of the Forked Deer. From the central of the north part are Sandy and Beaver Creeks. The ridge above mentioned forms a water-shed between the Tennessee and the Mississippi systems. The soil in the valleys of the various streams is very fertile, while the higher lands have a much lighter soil which, owing to the amount of sand, washes easily, and where it has been in cultivation long is badly washed. Until worn and washed even the uplands are highly productive. From a want of proper care in the growth of grasses and fertilization these lands have greatly depreciated in value. Perhaps the most valuable lands are found along Beech River. Geologically the formation is later than the subcarboniferous or even the carboniferous period but belongs to the cretaceous period. There is little, if any, of the coffee sand, but the rotten limestone, or green sand, and the Ripley group make the principal formation. This is followed by the Flatwood clays and the La Grange sands of the Lignitic period. Immense beds of the orange sand appear mixed sometimes with gravel but all unstratified. The whole surface shows evidence of drift formation containing lignitic beds, red and white sand intermingled with various marine shells. The water is generally freestone and is obtained by digging or boring, or from natural springs. White Fern Spring, in the western part of the county, and Henson Springs, about three miles west of Lexington, are both reputed to possess highly medicinal qualities, and are favorite summer resorts. No minerals of any value are suffered to exist in the county, a soft sand rock being the only thing of any quantity found in the county. In the valleys of the streams, and even on many of the ridges, large quantities of valuable timber are yet to be found; the most valuable of this is the oak, consisting of the various species also hickory, beech, pine and many other. Formerly cotton was the staple production and is yet an important factor, but its exhaustive nature has led farmers to give more attention to stock, grain and fruits. The main hindrance to these things is the want of a railroad for transportation to the great commercial centers. As the county has no navigable streams, turnpikes nor railroads, it has always labored at a disadvantage in regard to markets. The building of Virginia Midland Railway, for which the county is asked $75,000, will, if completed, open up a new field of enterprise. The county is surrounded almost entirely by counties having lines of railroads, and, in consequence, its resources are shown at a disadvantage, as the more favored places tend to sap the county and to rob it of its most enterprising and energetic business men.

The settlement in Henderson began almost immediately after the Chickasaw treaty of October 19, 1818. The majority of the early settlers were from Middle Tennessee, East Tennessee and North Carolina. Not a few were from Alabama, some were from Virginia and a few from Kentucky. Some traveled by land, driving their flocks and hauling their little household plunder in a wagon or carrying on jack horses. Those coming by water either came down the Tennessee to some favorite landing place, and then across the country or down the Cumberland, the Ohio, and then up the Tennessee. The peculiar characteristics of the natives of the respective States whence these settlers came were implanted in the settlers of Henderson County, and as the whole western district was settled mainly by the same class of people, we see a very great homogeneity in society. Immigration to Henderson County did not become general till 1821-22. A few came as early as 1818. Joseph Reel is claimed to have been the first settler in the county. He came to the county in 1818, and settled on Beech River, about five miles east of the site of Lexington. Here he opened up a farm, where he and his family remained. Samuel Wilson settled on a 726-acre tract of land, where Lexington stands, in the spring of the year 1822. The site for the town was obtained from him as stated elsewhere. Dr. John A. Wilson was also a resident of the county near Lexington at the time of the organization of the courts. He was elected county court clerk in 1822, and held the office till 1835. Abner Taylor, who was one of the first town board, settled a short distance from Lexington as early as 1822. Maj. John T. Harmon settled at the headwaters of Big Sandy about 1821. He was appointed surveyor and surveyed the original plat of Lexington. He was, perhaps, the owner of the first cotton-gin in the county. Jacob Bartholomew and William Hays settled near the headwaters of Beech River. William Cain and George Powers settled near what was called Pleasant Exchange. Wm. Dismukes settled on the north fork of Forked Deer River, and Joseph Reed about eight miles from Lexington, on Beech River. John Purdy settled near Jacks Creek. He was deputy surveyor for a time, and he gave name to the town of Purdy. James Baker settled about eight miles from Lexington, and Jesse Taylor near the place. Other early settlers were the McClures, Brigances, Trices, Strongs, Shackelfords, McGees and others. The census for 1830 shows a population of over 8,000. In consequence of the rapid immigration into the county it developed rapidly.

The fresh lands of the county yielded rich harvests for the planter and the forest was cleared away rapidly. The primitive hand-mill and mortar were resorted to at times in the first settlement of the county for meal, as little flour was then used. A mill was built on Mud Creek in 1821 by John and William Brigham, and another was built on Forked Deer by Daniel Barcroft about the same time. A horse mill was built on the road between Lexington and Trenton about 1822. Maj. John I. Harmon built the first cotton-gin in the county on Beech Creek in 1823. Shackleford's mill, about five miles east of Lexington, was built between 1823 and 1830. McGee's mill, near Lexington, and Trice's mill near the same place, also McClure's cotton-gin, were all built before 1830. At one time an extensive cotton factory was running with a large force of hands near Lexington. This was owned for a time by John and William Brooks.

The first marriage license in the county was issued to H. H. Hopkins and Sophia Greer, and bears date January 8, 1822. Others were John A. Null and Hester Humphreys, December 22, 1822; Calvin Gillum and Susan Reeves, 1823; B. H. Tate and Polly Chambers, July 26, 1825; James Phillips and Martha Rutledge, 1826; Robert Carter and Lydia Mathews, 1826; Wm. Potts and Elizabeth Rodgers, October 24, 1823; Robert Rhodes and Lucy Redges, January 24, 1823; Silas Mathews and Elizabeth Snell, January 24, 1824. The minister officiating most frequently was John Darnett, a Cumberland Presbyterian.

Henderson County was created by an act of the Legislature, on November 16, 1821. It was carved out of the Western District and placed under the control of Stewart County until the formal organization in 1822. The county is bounded on the north by Carroll County, on the east by Decatur, formerly Perry, on the south by Hardin and Chester, and on the west by Chester and Madison Counties. The county was reduced in 1845 by cutting off a strip about three miles wide and attaching the same to Decatur County, and a small fraction lying west of Forked Deer River was attached to Madison County in 1868, and a considerable portion of the southwestern corner was attached to Chester County in

1882. The County was named in honor of Col. James Henderson, of North Carolina, of Revolutionary fame. On the creation of the county Sterling Brewer, James Fentress and Abram Maury were appointed by the Legislature to select a site for the county seat. The place selected was the present site of Lexington, on Wilson Spring branch. The land embraced sixty-three acres of a 726-acre tract deeded by the State of Tennessee to Samuel Wilson, April 12, 1822, and was by Wilson conveyed to the commissioners as above on August 14, of the same year. For the consideration of $100 and one choice lot on the square—Lot No. 20—on the above date Wilson did "give, grant, bargain, sell, alien, enfoeff, convey and confirm" the tract to said commissioners. On the same day Brewer, Fentress and Maury conveyed the same by deed to Job Philpot, J. J. Hill, Abner Tyler, James Baker and John Purdy, who were selected as the first commissioners of the town. The place was surveyed by John T. Harmon, who laid out the place, giving the streets a bearing north 47° east. A public square containing four acres was reserved in the center for a courthouse, stocks and jail. The town commissioners were authorized and empowered to sell town lots, and with the proceeds of the sale to erect a courthouse and other public buildings. The first courthouse was a small log house one story high, and stood on the square near where the present house stands. It was built in 1822, at a cost of $142, and did not last long. The second house, which was of brick, was built about 1827 by Samuel Wilson, at a cost of $4,595.97. This house was not a good one and in 1832, Robert Baker, E. H. Tarrant and G. Kerherdon were selected to let out the contract for remodeling the house. It was let to James Baker for about $1,000, and completed October 1, 1833. In 1844 the walls of the house were taken partly down and rebuilt. This work was done by James H. Watson. The courts in the meantime met at the Masonic Hall. This house stood till 1863, when it was accidentally fired by some of the Third Michigan Cavalry, who were quartered in the house. The most of the county records were consumed in this fire After the war the courts met at the store house of Wm. Brooks, the office of T. C. Muse and other places till 1866, when H. G. Threadgill, A. H. Rhodes, J. P. Fuller, J. R. Teague and Samuel Howard were appointed a committee for the erection of a new courthouse. The contract was let to Robert Dyer for $7,450, to be completed October 1, 1867. The building is a two-story brick with double gables having offices on the ground floor for the register clerk and a large court room above. The court yard is one of the finest in the State.

The first jail was a temporary log jail, and was built by William Patton, at an expense to the county of $83. This served until about 1827, when a new brick jail was erected on Purdy Street near the Kizer Hotel. This was used as a jail till 1881, when it was sold to E. Flake for $480 and he sold this to Mr. Elkins who now occupies it as a private residence. In 1881 a new brick jail was built which stands in the eastern part of town. This was built at a total cost of $8,400.66. The contractors were L. A. Stanford and M. A. Hare.

Previous to 1851 the poor and unfortunates of the county were taken care of by private parties, or were farmed out to the lowest and best bidders. But few were taken care of by the same individual. In the year above named a deed was made by Absalom McGee to J. S. Priddy, Stephen Massengill and A. S. Johnson as commissioners of the poor for 273¾ acres of land. This lies about three miles south of Lexington on Beech Creek, and is a part of a tract entered by Solomon West. The cost of this land was $900. The paupers are kept on this farm while the products of the farm with about $5 per capita pays the steward for his services and supports the paupers.

The various assessments show quite a diversity in area, wealth and other items. The assessor's reports for 1836 show 108,123 acres of land (in cultivation?) valued at $450,469; eighty-six town lots valued at $30,880; 858 slaves valued at $525,000, only nine carriages and 1,230 white polls. In 1839 the lands were 114,520 acres valued at $463,836; town lots were 131 and valued at $47,875; slaves were 880 and valued at $489,680; pleasure carriages seven, and the total taxables $1,262,236. In 1852 the land was given in at 369,777 acres and valued at $825,339; town lots at 152 and valued at $54,319. The slaves were 1,339 and assessed at $796,945 and the total taxables at $2,335,000. The assessment for 1854 when slave property reached its maximum, the lands were given in at 309,700 acres and valued at $1,134,021; town lots at 144 and valued at $69,820; slaves at 1,419 and $1,001,075 in value. In 1868 the land was given in at 273,100 acres, and valued at $1,432,528, and a total of taxables $1,983,419. In 1870 the land, according to assessment, was 370,768 acres, and valued at $1,642,144, and the total property at $1,850,687. In 1882 the land was 373,390 acres, valued at $1,584,820, while in 1886 the land was given at 312,480 acres, and valued at $1,090,227; town lots were 81 and valued at $47,090. The total value of all property was $1,198,998. The variation in area is accounted for in incorrect assessments and in the reduction of the area by new counties and additions to old ones.

The first court in the county met on the fourth Monday in December, 1821, at the house of Samuel Wilson. What was done at this court, or of whom it was composed can not now be learned, as all records previous to 1840 have been destroyed. The appointment of county officers and the approval of their bonds doubtless received their first attention. John A. Wilson was chosen the first county court clerk, and he held that position till 1835, when he was succeeded by Jesse Taylor, who held the position until 1859, when he gave place to A. H. Rhodes who held the office until 1878, when C. R. Scott was elected and held the office until 1886, at which time J. A. Teague was elected to that office. These men were all so long connected with the office that a mere mention of their names is a sufficient history of them.

The first county register was, perhaps, O. H. King, who served until 1832, when he was succeeded by S. A. Orton who in turn was succeeded by John H. White, but just what date is not clear. White served till 1844, when he gave place to John Smith who served till 1856, when J. A. Henry was elected and served till his death, in 1884, thus serving twenty-eight years. On his death Maj. T. A. Smith was appointed to fill the vacancy, and was elected to the place in 1886. E. H. Tarrant was, perhaps, the first circuit clerk and served till 1836, when he was succeeded by Addison Pyle, who served till 1840, when R. B. Jones was elected and held the office till 1865. James Priddy was then elected and served till 1870, when E. J. Timberlake held the office till 1874, and was succeeded by I. T. Bell, who held the office until 1878. J. A. Teague held the office from 1878 till 1882, when W. R. Britt was chosen and held the office till 1886, and then gave place to J. R. Wilkerson, who was elected at that time.

John T. Harmon was chosen sheriff at the organization and served till 1826, when he was succeeded by Robert Marshall, who held the office probably till 1830 when S. M. Carson was elected and held the office till 1837, when R. B. Jones was elected sheriff and held the office till 1840, when John Howell was elected and served one term. G. H. Buck was sheriff from 1842 to 1844. John Howell was again elected and served until 1846, when W. B. Hall was elected and served one term. W. H. Shelby became sheriff and served from 1848 to 1852, when A. H. Rhodes was elected and served two terms. J. H. Gilbraith was elected in 1856 and held the office till 1860, when Levi McEwen was elected and held it till the war. A. E. Aydelott was elected sheriff in 1864 and was succeeded by R. J. Dyer in 1866, who served till 1868, when G. W. Moss was elected, but resigned in April, 1869, when J. A. Teague was elected to fill the vacancy. A. E. Aydelott was again elected in 1871 and served till 1774. J. M. Wadly was then elected and served till 1878, when he was succeeded by A. G. Douglass, who gave place to G. W. Essary in 1882. The latter served till 1886 and was succeeded by H. C. Lindsey.

Joshua Haskell was, perhaps, the first circuit judge. In 1838 John Read, of Jackson, became judge and served till 1861, when he resigned on account of failing health. Courts were held by special judges till they were closed by the war. On the reorganization Fielding Hurst was made judge and was succeeded by F. P. Bond, who in turn was succeeded by L. L. Hawkins in 1867. In 1873 T. P. Bateman became circuit judge and served in that position till 1886 when he was succeeded by Levi S. Woods, the present judge.

The Chancery District, composed of Henderson, Perry and McNairy Counties, was established May 6, 1844. Judge Andrew McCampbell was made the chancellor and served till 1848, when he was succeeded by Calvin Jones who held the office till 1854. Stephen C. Pavatt then became chancellor and served till August, 1861. R. H. Rose held the office of chancellor from 1866 to 1868 when he was succeeded by J. W. Doherty. G. H. Nixon was elected in 1870 and held the office till 1886, when he was succeeded by A. G. Hawkins. On the organization of the chancery court J. W. G. Jones was appointed clerk and master and held that place till 1866, when Owen Haney was appointed to the place and held it till 1872, when Jones was again appointed to the place, which he held till 1878. In 1878 W. F. Brooks was appointed to the place, which he has since held.

The first lawyers whose names appear were H. H. Hopkins, Wm. L. Petty, and James A. Heaslet. In 1826 or 1827 Micajah Bullock began practice at the Lexington bar, where he was prominent for nearly half a century. The first criminal execution in the county was the execution of a slave woman for the drowning of a child of Dr. John A. Wilson. The woman was his own slave. A very exciting trial was the case of the State against Milton Reiley for the murder of William (Bud) Willis. The killing occurred at Independence. The trial was moved to Jackson, where he was convicted and executed on June 9, 1849. The lawyers prominent before the bar at this time were the Hawkins', Bullock, Allen, Brasher, Adam Huntsman, Samuel McClanahan, A. G. McDougal, James Scott, Elijah Walker, T. P. Scurlock, J. C. Totten, Milton Brown, W. F. Doherty, J. H. Swayne, W. Beloate, H. Foster, Williams, Gillespie, A. G. Shrewsbury and others. Hon. John M. Taylor began the practice of the law about the opening of the war. A case of some interest occurred in December, 1859, in which Ben F. Page, by his next friend Sam. N. Anderson, sued Sam. C. Wheatley for slander. The jury, N. T. Buckley, J. P. Cross, J. M. Stubblefield, T. Barr, A. B. Jones, W. H. Jordan, J. N. Small, N. C. Epay, T. N. Black, S. H. Holmes and Wm. Wood, gave judgment for $2,344.58¼. Aaron Curtis was convicted of manslaughter for killing Calvin Barnett, and given a sentence of seven years to the penitentiary. In 1860 Wilson Tidwell and John Barnett each received three year sentences for larceny, and Columbus Phillips the same time for mule stealing. A number of suits were brought against parties for killing during the period of the war. These parties were generally acquitted or driven from the country by the indictments standing against them. A very interesting suit in the chancery court was brought by Brown & Parrish enjoining the formation of the new county, Chester, which was attempted to be established in 1872. A case of much local interest began in 1883 on the repealing of the old charter and the attempt to establish a taxing district at Lexington. Without going into details, it need only be said no taxing district was formed, and that the city is without a charter. The fight grew out of the question of whisky or no whisky. The attorneys of Lexington now are Hon. John M. Taylor, Judge L. S. Woods, R. H. Thorn, W. T. Logan, W. B. Ware, T. Davis and Arthur Pearce.

The military history of Henderson County properly begins with the late civil war although quite a number went from this county to the Mexican war.

At the election held on June 8, 1861, Henderson, Carroll, Decatur and Weakley were the only counties in West Tennessee that voted against secession. The vote of Henderson County was 810 for "separation," and 1,013 for "no separation;" but when the final clash of arms came the county was largely in sympathy with the South. The first full companies for the Confederate service were four companies raised for the Twenty-seventh Tennessee (Confederate) Regiment. This regiment rendezvoused at Trenton in the summer of 1861. B. H. Brown, it is believed, raised the first of four companies from Henderson County for this regiment. His company was known as the sharpshooters. The captains of the four companies were C. H. Williams, whose company was called the "Felix Rebels," B. H. Brown, of the sharpshooters, Richard Barham and S. A. Sayle. On the organization of the regiment C. H. (Kit) Williams was elected colonel; B. H. Brown, lieutenant-colonel; Samuel Love, major; — Smith, adjutant; Robt. Wilkerson, sergeant-major; D. A. McKamey, surgeon and J. R. Wingo, assistant surgeon. On the election of Williams to be colonel, W. P. Timberlake was elected captain of his company, and on the election of Capt. Brown to the lieutenant-colonelcy, John M. Taylor became captain of his company. The regiment numbered about 1,000 men and was put in camp of instruction at Trenton for a time for discipline, but soon moved to Henderson Station on the Mobile & Ohio Railroad for sanitary reasons. Here it remained till the battle of Belmont, when it was ordered to Columbus, Ky. The next troops were one company for the Thirty-first Tennessee (Confederate) Regiment. This regiment also organized at Trenton in the fall of 1861. A. H. Bradford was elected colonel; C. M. Cason, lieutenant-colonel, and John Smith, major. The remaining troops from this county were members of the Fifty-second Tennessee (Confederate) Regiment. This regiment was organized at Henderson Station January 4, 1862. It was composed of the companies of Capts. Wesson, Russell, Wilson, Akin, Thomasson, McCullum, Thomas, McMillan, Estes and Williams. The operations of these regiments are given under the histories of these regiments elsewhere.

The Seventh Union Regiment of Tennessee Cavalry was raised mainly in Henderson and Carroll Counties. Three full companies were raised in Henderson County. The first of these was raised by T. A. Smith, whose lieutenants were A. T. Hart and Frank Reed. The second company was commanded by Capt. A. N. Hays, whose lieutenants are not remembered. The third company was that of Capt. J. W. Beatty. His lieutenants were J. J. Wallace and — Helme. A part of a company consisting of twenty-nine men was raised by Capt. Derryberry. This regiment was mustered into the service November 14, 1862. The regiment organized by electing Isaac R. Hawkins lieutenant-colonel and T. A. Smith, major. The regiment numbered 650 men. Their work was confined almost entirely to guard duty along the line of the Mobile & Ohio Railroad and the Memphis & Charleston Railroad. In addition to the guard duty they scoured the country, picking up deserters, stragglers, and preventing recruiting for the Confederate Army, and fighting guerrilla bands. A portion of the regiment was captured by Forrest at Trenton in 1862, and on March 24, 1864, nearly the entire regiment was captured by Forrest's men at Union City.

The Methodist Episcopal Churches South are a part of the Jackson District of the Memphis Conference. They are mainly embraced in the Lexington Station, Lexington Circuit and Scott Hill Circuit. The three above mentioned embrace fifteen churches or classes, and a membership of 671. The first class was organized in Lexington about 1840 and a house soon after erected. The old register having been lost, it is impossible to ascertain the names of the first class or the date of the organization. The oldest member now living is Mrs. Elizabeth Ewing who joined the church at Knoxville in 1824. The names of others who joined the church early, are R. B. Jones, in 1839, under the preaching of Rev. Renshaw; Mrs. A. A. Warren, in 1838, under Rev. J. Kelsey; Bettie Bell, in 1840, under R. S. Swift, and E. E. Smith at the same time; J. W. G. Jones, in 1847, under A. D. Bryant. These are all the names of members that are preserved previous to the war. Among the ministers of the Lexington class since the war may be mentioned R. S. Swift, J. G. Harris, T. G. Whitten, J. J. Brooks, J. A. Moody and W. T. Lock. This class now numbers fifty members and has a new house of worship and maintains a good Sunday-school. Perhaps the first Methodist Church built in the county was the one at Olive Branch in 1832. This was built on a two-acre lot deeded by Solomon Milam to Ramsom Cunningham, John Cooper, Jas. Hart and Thomas Johnson on July 29, 1832. Shady Grove was another one of the early Methodist Churches of Henderson County. Here was a well known camp-ground and church, which were established between 1830 and 1840. Among those connected with this church were the Renshaws, Andersons, Corbets, Hunts, Cogdills, Sherwoods, Hamlets, Youngs and others. The church at Holly Springs was built in 1845, New Hope in 1855, Barren Springs in 1857, Hepzibah in 1855, New Prospect in 1850, Bethel about the same time, Mount Pleasant in 1872, Poplar Springs in 1873, and many others at different dates. The early revivals were largely due to the zeal of the members at the annual camp-meetings that were formerly held in every county and in almost every neighborhood.

The Missionary Baptist Church was built in Lexington in 1847. This stood till the war when by neglect it was allowed to go to decay. In 1880 another lot was purchased of J. S. Fielder and the present brick house erected thereon. This church has a good membership and maintains a Sunday-school. Other Baptist Churches are Piney Creek, Union Church, Scarce Creek, Ridge Grove, Bible Union, Pilgrim's Rest in Zion, Hopewell and a few others. The membership of this church is quite large in the county.

HENDERSON COUNTY.

John Barrett, a Cumberland Presbyterian minister preached in Henderson County in 1824. He was, perhaps, the first to preach the doctrine of this church in the county. Some of the first churches in the county were built by the Cumberland Presbyterians. There is a small congregation of Presbyterians at Lexington, but they are without a house of worship at present, although they own the old Lexington Academy which was purchased recently for church purposes. Palestine is the place of an old church and camp-ground. The membership at this place is twenty-one. Spring Hill is another Cumberland Presbyterian Church. Its membership is forty-eight. Mount Gilead Church was built in 1856. Its membership is now about twenty. Besides these churches there is one Methodist Protestant Church, a United Baptist Church, at Masyer's Chapel, a Freewill Baptist Church at Shady Grove, and one on Steele Creek, and a Christian Church in the Fifteenth District.

The first school established in the county was the Lexington Academy, which was authorized October 18, 1825, at which time John T. Harmon, J. W. Philpot, John Purdy, Richard McCree and James A. Haslett were appointed trustees. In 1826 J. T. Harmon, C. H. Miller, J. J. Hill, Reuben Wilcox and James A. Haslett were authorized to form a lottery for the purpose of raising a sum, not to exceed $20,000, for the academy. The academy trustees were to have perpetual succession till 1865. In 1827 M. B. Cook, W. M. Haskins and Samuel Wilson were added to the trustees. Previous to this, schools of an isolated character had been taught in the various neighborhoods of the county. Sometimes they were in schoolhouses built for the purpose, sometimes in churches, and not unfrequently under church patronage. What was the result of the lottery scheme is not now known. The trustees acquired considerable property in the name of the academy as will be seen from the following purchases and sales. In 1832 they sold a house and lot in Christmasville for $600, and in the same year they bought of R. C. Blair fifty acres on Brigance Creek for $1,500, and another body of fifty acres of S. B. Orton for $440, and another body in Carroll County for $1,000. They purchased fifty acres of S. M. Carson for $1,000, 220 acres of B. Gillespie for $550 and of R. A. McCree — acres for a small sum. The first house was built in the eastern part of town on a lot purchased of Samuel Wilson in July, 1832. A brick house was here erected which stood till 1852–53, when from decay and want of capacity it was sold and the proceeds invested in a lot and building in the north part of Lexington. The trustees making the last purchase were W. H. Warner, John Brooks, R. B. Jones and Wm. Brooks. On the lot purchased were erected good brick buildings with two rooms. In these academies and two or more church-schools and numerous private schools the majority of the boys and girls of Lexington were educated. At one time Lexington was quite an educational center having its church-schools and the academy. The academy fund alone at one time amounted to over $1,000. The old academy was used for the public school till 1885, when it was sold to the trustees of the Cumberland Presbyterian Church and a new site purchased southeast of town for a new building. The trustees now own four acres of ground on which they have erected a new frame building two stories high, containing a study hall and several recitation rooms. The trustees realized $250 on the old buildings and had on hand about $300, and in addition to this a sufficient subscription was obtained to raise the amount to $1,500 with which the new site was purchased and the building erected. The present trustees are C. R. Scott, president; P. J. Dennison, treasurer, and J. N. Hall, W. F. Brooks and L. A. Stanford. The present board of management was organized in January, 1885, and the present building erected in 1886. The school work is under S. A. Mynders, A. B., who is principal of the school. The school is recognized as the County High School and the trustees are elected by the county court. The course of study embraces English language and its literature, pure and applied mathemathics, natural sciences, ancient and modern languages and bookkeeping, with a special course for teachers. The course is intended to fit pupils for the university and for practical life. About forty public school-teachers have been in attendance the present year, and the whole number enrolled is about ninety-five. Diplomas are awarded those completing the course.

The first of anything like a systematic course for the common schools grew out of the act of 1839. The first reports in this county were made in 1844. In that year the school directors or commissioners were elected in each civil district, and the school districts were made to correspond with the civil districts. The whole number of children of school age was 2,058. The length of school term varied from forty to sixty days. The school fund averaged about 50 cents to each pupil. This plan of management was continued with little variation till the whole was broken up by the war. The present system was adopted in 1872. The school districts still correspond with the civil districts. Owing to the facts that official reports of the schools have not been preserved it is impossible to trace their growth and development. A partial report of 1885 shows that the white scholastic population for that year was 4,514; colored, 683, or a total of 5,197. The whole number of white teachers employed was 81; colored, 7. The number of consolidated schools was 3. The enrollment in the schools was 2,250 white, and 350 colored children, and a total average attendance of 1,350. The total amount paid in salaries was $7,329.60, and a total expenditure for schools of $9,381.25. The average length of school term was 57 days and the average salary per month was $28.

The county seat, Lexington, is one of many towns in the United States named in honor of Lexington, Mass. It is near the center of the county. It is 720 feet above sea level, and is in latitude 83° 40' north and 11° 12' west of Washington. As elsewhere stated it was selected by the commissioners in 1822. The streets were made eighty feet wide with the alleys forty-two feet. The lots were laid off in rows around the square, beginning at the northeast corner, and numbered 1, 2, 3, and around the square to the place of beginning, and then another row started and numbered in the same order, the whole amounting to 104. The first purchasers of lots were John A. Green, John Brooks, Samuel C. Wilson, James Wright, J. A. Wilson, W. L. Petty, Samuel G. Tate, William Stoddert, Daniel Thomas, James Jordan and William Edwards. The lots were sold at auction, the auctioneer being R. Marshall, for which he was allowed $50. John Purdy was also allowed $50 for assisting in the survey. By the report of John Stewart and Micajah Bullock the entire sale of lots amounted to $6,285.40½, and the expenses of sale, survey, public buildings, amounted to $5,453, with some incidentals, which left a surplus of $529.03¼ on hand. Before the entering of the land of Samuel Wilson, in the spring of 1822, where Lexington now stands, the forest was unbounded by a single woodman's ax, it was as nature had planted it, the surface of the soil was unbroken by a single furrow of the plowman, the flowers were seen almost "to bloom and waste their fragrance on the desert air." James Strong, who settled about three miles north of Lexington, once killed a fine buck within the limits of the public square, while on his way to mill in the southern part of the county. Lexington was first incorporated by an act of the Legislature October 9, 1824. Its charter, which was to run fifty years, has been allowed to lapse, and has been renewed a number of times, but it is now without any charter. Under the present management no intoxicating liquors are sold. Under an act of 1839, the county surveyor, J. M. Galloway, in March, 1841, laid off "prison bounds" for prisoners for debt. The limits were one mile square, of which the courthouse was the center. According to the chartered rights Lexington was allowed the same powers and privileges as the town of Winchester. Samuel Wilson was doubtless the first resident of Lexington. It was at his house that the first court of pleas and quarter sessions was ordered to meet for organization. Among the business men in building up the city may be mentioned Gladin Gorin, who did considerable business in Lexington for a time, and then went to New Orleans to engage in the wholesale trade. R. W. Hall, James E. Glass, William and John Brooks, Dr. John West, J. S. Fielder and William Collins were identified with the business interest of Lexington before the war. Before the breaking out of that unhappy event the business of Lexington was quite extensive.

The present business men of Lexington are G. W. Florence, J. N. Hall, F. W. McHaney, John McHaney & Co., T. Edwards, Scott & Stanford, Dennison & Muse, W. R. Elkins, Boswell, Fielder & Co., and J. H. Lofton. The hotels are the Kizer House and the Scott House. Dr. Warren has been longer before the public professionally than any other man in the county. His professional work began about 1838-39. One of the most remarkable men physically that ever lived in Lexington, or any other place for that matter, was Miles Darden, commonly called Durden. He was a native of North Carolina, and moved to Lexington and kept hotel at the corner of the square, where T. Edwards' grocery store now is. Before his death he moved to the county in the vicinity of Jacks Creek. His death occurred in 1857. His measurement, which is attested by the best authority, was as follows: Height, seven feet six inches; circumference of the waist, six feet four inches; weight, over 1,000 pounds. He was very sensitive about his weight, which was never known exactly, but estimates put it at all the way from 800 to 1,000 pounds; the latter weight was ascertained by measuring the spring of his wagon while he was in it, and then secretly weighing them down to the same tension, and then calculating the amount of weight thus required.

Lexington has usually been favored by a newspaper but as the changes have been frequent and no files have been preserved it is impossible to follow the changes. The Lexington *Dispatch*, of which H. C. Henry was editor and proprietor, was established about 1857. This paper was continued till the war. The *Advance* was published by G. B. Davis and later the *Advance-News* by W. T. Hawkins. The Lexington *Progress* will have been established three years in April, 1887. W. V. Barry is its publisher. The *Progress* is strictly a home paper and is independent in politics.

Constantine Lodge, No. 64, F. & A. M., was chartered October 11, 1828. The charter was granted to James Hart, W. M.; J. A. Henry, S. W.; J. E. Weathers, J. W. and other brethren. The Grand Master of the State at that time was C. H. Fuller. The membership at present is thirty-two. It numbered at one time sixty-nine but the formation of a lodge at Juno, Ebenezer and one or two other places cut off a portion of the membership. The present officers are J. A. Teague, W. M.; T. A. Smith, S. W. and A. M. Stewart, J. W.

The charter was granted to the present chapter on October 14, 1867. A. H. Rhodes was then H. P.; J. L. Reed, King and Adam Harmon, Scribe. The original charter to this chapter or to a chapter at this place was granted at an earlier date but surrendered. The present style of the chapter is Lexington, No. 37. The officers are A. Fesnure, H. P.; T. A. Smith, King; M. L. Galloway, Scribe. The membership is nineteen.

Lexington Council, No. 66, was granted a dispensation November 7, 1871, and a charter November 4, 1872. J. L. Phelps, John M. Taylor and J. A. Teague rank in the order named. The membership is sixteen.

Sardis has a population of 160. It is located in the southeast corner of the county in the Thirteenth District, eighteen miles from Lexington. It was named from an old Methodist camp-ground which was one-half mile east of the village. The place was named Sardis in 1875; Isaac W. Hassell was the first postmaster and merchant. There was, however, a stock store started at the place about 1870. The present business men are Fields, Moore & Co., N. T. Stone, J. G. Ricketts and J. C. Lewis; mill, Fields, Powell & Co.; cotton gin, Grier & Colter. W. G. Moore is postmaster. J. H. England is physician. There are two churches, the Methodist Episcopal Church South and Methodist Episcopal Church.

Scott's Hill is situated about fourteen miles southeast of Lexington near the Decatur County line. The village contains about 200 inhabitants and was named from Micajah Scott, the first settler near the place. Dr. Wm. Brigance was the business man of the place, he was also the first postmaster. The present business men are Holmes & Son, Woodward Austin & Co., Brown & Co. and F. M. Volner; J. H. McKenzie, druggist; H W. Austin is postmaster. The physicians are P. M. Austin and Bevel & S. P. Winston. The hotel is kept by R. G. Kelley. The only church in the place is the Methodist Episcopal South.

Juno is eight miles west of Lexington in the Seventh District. The population of the place is about thirty. The village had its origin about 1846 or 1847 and was named by Dr. J. C. Hollam, who was the first postmaster of the place. The first merchants were J. W. Anderson and G. W. Stewart. The business men of the place are Wm. Antry & Bro., who have also the postoffice, and J. B. Williams. The professional men are Dr. Joseph True and Dr. Benj. Howard.

Independence, a once flourishing village, stood twelve miles northwest of Lexington.

It was named in 1832 by Isaac Hall. A postoffice was established about that time with Wm. Hewitt as postmaster. The first business men were Joseph Hall and Wm. Hewitt. The place went down about the time of the war and is now known in name.

Barren Springs was formerly called Barren Springs, but is now known as Reagan. It is in the Twelfth District and lies eleven miles south of the county seat. The village was named in 1881 and on the establishment of a postoffice in 1884 it was changed to Reagan. The population of the place is about fifty. The business men are J. D. Scott & Co. and R. R. Taylor. The steam-mill, gin and saw-mill is owned by G. W. Hodgin & Co. There are two churches, the Primitive Baptist and the United Baptist.

Long had its origin in 1878. It was then called Middelbury being about half way between Lexington and Decaturville. In 1880 the name was changed to Long in honor of W. B. Long who was made postmaster. The place contains sixty-five inhabitants. W. B. Long is the principal business man of the place.

Crucifer is located in the Second District, nine miles west of Lexington. It was formerly called Cross Plains. It was named by Anderson Mitchem about 1835 or 1840. When a postoffice was established at the place it was changed to Crucifer. Joseph Smith was the first postmaster. The first merchants were Barnett & Bro. Wm. H. Threadgill is now merchant and postmaster. Dr. M. B. Outlaw is physician.

Lone Elm took its name in 1869. It was so named by P. J. Howard, Jr., for an elm tree which stood near. The place is eight miles east of Lexington and contains sixty-five inhabitants. The first merchant was P. J. Howard, the postmaster was F. R. Bray. The present merchants are F. R. Bray & Co., and Duke & Sullivan. J. P. Duke is the present postmaster. The professional men are Drs. W. T. Watson and P. Mackey. There are also business houses at Shady Grove, Poplar Springs, White Fern, Pearcy's Mills, Wildersville and at other points in the county.

CHESTER COUNTY.

CHESTER COUNTY embraces an area of 167,000 acres and is on the water-shed between the head waters of South Fork of Forked Deer River and the small tributaries of the Tennessee. It is surrounded by the counties of Madison, Henderson, Hardin, McNairy and Hardeman. The surface is comparatively level and has an elevation above the sea level of a little over 400 feet. The only broken parts of the county are in the eastern and in the western parts. The drainage is almost entirely through the Forked Deer River. The tributaries of this river are Ozier Creek, Horse Creek, Turkey Creek, Sugar Creek, Clark Creek and Jacks Creek. Middleton Creek flows east into the Tennessee, and Clover Creek west into the Big Hatchie. Owing to the level surface of the country these streams are generally sluggish and frequently are clogged by drifts of logs and brush. The channels of these streams are shallow and frequent overflows follow heavy rains. Sand Mountain in the northeastern part is the highest point in the county and is probably the highest point between Henderson and the Tennessee River. This is rather a bold knob of a hundred or more feet in height and is covered with a growth of "black jack" and other timber. The soil is generally of a light clayey formation, intermixed with sand. Vertical borings show the formation below the surface to be mainly orange sand or rotten sandstone. The entire formation is comparatively recent. Water is obtained mainly by borings made; this is found in abundance and of good quality. A few chalybeate springs are found, but none of any reputed merit for medicinal qualities. The soil is well adapted to the growth of cotton. The quantity of cotton raised is not as great as in other counties, yet the quality is excellent. It also produces an excellent quality of sorghum. Corn and the other cereals do well, yet they are not considered staples. The land is also well suited to the growth of the grasses and for pasturage. Some of the ridge lands of the western part are covered with pine, while those of the east have oak, hickory and other hard woods. Along the streams are found cypress, poplar, elm, maple, gum, beach, holly and sugar maple. There is also in some parts black walnut and the several varieties of the timbers before mentioned.

The first settlers in what is now Chester County came to the county about 1820-24. These were from Virginia, North Carolina, South Carolina, and a few from Alabama. Many came from the States above mentioned to Middle Tennessee, and afterward moved to West Tennessee. The first settlement in the county was made in the vicinity of Mifflin about 1821. Col. J. Purdy, father of Robt. Purdy of Henderson, came to the vicinity of Mifflin about 1821. He was from Pennsylvania, and the village of Mifflin was named by him in honor of a town in his old State. He was a surveyor, a prominent business man, and a member of the Constitutional Convention of 1834. Within a few miles of Mifflin James Thomas settled in 1824. He was originally from Virginia, but moved to Alabama and thence to Mifflin. James Clifford came at the same time and settled down—a near neighbor to Thomas. Jere Hendrick and Micajah Jones also opened farms in the same neighborhood. The former came from Virginia about 1822; the latter left three sons, all of whom lived to be quite old. Wm. Phelps, now about seventy years old, has spent nearly all his life in the vicinity of Mifflin. A little south and west lived Stephen Beaver, Samuel Neill and James Neill. It is believed they were from North Carolina. Robt. Junell came to the county about 1825; he opened a farm and left a large family. The names of Wm. Rush, John Hubbard, Wm. Hall, Lemuel Deberry, John Halton and Peter Collins are closely related to the history of the Mifflin neighborhood. James Brown, from North Carolina, settled a short distance east of Mifflin. Wm. Spencer was from the same State and settled near Brown. Robt. McRea and Charles J. Allen, a relative of McRea, settled north of Mifflin. McRea built one of the first mills on Forked Deer River. Wm. Billingsly settled within one and a half miles of Mifflin about 1821. James and Richard Shackelford, Wm. Arnold and Charles Riddle all settled southeast, within four miles of Mifflin. The latter was a "Hard-shell" Baptist preacher and a celebrated hunter. As game became scarce he moved to Mississippi, where it was more abundant. George Still, a pioneer, was a surveyor; he moved to Texas in 1838. James Glass has the honor of having taught the first school in the new settlement in 1828. He afterward moved to Center Grove, thence to Lexington, Jackson, and is now living in Louisville. Thomas Garland, the first circuit rider, west of the Tennessee, formerly preached at Holly Springs. Job Dean, a soldier of the Creek war, was a settler of the neighborhood above mentioned.

In the vicinity of Jacks, Hugh Ross settled at a very early day. He was the father of S. L. Ross, and was a member of the State Senate at one time. J. F. Hamlett, John Brummer and John Crook, father of Dr. Crook, of Henderson, settled about 1830. John Kootz is said to have built his own house with the aid of his wife and a yoke of cattle. Job Trice, who is still living, reared a large family. John M. Hart, father-in-law of Mrs. Hart, of Henderson, was an early settler of Jacks Creek. Maj. Neeley, a prominent citizen, came to Jacks Creek about 1825. Robert McCorkle, a Methodist Episcopal preacher, Norman McLeod, and Dr. Alfred Tabler were among the earlier settlers of the place.

In the vicinity of Montezuma Joseph Johnson was perhaps the first settler. He was from North Carolina, and settled near Montezuma about 1826-30. Wesley and Nehemiah Burkhead and C. H. O'Neal were from the same State and settled in the same neighborhood. Wm. Cason, father of Col. Cason, came from Middle Tennessee and settled near Montezuma in 1826. William McKnight arrived about the same time. The Steeds and Barretts came to the same neighborhood a little later.

The first road cut through the country was from Lexington, by way of the Jacks Creek and Mifflin neighborhoods to Montezuma, thence to Bolivar. Meats were largely of game, such as turkey and deer, which were then numerous. The first mills in the country were those of Jere Hendricks and Richard McCleary, on Forked Deer, and that of

Stephen Beaver on Clark Creek. As an illustration of the capacity of these mills it is said Hendricks was in the habit of putting a turn of corn in the hopper and then turn on the water, when he would go about his farm work, and at noon he would put in a new grist and again return to his work till night. If not speedy it was not expensive.

The enabling act, creating Chester County, was passed March 1, 1879. Section 1 of the act called for portions of Madison, Henderson, McNairy and Hardeman Counties to be cut off and to be erected into a new county to be known by the name of Chester. This name was given as a compliment to Col. R. I. Chester, of Jackson, who was at that time representative from Madison County. The same section further designated what portion of the respective counties should be attached to the new county. Section 2 of the Act named J. F. Hewlett, Robert Long, B. H. Brown, J. H. Fry, B. J. Young, A. B. Patterson, J. W. Perkins, J. W. Mitchell, J. M. Simmons, John Parham, J. W. Sherrell, W. L. Stegall, William Rush, J. M. Reams, M. D. Pare and Abel Stewart as commissioners to run the boundaries. Section 4 called for an election in the several factions, which required a two-thirds vote of all the voters in the faction to vote "new county;" those opposing were to vote "old county." Section 8 required the new county to be divided into ten or twelve civil districts. Section 9 appointed persons to hold election of county officers, and 10 selected commissioners to select a site for a county seat. They were ordered to select a place not more than three and a half miles from the center of the county, and were to have regard to health and convenience. Section 11 provided for the purchase and erection of public buildings; and 12 required the voters of the several factions to vote at their old places until authorized by further instruction. The commissioners met and organized by electing William Rush chairman and John Parham secretary. Long, Pare and Stewart had moved away and their places were filled by W. L. Cherry, J. M. and J. W. May. The first meeting of the commissioners was at Montezuma on June 13, 1879. The result of the elections on the question of the new county, on September 6, 1879, resulted in a vote of 263 out of 316 for the new county in the Madison faction, 408 votes out of 506 in the Henderson faction, 392 votes out of 510 in the McNairy faction, and 80 votes out of 103 in the Hardeman faction. The organization of the new county was delayed by an injunction suit filed by J. D. Brown, John Brown and Isaac Parrish of the Henderson faction. The suit was brought before Chancellor Nixon and the suit sustained. An appeal was taken to the supreme court and the case brought before that body at Jackson at the April term, 1882. The judgment of the former court was reversed and the injunction dissolved. The elections held on May 29, 1882, for choice of county officers resulted in the election of Robert Criner for sheriff by a majority of 173 votes; of Ed Estes for circuit court clerk by a majority of 285 votes; of John Parham for county court clerk by a majority of 84 votes; of W. S. Rhodes for trustee by a majority of 94 votes, and of C. M. Cason, register, by 38 votes. The permanent organization was effected June 3, 1882, at the Baptist Church. On motion by John Parham and by order of Judge T. C. Muse, who stated the customs of colonial times, the audience were led in prayer by Rev. J. H. Garrett, after which the congregation joined in singing, "O, for a Thousand Tongues, etc."

The question as to the county seat was left to a popular vote. The only two places in nomination were Henderson and Montezuma. It was decided in favor of the former place by an overwhelming majority.

At the meeting of the commissioners in June at Montezuma, in 1879, A. B. Patterson, B. J. Young, J. H. Mitchell and J. W. Sherrell were appointed to receive donations for public buildings. Several conditional bonds were tendered on condition that the new county should be made and that certain lots should be chosen. The injunction suit having been filed and the matter delayed, these could not be acted upon. The courts met at other places till April 13, 1883, when the county court, after receiving many propositions, finally accepted the proposition of Mrs. Hattie E. Duckworth. This was for the residence and grounds of the late Dr. J. A. Crook. This included the residence and grounds containing about four acres. The sum asked was $3,000, payable in one, two and three years, with interest at six per cent.

On July 2, 1883, W. L. Messinger, Wm. M. Senter and J. A. Miller with the county surveyor were ordered to lay off the square and to examine the buildings. The building purchased is a large two-story frame building, having a court room and offices for the county officers.

The bell for the courthouse was received as a donation from Col. R. I. Chester, sent as a compliment in return for perpetuating his name in the county.

In January, 1886, the county court appointed Dr. J. A. Crook, N. T. Buckley, Wm. Rush and C. G. Terry a committee to select a site for a jail and to confer with builders for its erection. The place chosen lies a little north of the courthouse and embraces a portion of the lands purchased with the courthouse. The contract was let for the building on April 5, 1886. The building is a two-story brick about 48x20 feet. It contains two cells and the sheriff's residence. The contract was let to J. M. Wheatley for $1,650. On the report of a committee, it was decided to build a cook and dining-room to the jail. This, with some trifling changes made in the original contract, brought the cost up to $1,900, which was paid in county warrants of $900 and $1,000 each.

The paupers of the county are so few, that as a matter of economy, they are farmed out to the lowest and most responsible bidder. The average number does not exceed five.

The outlet for the produce and travel of the county is the Mobile & Ohio Railroad. This road extends through the central part of the county, a distance of twenty-nine miles. Its assessed value is about $166,000 or nearly $5,500 per mile. This road was built in 1856-58.

The total value of taxables for 1883 was $858,503 for 1884 $852,051, for 1885 $776,425, and for 1886 it was $704,435 exclusive of the railroad.

Henderson, the county seat of Chester County, is situated on the Mobile & Ohio Railroad near the center of the county. The place is supposed to have been named from Henderson County. The town was not laid out until after the building of the railroad. The first lots were sold in 1857-58. The land was owned by J. D. Smith. At this time the only cleared lands were the places of B. A. Hicks one and a half miles west; Jack Garland's place known as the Murchiser property a little southwest; and that owned by the Jordan H. Garland's heirs, and the Simmons' heir east and north of Henderson. The place was originally called Dayton but the name was soon changed to Henderson. Gholston built the first house in the place which stood just opposite the postoffice. Dr. T. A. Smith, Polk Bray, H. D. Franklin, A. S. Sayles and John West were among the first business men of the place. Like most other towns, Henderson received a check by the war but soon recovered its normal state. Henderson has had a steady and healthful growth but not rapid. It does not operate under a charter and thus avoids the sale of intoxicating beverages. From a moral standpoint few places reach the standard of Henderson. The business is largely of the cotton trade, this amounting to the sum of 5,000 bales some years. Cotton is by far the largest item of produce handled, yet there is a general line of produce handled every year which amounts to thousands of dollars. Henderson contains 227 lots which are assessed at $87,435. The business of the place is done by the following business houses: General stores: J. F. O'Neal & Co.; I. G. Galbraith & Co.; Cason, Estes & Co.; L. C. Rhodes & Co.; Ashcraft & Co.; W. C. McCullum & Co.; W. M. Bray & Co.; and Rowsey, Robins & Co. Grocery stores: J. M. McCulley & Co.; G. L. Priddy & Co.; Estes & Ozier; W. H. Thomas; P. J. Howard & Co.; and W. C. Crittenden. Drug stores: W. B. Shannon & Co.; Baird & Bro. Jeweller: A. H. McKinnon. Hardware: Carroll & McLeod. Henderson also contains several good livery stables, hotels, boarding-houses, shops and is well supplied with professional men.

Mifflin is the oldest town in the county. It was laid out about 1828 by Col. Priddy who, with James Bank, opened a business house there about that time. James Smithers sold goods there possibly a little before the others. Spencer and Glass built a cotton-gin and a store about a mile and a half east of Mifflin, in 1832. From 1830 to 1840 Wm. Priddy, Ezekiel Halton, William and Henry Collins, and Wm. Watkins did business in Mifflin. Among the later ones were John West, Beaver, Carver & Co., John Smith and J. M. Priddy. Following the war were Beaver & Carver, Ashcraft & Co. The late business men are Wheeler & Edwards, Beaver & Son, Bell & Bros. and R. C. Cooper. Mifflin is surrounded by a good farming community and contains about 100 inhabitants, also a Methodist church and a schoolhouse.

Jacks Creek was named from the creek on which it stands. The first business house was opened there about 1830 by Col. Samuel Wilson and B. Gillespie. W. B. Terry followed later. He became wealthy from trade in Henderson and McNairy Counties. About 1840 Crook & Keeland opened a store at Jacks Creek. The latter was afterward a magistrate and died at Denmark. R. Anderson did business there about 1850. Gov. Stone, of Mississippi, taught school at Jacks Creek; he also clerked for Crook & Thomas before removing to Mississippi. The principal business of the place between 1850 and 1860 was done by A. C. McCorkle, and Hollis, Skinner & Co.; from 1870 to 1880 by R. J. Howard & Co., McCorkle & Thompson, W. S. Rhodes and J. M. McCullum. The present business is done by C. M. Kee & Co., J. M. McCorkle & Co. Jacks Creek, like Mifflin, is an old place and has but little growth. The Masonic Hall was erected in 1854–55. The lower part of the hall is used as a church. Friendship Lodge, No. 229, was organized in 1849–50. A. N. Tabler, Richard Barham and H. D. Crook were among the first members.

Montezuma is supposed to have been named from the ancient Aztec capital. It lies about four miles west of Henderson. J. R. Wambler is believed to have been the first merchant in the place. He began about 1830, and continued for many years. Halton & Cason began business there about 1848 and continued till the war. Estes & Randolph also sold goods a number of years before the war, and E. Estes & Co. were there a short time. The business of the place is now done by George Brown.

The following magistrates who composed the first county court met at Henderson on June 3, 1882: P. McNatt, J. D. Shelton, R. N. Reed, H. L. Massengill, Benj. Robertson, M. D. Davis, N. T. Buckley, H. C. Trice, C. R. Narborough, J. H. Fry, Hiram Johnson, F. H. Weir, J. S. White, A. L. Bean, W. M. Senter, R. M. D. McNatt, Wm. Kerr, Martin Reams, Wm. Rush and P. Gatham. The court organized by electing Wm. Rush chairman, and proceeded to make the bonds of the several county and district officers. R. L. Hendricks was then chosen surveyor; F. M. Ballard, ranger; J. S. Jester, coroner; J. N. Wheatley, scaler of weights and measures, and W. R. McNatt, superintendent of public instruction. The constables first chosen were N. Shelton, Calvin McCann, J. T. Stansill, R. D. Bell, J. D. Smith, C. C. Jones, M. M. O'Neal, Robert Mitchell and S. H. Moore. July 24 the court canvassed the vote cast for the location of the county seat. It was found there were 796 votes cast in favor of Henderson and fifty-five in favor of Montezuma. The county court, January 1, 1883, memorialized the General Assembly, asking that Chester County be allowed to remain in the Eleventh Judicial Circuit and in the Tenth Chancery Circuit. The first *venire* summoned by the county court called for John Short, S. J. Thompson, J. R. Bland, John Newsom, J. H. Deberry, Stanton Lee, W. B. Fry, J. W. Ozier, J. R. Edwards, J. F. Holloway, Benj. Rhodes, W. C. Christopher, E. C. Wamble, R. C. Ball, F. M. Putnam, A. D. Barnett, Wm. Senter, N. C. Caygle, Martin Reams, K. S. Jackson, Henry Garner and J. Rush. The first court also fixed a schedule of privilege taxes, these ranging from $5 to $150, the amount charged for circuses. The first marriage license issued in Chester County was to Joe Glover (colored) and Rachel Sandford. This was June 5, 1882. The minister officiating was Rev. Henry A. Jackson. The second license was to R. B. West and M. A. Perkins June 6.

The first circuit court (Eleventh Circuit) met at Henderson on July 17, 1882, Hon. Thomas P. Bateman presiding. The other officers present were Robert Criner, sheriff, and E. A. Estes, clerk. The first *venire facias* embraced the names of Wm. Cash, W. C Johnson, John Criner, G. W. Smith, T. J. McCorkle, B. Robertson, Jacob Young, R. P. Hunter, S. J. Bishop, H. J. Dean, A. J. Peddy, John McCall, J. R. Bray, J. W. Shull, J. P. Thomas, G. J. Patterson, J. C. B. Nailer, F. M. Cherry, R. M. D. McNatt, W. C. Caygle, C. Wilson, G. C. Butler, L. D. Simmons, J. H. Mitchell and James Fry. The grand jury chosen was composed of L. D. Simmons, R. P. Hunter, W. J. Young, F. M. Cherry, J. C. B. Nailer, A. J. Peddy, H. T. Dean, J. A. Criner, T. J. McCorkle, S. J. Bishop, W. C. Johnson, C. Wilson and J. R. Bray. This court did no further work than to approve the several official bonds and adjourn till September at a special term. Said term met at the appointed time with Judge T. C. Muse on the bench. The other officers at this time were A. A. Anderson, sheriff; A. E. Estes, clerk, and M. H. Meeks, attorney-general. The first civil suit was the case of B. S. Hite against N. P. Ingram on a note; a similar one was brought by H. G. Hollenburg against J. F. Newsom. Fines of $50 were assessed against George Greer and J. Christopher for carrying concealed weapons. At the January term, 1883, Will Willoughby (colored) plead guilty of involuntary manslaughter for the killing of Will——, on December 24, 1882, and received a sentence of three years to the penitentiary. At the August term of the same year, M. Prewitt was fined $50 for carrying weapons, and Frank Combs one cent and costs for maintaining a nuisance. Charles McLellan received a sentence of one year to the penitentiary for petit larceny. Willis Richardson was fined $100 for selling goods without license. The first case to the penitentiary was Ben West (colored) for stealing a $10 bill, and the last was Oliver Garland for a similar offense.

On the organization of the county it was directed that Chancellor H. J. Livingston should open the chancery court of Chester County on July 10, 1882. Five weeks notice had previously been given in the Brownsville *Democrat*. On the meeting of the court Dr. Joseph A. Crook was appointed clerk and master. The solicitors appearing before this court were J. M. Troutt, M. F. Ozier, J. W. Pace, A. W. Stovall and J. S. White. The Court ordered this rule, that all processes except final processes should be filed on the first Monday in each month, and that the clerk and master should open such processes accordingly. After fixing the bonds of the several officers, the court adjourned to meet in special session in December, 1882. Suits of divorce came up at this court before Chancellor Livingston. Abel Cook had the bonds of matrimony between himself and wife, Nancy, dissolved, also J. S. Barrett was divorced from Sallie Barrett. The Court again met in regular session in May, 1883, before Chancellor T. C. Muse, of Jackson. A very interesting and peculiar suit is pending in the chancery court, involving an estate of $25,000. It is the suit of Carroll Beaver against Nancy Beaver for divorce on the alleged grounds of impotency on the part of defendant. A suit to which Chester County is a party is now pending in the supreme court of the United States. It is the suit of the several counties through which the Mobile & Ohio Railroad passes against that road and the Farmers' Trust Company of New York. The suit was begun in the chancery court at Humboldt. The suit was brought to recover taxes against the road amounting to the sum of $150,000. Chester County's apportionment is $16,000. This road was chartered in 1852, and was granted immunity from taxation for twenty-five years, or until it could show a dividend of 8 per cent on its stock. It is claimed that the giving the mortgage to the above trust company was done to defraud the counties out of their just dues.

The common schools of Chester County operated under the counties to which the respective factions belonged until the organization of the county was effected in 1882. Public and private schools supplied the wants of the people until the organization of the public schools after the war and the more perfect organization on the adoption of the new constitution in 1872. On the organization of Chester County the schools were put under the superintendency of R. McNatt who was followed by W. D. Ross, who was succeeded by J. S. White. The county is divided into thirty-two school districts and has about sixty schoolhouses. Two of these houses are brick, a few frame and the remainder are log houses. The scholastic population by the last enumeration is 3,135. The male white population is 1,270, the female 1,270; the colored male population is 334, the female is 304. There are from sixty to seventy teachers employed and the average length of school term is only about fifty days. Owing to the fact that many of the schoolhouses are not in a condition suitable for cold weather the schools are taught out in the summer months. A natural result follows—the attendance is not good nor is the work effective. The two schools at Henderson take the place of the public schools and are run partly as consolidated schools. The public funds are divided between the two in proportion to their attendance. The matter of attendance at either school is optional with the parent or guardian. There is a consolidated school at Montezuma—the old Jackson District High School, and two in the Second District, the Howard Seminary and the Clear Springs Academy. There is also a consolidated school at Mifflin. The short term of school and insufficient schoolhouses have caused a great number of persons to sell out their farms and move elsewhere to have better school advantages. The operations of the four mile law have effectively driven the sale of whisky from the county.

West Tennessee Christian College is a continuation of a school begun in 1869 by Miss Helen Post and A. S. Sayle. The school thus started was afterward incorporated as the Masonic Male and Female Institute, which won an extensive reputation during its fifteen years existence. The name Masonic in connection with the institute was merely nominal. This school was under the management of Prof. Geo. Savage, now of Eagleville. On August 4, 1885, the school was incorporated as the West Tennessee Christian College by I. J. Galbraith, John Parham, L. G. Thomas, H. Robertson, J. W. Galbraith, W. L. Hill, E. B. Fuller, J. B. Inman, R. J. Parham, J. W. Ozier and J. A. McCulley. The officers of the executive board are I. J. Galbraith, president; J. H. Fuller, secretary, and J. W. Ozier, treasurer. The faculty consists of J. B. Inman, president; J. H. Fuller, A. M.; R. J. Haynes, A. M.; Miss Sue Inman, Miss Mattie Boothe and Miss Laura Ivey. The corporation owns good buildings and campus. A boarding hall for young ladies is under the care of the president of the college. The curiculum embraces the usual college course. The attendance at the college is about 100. The ability of the faculty, the cheapness of living, the healthful moral and physical atmosphere make the West Tennessee Christian College a desirable place at which to educate young ladies and young gentlemen.

Henderson Male and Female College. The Jackson District High School was established at Montezuma about four miles west of Henderson in 1874-75. A good two-story brick building was erected at that place and a good school maintained there till 1885. The building erected was a stock concern and is still used for school and church purposes. The necessity of having railroad communication led to the erection of the college at Henderson. The present college building was erected in 1885. It is a two-story brick building, and well adapted for school purposes and was erected at a cost of about $2,500. It was built by a stock company, the shares being $25 each. It was incorporated in September, 1885 as the Henderson Male and Female College by J. F. O'Neal, H. C. Ashcraft, W. T. Cason, J. M. Troutt, T. A. Smith, J. M. Cunningham and J. D. Johnson. It is recognized as the school of the Methodist Episcopal Church South, yet it is not rigidly denominational. Its aim is to enlighten, to make pupils wiser and better. The school is under the management of a board of trustees who look to the interest of the pupils. The faculty consists of Rev. G. W. Wilson, A. M., president; Rev. H. S. Taylor, A. M.; Miss Sue Cason, Mr. W. T. McGee and Mrs. H. S. Taylor.

The curriculum embraces a full course in English, Latin, Greek, French, bookkeeping, mathematics, natural sciences, etc. The classic course is divided into the freshman sophomore, junior and senior years. The degree of A. B. is conferred on those who complete the entire course; B. S. on those who complete all except the Greek, and certificates of proficiency on those who complete parts of the course. The enrollment of the school is now over 100, which is considered flattering for the first year's work.

The Missionary Baptist Church was organized at Henderson by a Presbytery consisting of Revs. William J. Hodges, Samuel Bray and David J. Franklin, on August 15, 1867. The following names were enrolled as members of the first organization: Hugh McKnight, A. B. Crook, John D. Smith, David J. Franklin, A. S. Sayle, L. J. Anderson, Mary V. Crook, Melvina McKnight, Sarah B. Franklin, Rhoda F. Ewing, S. E. Anderson, M. C. Smith and Rosa F. Graham. W. J. Hodges was elected moderator, A. S. Sayle clerk, and A. B. Crook deacon. A. B. Crook was ordained deacon by W. J. Hodges, Samuel Bray and D. J. Franklin in accordance with the customs of the church. After appointing delegates to the Unity Association the church adopted the articles of faith of the church. The first additions to the church were M. McKnight, John D. Smith, Amanda F. Smith, Robt. W. Smith and C. T. Lovelace, all by letter in September, 1867. The church house was begun in August, 1867, but not completed till some time in 1868. The lot was deeded by J. D. Smith to A. B. Crook and Hugh McKnight as trustees. The building committee consisted of A. B. Crook, D. J. Franklin and A. S. Sayle. The value of church property is estimated at $900. The membership as reported to the last association is seventy-seven. A Sabbath-school is maintained by this church, numbering sixty-four. H. D. Franklin is both church clerk and Sunday-school superintendent. The pastor is Rev. W. G. Inman.

The Church at Cave Springs was constituted in 1866. The membership is forty-four. The church property is estimated at $500. M. V. Davison is church clerk. The church at Friendship was constituted in 1846. The present membership is seventy-two. J. S. McGraw is pastor and D. M. Marsh is clerk. The value of the church property is $300. The church at Hopewell has a membership of thirty and church property worth $100. This church was constituted in 1860. L. D. Nash is church clerk and John Henry, pastor. The church at Woodville was constituted in 1885. The membership of the church is forty-nine. The pastor is Abner Lambert, and J. M. Gratham is clerk. There are also churches at Mount Gilead, Hepsebah and Bethel, but their strength is not reported.

The Methodist Church was organized at Henderson about 1874-75. The pastors, in order, have been R. A. Umstead, George W. Wilson, from November 28, 1874, to November 23, 1875; B. F. Blackman, November 23, 1875, to December 9, 1878, to November, 1879; Richard W. Newsom, 1879 to November, 1881; John H. Garrett, November, 1881, to 1882-83; James Perry, 1882-83 to 1884; B. A. Hays, 1884; — Blackard, 1885; G. W. Wilson. The church was built in 1882. The first trustees were C. M. Cason, W. C. Walsh, M. F. Ozier, F. A. Smith and Hiram Johnson. Among the first members were Henry C. Ashcraft, Mattie M. Ashcraft, A. Brashears, Mary C. Bland, William Cason, Mary Cason, Caleb M. Cason, Mary H. Cason, William T. Cason, Charles M. Cason, William Cason, May J. Campbell, Hattie E. Crook, Alice C. Cauthorn, Harriet A. Conner, Sophia V. Davis, Fannie Ewing, Mary H. Hamilton, Hiram Johnson, J. T. Jester, John H. Hendrick, Mary J. Mason, Bettie Ozier, Mary C. O'Neal, Robert Purdy, Rebecca Purdy, Margaret J. Priddy, T. A. Smith, Elizabeth E. Smith; Martin, Mary, Joseph W. and Mary C. Stewart; Mary C. and Hugh N. Sherrill, Mary E. Simmons, Ann Spencer, Joseph W. and Hattie E. Temple, Catharine Vance, William C. and Hattie Walsh, J. A. and Maggie Worley, and Thomas and M. J. Worsham. This church has a good house of worship, and a membership of over 100. A flourishing Sabbath-school is also maintained.

The church at Montezuma was organized about 1830. To this church belonged the families of the Burkheads, Casons, Wamblers, Steeles and some others. The first was a log house, which was afterward supplanted by a frame building. This frame building served until a few years ago, when the institute which had been erected for the Jackson District High School began to be used as a church. This is a brick building and is very well suited for church services. This church has a good membership.

The Methodists also have churches at Mount Pisgah, Big Springs, Mount Pleasant, Mifflin, Mount Gilead, Holly Springs, Burkett's Chapel and Holton's Chapel. The whole membership in the county is nearly 600.

The only Christian church in Chester County is at Henderson. This was organized at Jacks Creek in 1871 by Rev. R. B. Tremble, of Mayfield, Ky. The first members were R. J. Barham, John Barham and wife, Holcombe Robertson and wife, John McCully and wife, I. J. Galbraith and wife, J. N. Galbraith and wife, W. A. Brummer and wife, James Wheatley and wife, W. J. Hodges and wife, R. I. Stow and wife, Miss Lou Ross and Miss Bettie Ross. The first elders were R. J. Barham and H. Robertson; the deacons were John Barham and John McCully. The organization was moved to Henderson in 1883, and a nice new frame building erected for church services at a cost of about $1,500. The present elders are R. J. Barham, H. Robertson and E. B. Fuller. The deacons are J. W. Ozier, J. N. Hodges, I. J. Galbraith, S. G. Thomas and Hugh Ross. The church maintains an excellent Sabbath-school. The church register shows a membership of 292 since its organization; of these, seventy-two have moved away, died or have been dropped from other causes. J. B. Inman, president of the West Tennessee Christian College, is pastor.

DECATUR COUNTY.

DECATUR COUNTY has an irregular surface broken by deep ravines and hollows without any seeming order or system. The general slope is toward the Tennessee into which the entire drainage of the county empties. The water-shed between the Tennessee and Mississippi lies west of the county. The only stream of any considerable size flowing through the county is Beech River, which empties into the Tennessee near the center of the county. Numerous smaller streams empty into the Beech. These received their names from early settlers who opened farms on or near these streams. Branches and creeks empty into the Tennessee every few miles from the southern to the extreme northern limit of the county. The valuable farming lands are found on the banks of the Tennessee, Beach River, and the smaller streams. The frequent inundations of the Tennessee render the land on its banks highly productive yet the farmers suffer at times from these overflows. Perhaps the largest area of valuable land is on Beech River. In addition to the excellent soil along this river it affords fine mill sites which have been used since the early settlement of the county. Very valuable timber abounds in great abundance in this county. Being isolated as it is, this product has not been exhausted as in many places. The most valuable of these timbers is the oak in its various varieties. Beech and other timber is also found. The getting out of cross-ties has recently developed into an extensive industry, perhaps the most valuable of any in the county at the present. The soil on the stream above mentioned is dark and well suited for the growth of corn and other cereals while the soil on the ridge is much lighter and partakes of the general character of the soil of a large area of West Tennessee known as the sandy lands. These lands yield corn, wheat, oats, etc., but are liable to wash and without great care soon become badly worn and almost worthless. Considerable mineral wealth is found in this county. It consists of fine grained sandstone from which grindstones and whetstones are made; also there are deep ledges of limestone well suited for building material. Siliceous, cherty, flinty soils are common and numerous beds of fossil remains, crinoidal stems etc., are found. Deposits of galena have been found in some parts of the county but no effort has been made to develop these; also deposits of marble are to be found. The most valuable mineral which promises much profit is the iron ore. This deposit belongs to the immense area of Hardin, Wayne, Hickman and other counties of western Middle Tennessee. The Brownsport Iron Company own 12,000 acres of land about the old Brownsport furnace. The company consists of Napoleon Hill, G. M. Trigg, G. P. Thornton and others. Napoleon Hill is president of this company. The furnace was operated successfully for a time and ore of fine quality and of great abundance was found, but an extensive lawsuit has involved the company in trouble, and work at the furnace has been suspended for a number of years. The richness and abundance of the ore and the great quantity of timber near, it is claimed will render this one of the most profitable of mines.

The county originally belonged, or was a part of Perry County, which was cut off of Hickman County in 1819, and named in honor of Com. Oliver Hazard Perry. Owing to the inconvenience of having to cross the river in attending court, it was determined to form a new county out of that portion lying west of the river. Mr. Brasher was largely instrumental in forming the new county. The act creating the county passed the General Assembly in November, 1845. It was to form a new county out of "that part of Perry lying west of the river, to be known and distinguished by the name of Decatur County, in honor and to perpetuate the memory of Com. Stephen Decatur, of the United States Navy, of whose services our nation should be proud and whose memory should be revered." The county is bounded on the north by Benton County, on the west by Henderson County, on the south by Hardin County and the Tennessee, and on the east by the

Tennessee River. The area as given by the assessors is 202,043 acres, valued at $645,750. This area seems to vary about 50 per cent from that indicated by the boundaries. The committee to run the boundary line consisted of J. C. Barbrough, W. J. McGee, J. S. Walker, Samuel Brasher and D. B. Funderburk. The county seat was selected by Samuel McLoed, Samuel Brasher, Balaam Jones and D. B. Funderburk, on the lands of John McMillan, from whom they obtained twenty-five acres, and ten acres was obtained from Burrell Rushing, making thirty-five acres in all The deed to this land was made May 7, 1847. After the division of Perry County, the new county was allowed the jail and the court square in Perryville for public purposes until a new site should be selected and new buildings erected. The first court met, it is said, in Decaturville in 1848, in a cabin on the west side of the square. This was used a short time till the erection of a two-story frame courthouse, which was burned July 3, 1869, with all the records except those in the register's office and the clerk and master's office. It is claimed that the fire was the work of an incendiary for the purpose of destroying the records On July 12, 1869, the county court appointed J. W. Mayo, W. C. Fryar, D. M, Scott and others a committee on plans and specifications for the erection of a new courthouse. This contract was let early in October. The house is a two-story brick, having offices for all the county officers on the first floor and the court room above. This house was erected at a cost of about $9,000. The county was allowed the use of the old jail as before stated, at Perryville, till the removal and establishment of the new seat of justice. The first jail stood on the present jail lot and was constructed of brick and logs. It was burned in 1855, and a new one after the same pattern erected in its place. A committee in 1869 reported this jail badly out of repair, and that the county was in need of a new one, but no definite action was taken till 1883, when J. W. Wiley, J. G. Hardin, W. H. Fisher and others were selected to supervise the erection of a new jail. Their report was filed April 7, 1884. A new jail was ordered. This is a fine brick structure and is used as the sheriff's residence as well as the jail. The cells are of the most improved pattern and are deemed entirely safe. The whole cost about $9,000.

The poor that were not farmed out to individuals were kept at a small place on the original town plat till 1878, when a farm lying in the Fourth Civil District was purchased by J. Garret, D. M. Scott, James Jennings and George Morgan from Robert S. Brasher and others. The farm consists of 200 acres and was purchased for $500. The only outlet for market for the product of Decatur County at present is by way of the Tennessee River, as the county has never had a railroad or turnpike. A proposition is now before the county asking for $25,000 stock in the Tennessee Midland Railroad, which, if built, will greatly enhance the value of the property of the county.

The settlers in this county were mainly from Middle and East Tennessee or North Carolina. These began to arrive soon after the extinguishment of the Indian titles in 1818. A few perhaps came earlier as hunters and trappers, but were not permanent settlers, as the possession by the Indians would preclude a permanent residence. Traditions among old residents make the first entry into the county as early as 1808 or 1810, but this is hardly true. In 1822 Thomas Shannon with his wife, five sons and three daughters, left Davidson County for West Tennessee. Mr. Shannon himself, four negroes and two white men passed down the Cumberland and Ohio Rivers and up the Tennessee to the southern part of Decatur County. The family came through by land and crossed the Tennessee at Shannonsville. Mr. Shannon settled near what is now called Point Pleasant. This portion of the county was a portion of Harden County till 1856. Uncle Jimmy Harris came down the Tennessee and landed at the mouth of a little stream which he named Cub Creek, doubtless from the number of young bears killed there. The date of his arrival is not known, but he is generally conceded to have been the first settler in the county. He was soon followed by others who settled in different parts of the county. They usually chose sites near the Tennessee or the smaller streams of the county. Ephraim Arnold settled in the vicinity of Harris a few years later than Mr. Harris. Reuben White, Wm. Yarbro or Yarbrough, the Rushings, Smiths, Dennisons, Pettigrews, McMillans, Houstons, Rains and others soon followed. These families have been identified with the county since its first settlement. Others soon followed but it would be impossible to fol low all as the increase soon became rapid. The names of the first settlers at Carrollville, Shannonsville and Perryville are given in connection with these places.

As Decatur County was a part of Perry County until the organization in November, 1845, the records of the county to that date were a record of Perry County and the destruction of nearly all since that date up to 1869 renders a review of the courts impossible. Judge James Scott was doubtless the first circuit judge after the division of the county and Robert A. Hill, the attorney-general. Judge Scott was followed by Judge Elijah Walker. Both Judge Scott and Judge Walker were from Savannah. The former died, it is believed, in 1850, and the latter in 1873. Both men were recognized as men of ability and integrity. Judge Walker served as judge till the outbreak of the war. Robt. A. Hill was succeeded as attorney-general by Lee M. Bentley. Fielding Hurst was from McNairy County and was appointed circuit judge at the reorganization after the war and served till 1867 and J. W. Doherty till 1869, when Judge Walker was again elected and served till his death in 1873, when he was succeeded by Judge T. P. Bateman, who served till 1886. Among the later attorney-generals are J. W. Doherty and John M. Taylor. The chancery court was established at Decaturville in 1854 with Stephen C. Pavatt as chancellor, who served till 1866 or till the close of the courts by the war. R. H. Rose was chancellor from 1866 till 1870, when Geo. H. Nixon was elected and served till 1886, when he was succeeded by A. J. Abernathy, the present chancellor. Judges Rose and Nixon are both residents of Lawrenceburg and Judge Abernathy is a resident of Pulaski. D. B. Funderburk was appointed clerk and master and served till 1872, when D. C. Kennedy succeeded him and served till 1879, when J. A. English was appointed and still holds the office. The first county register was John A. Rains, who was defeated for re-election in 1848 by A. M. Yarbro, who served till 1856, when he was succeeded by W. B. Bright and he by J. J. Lacy and he by W. H. Milam. Then came Wm. Pratt for three terms, when he was succeeded by P. R. Brasher, who gave place in 1886 to G. B. D. Rushing. The first county court clerk was Samuel Yarbro, who served till 1856 and was succeeded by M. J. Fisher, who served one term and was succeeded in 1860 by J. R. Carmack, who served till the outbreak of the war. J. C. Roberts served from 1866 to 1868, when he was succeeded by J. P. Rains, who served till 1870. John McMillan was then elected and held the office till 1882, when the present incumbent, J. E. Dees, was elected. The first circuit clerk was D. B. Funderburk, who served till 1856, when he was succeeded by Hiram Lacy, who held the office till 1860. Samuel Akin was then elected and held the office till the war. After the reorganization C. S. Brandon and P. O. Roberts held the office until 1870, when D. N. Scott was elected the two following terms. J. P. Rains was elected to the office in 1878 and still holds it.

The first county sheriff was Hiram Lacy, who held the office from 1846 to 1852. John McMillan then held the office from 1852 to 1858, and G. W. Hanes from 1858 to 1862. Benj. F. Tuton was sheriff from 1865 to 1866 and J. C. Barnett from 1866 to 1868. J. B. Houston served from 1868 to 1870, when D. C. Kennedy was elected for one term. Isaac McMillan served from 1872 to 1874 and W. R. Tuton from 1874 to 1876. Isaac McMillan was again elected and served from 1876 to 1882, when he gave place to E. E. Arnold, the present incumbent. The majority of suits before the Decatur Courts have been comparatively uninteresting to the public; being as it is, away from the great money centers the suits have not involved vast sums of money. Peaceful as the county has been, the records show that about one indictment for murder has been returned every year since the organization of the county. This number is not over the average perhaps in the State, startling as it may seem. A case exciting considerable interest was the killing of M. J. Fisher by Carroll Graves in October, 1862. This grew out of political differences and Graves made his escape and has never been brought to justice. On November 30, 1875, Geo. W. Tate was killed by George Lyle or Lisle on the southeast corner of the public square. Lisle made his escape and first went to Kentucky, but was afterward apprehended in Missouri and brought back to Decaturville for trial. After a very exciting trial of several years he was convicted and sentenced to the penitentiary for a term of fifteen years. He is now doing his term of service. The present bar of Decaturville is composed of J. W. Doherty, John McMillan, J. A. England and D. E. Scott.

On the question of the war Decatur was much divided in opinion and sentiment. On the vote of the question of "separation" or "no separation" there were cast 310 votes for "separation" and 550 votes for "no separation." There was no such thing as neutral ground on the question of the war and few able-bodied men escaped the army either for or against the Union. The county being isolated from the great lines of travel except by way of the Tennessee River, it was comparatively free from the march of the armies, but what was worse it suffered terribly from predatory bands of irregular cavalry or roving bands—too often robbers under the name of soldiers The first troops raised for the Confederate service was the company of Capt. Isham G. Hearn. This company became Company F, of the Twenty-seventh Tennessee Confederates. This company was called the "Blind Tigers" or simply "Tigers." The regiment was organized at Trenton in 1861 by the election of C. H. Williams, colonel; B. H. Brown, lieut.-colonel; and Samuel Love, major.

The second company raised in the county was that of Jonathan Luton which company became part of the Thirty-first Confederate (West Tennessee) Regiment. The officers of this regiment were A. H. Bradford, colonel; C. M. Cason, lieut.-colonel; and John Smith, major. Four companies were raised for the Fifty-second Tennessee (Confederate) Regiment. These were the companies of N. A. Wesson, W. R. Akin, J. H. Thomas and John McMillan. The other commissioned officers of the last company only are remembered. They were J. L. Buck, first lieutenant; P. R. Brasher, second lieutenant, and S. L. McClure, third lieutenant. The regiment was organized on January 4, 1862, at Henderson Station by electing B. J. Lea, colonel; John Esle, lieutenant-colonel, and J. G. Rundle, major. After the battle of Shiloh, about the last of April or first of May, the Fifty-second was consolidated with the Fifty-first. Col. John Chester, of Jackson, became colonel of the consolidated regiment, and Col. Lea was assigned to duty elsewhere. Henceforth the consolidated regiments operated as one body

Decatur County furnished two companies for the Federal Army The first of these was raised by Capt. Elisha Roberts. This was done about the first of October, 1862. Elisha Roberts, Wm. Chandler and Wm. C. Webb, were each captain of this company in the order named. The lieutenants were J. L. W. Boatmare, first; Wm. F. Balright and Isaac J. Shull, second lieutenants. The operations of these men are given elsewhere in the history of the Sixth Union Regiment, Tennessee Cavalry. The second company was raised by Capt. Andrew Roberts. These men were a part of the Second Union Regiment of Tennessee Mounted Infantry. The nucleus of this regiment was Company A, which was mustered into service October 1, 1863. By February 1, 1864, at which time the regiment was organized, it numbered seven companies. John Murphy was then elected lieutenant-colonel. On the completion of the Regiment Lieut.-Col. John Murphy was promoted to Colonel. The operations of the Second were mainly in doing fort duty and scouring the country, in picking up stragglers, and in preventing recruiting for the Confederacy.

The principal church denominations in Decatur County are the Methodist Episcopal South, the Missionary Baptist and the Cumberland Presbyterian. The Methodists of this County belong to the Decaturville Circuit and the Jackson District and the Memphis Conference. In the Decaturville Circuit there are eight classes or church organizations and four local preachers. By the report for 1885 there were 755 members belonging to the Decaturville Circuit. Among the earlier churches of the denomination is Gray's Chapel, which was built in 1853: the trustees at that time were W. T. Brasher, Wm. Ivy, Wm. Brigance, Henry Jackson, Thomas Hays, Wm. L. McKenzie and Phillip Ivy The Methodist Church in Decaturville was built in 1854 in connection with the Masons. New Liberty was built on the land of Curtis O'Neal, in 1855. The trustees at that time were L. B. Stanfield, Lewis Garret, S. Singleton, Henry Singleton and Joseph Kelly. The most of the church house now standing has been erected since the war. A Cumberland Presbyterian Church was built at Mt. Joy in 1848. The trustees at that time were L. E. Davis, Wm. May and Robert Campbell. The church at Liberty was built in 1858. The trustees at that time were W. W. G. Rushing and John W. Bennett. The membership of the former congregation is given at twenty-eight, and of the latter at thirty-six. Perhaps the oldest and strongest denomination in the county is the Missionary Baptist, but no date of that church is at hand.

The schools of Decatur County were first organized while it was yet a part of Perry County. The academy at Perryville was built in 1825. Soon after the organization of the county Lot 99 was purchased in Decaturville, for the purpose of building thereon an academy. The trustees of the academy were J. L. Houston, J. A. Rains, H. C. Fryar, Wm. Henry and David B. Funderburk. A building was soon erected and a school opened. This institution has been under the control of the trustees appointed by the county court since its inception. Among the early teachers of the county may be mentioned Elias Blunt, familiarly known as "Gov. Blount," Elias Deaton, Geo. W. Beard, Green B. Rushing, Housten Roberts, Calvin Rushing, W. M. Dalton, B. H. Southerland. These men possessed the characteristics of early teachers—they had industry, knew how to wield the birch, and could teach the three "R's." The academy above mentioned was quite prosperous, and some able instructors taught in it. A college building was erected but was unfortunately destroyed by fire before ready for use. The scholastic population of the county is given at 2,929 white, and 540 colored. The enrollment for the year was 1,755 white and 251 colored. The length of school term is sixty days; the salary of teacher is $28 per month; the number of schoolhouses is forty-nine, and the total amount expended for schools was $2,815.31.

Decaturville, the present seat of justice was selected and deeded to Samuel McLoed, Samuel Brasher, Balaam Jones and David B. Funderburk in 1847. The site embraced an area of thirty-five acres. The first settler in the place was Gilbert McMillan, who built a house, where Decaturville now stands, in 1836, and it was known as McMillan's shop for a number of years. At the first sale of lots the following were purchasers: Pettigrew & Coats, John Garret, L. G. Friedley, Daniel McLoed, P. H. Fisher, E. E. Pate, Lawson Kelley, E. E. Jones, John McMillan, W. H. Bennet, J. W. Delaney, G. N. Gains, H. C. Fryar and a few others. Daniel McLoed built a house on the northeast corner of the square where the Dennison Hotel now stands, which was the first business house built in the place. Here he sold groceries for a time. Samuel Yarbro and Johnathan Luton were the first dry goods merchants. They did business where John Tate is now located. Soon after Young & Johnson opened business on the southwest corner of the square, and Pettigrew & Coats on the northwest corner of the square. Others were J. J. Sharp & Co., and later Storm & Smith, J. M. Fryar, Kendrick & Roberts and Blythe & Bondurant. The present business men of the place are Stout & Scott, Reuben Smith, J. L. Tate, J. T. Rodgers, Roberts & Moreland, W. F. Stout and J. L. Welch & Co.; hotel, the Dennison House. The Methodist Church and Masonic Lodge Hall, No. 218, was built in 1854. The town of Decaturville contains about 300 inhabitants, and is without a charter.

Perryville, the old county seat, was selected as the seat of justice in 1821. On November 14, 1821, the Legislature selected Charles Miles, John Reaser, James Dickson, Charles Graham, W. S. Britt and Wm. Patterson to locate said seat. The place selected was the present site of Perryville. The town was incorporated in 1825, and in November of that year Joseph Brown, Wm. Jarman, J. S. Allen, J. W. Crowder, Jacob Johnson, James Kelough and John McClover were made the town board and, also, trustees to establish an academy at Perryville. Samuel McClure was the first merchant in the place, and perhaps in the county. In 1821 he was succeeded in business by J. M. Pettigrew, a native of Ireland, but a man of great business ability. In the following year Pettigrew was joined by a brother, and in a short time by a half brother. Their business grew to immense proportions, and Perryville became one of the most extensive shipping points on the Tennessee River. While Perryville was the county seat it was not only the commercial but was also the political center of the county. Here met the early courts. The operations of the notorious John A. Murrell's band were through this portion of the county about 1830-32. While Perryville was still the political center it was visited by the great political lights such as James K. Polk, Andrew Jackson and a host of others. Among the early ones was the eccentric David Crockett. With the division of the county began the decline of Perryville so that now it contains but few houses, one commission or store house, one general store and one hotel.

On October 17, 1821, the Legislature appointed John Blackburn, John Johnston, Worley Warrington, J. W. Nunley and Wm. B. Ross commissioners to lay off a town "to be called Carrollville, in honor of His Excellency Wm. Carroll," at Reeves Ferry. This town was on the lands of John Blackburn, John Johnston and Worley Warrington. It lay a short distance above Perryville but is now a town more in name than in reality. At the time of fixing the permanent capital of the State, Carrollville was one of the many contestants for the honor of being selected as the fortunate place.

The place known as Shannonsville was laid out in October, 1824, on the land of Robt. Shannon. It contained twenty acres in the original plat, and was laid out by James Wright, Fred C. Holland and Jackson White. There is little left to mark the site of the old town.

McNAIRY COUNTY.

McNAIRY COUNTY occupies the water-shed between the Tennessee and the Mississippi Rivers. The dividing ridge extends nearly due north and south through the middle of the county. The waters on the eastern slope flow into the Tennessee, and those on the western slope into the Mississippi. The eastern portion of the county is comparatively hilly, but interspersed with some excellent farming lands. The soil is mixed with sand and clay. The southern part of the county is more level, and has excellent soil which is of a darker color. The western and northwestern portions of the county are comparatively level. Those portions that are too broken for cultivation, those that are too sandy, and some of the flat lands, such as cypress swamps, are the only unprofitable lands in the county. The surface soil varies in thickness from four inches to twenty-four inches, and where the subsoil is of the proper kind is highly productive. The average depth of the soil is about seven inches. Beneath the surface is found the green sand, or rotten limestone, the Ripley group and the Flatwood clays. The two former belong to the cretaceous period, and the latter to the lignitic period. The green sand attains its greatest thickness in this county, amounting to 350 feet. In this bed are found oyster shells and other marine animals, and bears positive evidence of marine and lacustrine formations. The principal streams of McNairy are Snake Creek, named doubtless from its serpentine course, which rises about twelve miles southeast of Purdy and empties into the Tennessee River; Oxford Creek, named in honor of Abel Oxford who settled near its banks, rises nine south of Purdy and flows southwest into Cypress; Owl Creek, named from its being the resort of that prophetic bird, rises eight miles south of Purdy and flows easterly, and empties into the Tennessee; Cypress, so named from the growth along the stream, rises about four miles northwest of Purdy and flows in a southwesterly direction into Hatchie River; Hatchie Creek rises about ten miles northwest of Purdy and flows into the river of the same name. The most of these streams, if not all, have their origin in some of the numerous large springs in which the county abounds. The valuable timbers are the oak, hickory, ash, chestnut, pine and cypress. On the west side of the ridge may be seen the bay and on the east the beech.

The following is the population of the county at each census since 1830: 1830, 5,697; 1840, 9,385; 1850, 12,864; 1860, 14,732; 1870, 12,726; 1880, 17,271. The valuation of property has varied much within the last few years. In 1871 the total value of property in the county was put at $1,492,530; in 1872 it was $1,757,233; in 1884 it was $1,158,497; in 1885, $1,095,135; in 1886, $1,200,815, and in 1887 it is $1,002,121.

McNairy County, like all West Tennessee, belonged to the Chickasaw Indians previous to the treaty of October 19, 1818. The first settlers entered the county about 1820. It is not known who was the first to enter the county. W. S. Wisdon, the great financier of the county, arrived in it in 1821. He was one of the most widely known men in the county. He was county court clerk from 1832 to 1836. He died in Purdy in 1871 "full of years and honors." Benjamin Wright, father of Gen. Marcus J. Wright and others of that distinguished family, came to the county in 1823. He was a soldier in the Creek war, also in the Mexican war. Maclin Cross was one of the earliest settlers of the county, and was circuit court clerk from the organization till 1836. He was a lawyer, business man and politician. He left several sons. Dr. William Barnett was a prominent physician of Purdy, and originally from Williamson County; Joseph Barnett, county court clerk from 1824 to 1828, was a brother of Dr. William Barnett. R. S. Harwell was one of the first business men of Purdy, and was for half a century identified with the commercial interests of the place. Daniel Hill with his eight sons and their families, two sons-in-law and families, Isaac Coffman and Thomas Griffin, old Ben Walker, William Beatty, Samuel Houston, the Wilson and Rankin families, all came to the county in 1828, and settled in what is known as the Hill settlement, north of Purdy. They were from Jefferson County, Tenn. These pioneers formed a neighborhood of excellent citizens. The Hill family were long known for their extreme longevity. Jacob Jackson, a North Carolinian, and a soldier of the Creek war, came to McNairy County in 1826, where he lived till his death in 1880. He was for thirty years a justice of the peace. John Hamm, originally from South Carolina, moved to Kentucky, thence to Middle Tennessee, and in 1826 to McNairy County, and settled in the neighborhood of Rumor. He left a large family, the most of whom settled in the same county, and have since been identified with its interest. The senior member of the above mentioned family served four years in the Revolutionary war.

Archibald Houston, another Revolutionary soldier, moved to McNairy County from Pennsylvania in 1822. He was a man of great moral worth, and remained in the county till his death in 1837. John and Samuel Chambers were natives of South Carolina, the former coming to the county in 1820, and the latter in 1821. John Chambers first settled on Owl Creek, and later on Chambers Creek, to which he gave his name. He was connected with the organization of the county. Samuel Chambers also settled on Chambers Creek in the south part of the county, where he resided until his death in 1858. John, the brother, died in 1857. Abram Lorance, a native of North Carolina, came to McNairy in 1824, and settled in the north part of the county. He was a farmer by occupation, of unassuming mien, but held several important offices. He lived to a green old age. John Weaver came to McNairy from North Carolina in 1824, and settled in the northwest part of the county; he was a soldier of the Creek war, and was one of the hardy pioneers who helped to clear away the forest; he raised a large family, the most of whom still reside in the county. Javan Cox came to the county in 1826; he, too, was a Revolutionary soldier. John Maxedon, son-in-law of the above, also came to the county in 1826, and settled first in the north part of the county, but in 1829 he moved and settled near Bethel Springs. William Cason came from Middle Tennessee, and settled in the northwest part of McNairy County in 1826. He opened there a farm, where he reared an intelligent and honorable family. William T. Anderson came to McNairy County in 1822, and settled in the north part of the county. He opened a farm, and for a time managed a small still-house. As prosperity smiled on him he increased his lands and opened a store. He was a man of sterling integrity, and, at the outbreak of the war, was quite wealthy. Lindsey Saunders was a native of North Carolina; he came to McNairy in 1825; he held several positions of trust and profit; he was an unconditional Union man, and was endowed with "vision prophetic" on the question of secession, as is shown from his will as given elsewhere. A. A. Saunders, the fifth county court clerk, was a prominent minister of the Missionary Baptists. Hon. James Warren came to the county in 1827, where he has since resided. He has lived longer in the county than any man now living in it. He has three times represented his county in the Legislature. The families of McCann, Beard, McCullar,

Walsh, Ferguson, Dorion, Wilkinson, Rains and Stovall, had all settled in the county before 1827. Since it is the province of this article to give priority rather than prominence, there has been no order followed in speaking of them. From an article on "early settlers" of McNairy County from the pen of Hon. James Warren, above mentioned, the following settlers are mentioned as prominent in the county in 1827:

East part of the county—Beck, Erwin, Gilchrist, Jones, Kerr, Suttrell, McKinzie, Sanders, Veal and Wilson. Southeast—Atkins, Burk, Braden, Black, Cunningham, Donald, Dameron, Ealum, Forris, Michie, Sharp, Stubblefield and Wardlow. South—Barnhill, Chambers, Graham, Hooker, Hamm, Houston, Huggins, Littlejohn, Prather, Ramer, Springer, Boatman, Darby, Jeans, Forsyth, Henderson, Horn, McCullough, Meeks, Rains, Rotin and Simpson. Southwest—Derryberry, Flowers, Ferguson, Gooch, Kirk, Lock, McGuin, Null and Young. West—Bradshaw, Dillon, Hornbuckle, Kernodle, Laughlin, Lockman, McIntire, Moore, Robertson, Saunders, Stovall, Turner, Weatherly and Wilson. Northwest—Clayton, Cobb, Clemons, Floyd, Garner, Hurst, Jackson, Merchison, Mauess, Rowsey, Rankin, Smith, Schoffield, Stewart, Burkhead, Bryant, Cason, Deaton, Estes, Hodges, Johnson, Muse, McIntire, O'Neal, Randolph, Wamble, Wade and Weaver. North—Beard, Bullinger, Fowler, Hallis, Ingraham, Jones, Kirby, Lawrence, McHolstead, Plunk, Putnam, Patterson, Robinson, Robbins, Sipes, Smith, Sells, Sedford, Walsh and Ward. Northeast—Blackshear, Basinger, Combs, Carroll, Cochran, Cox, Hardin, Kemp, Landreth, Merrill, Massengill, Phillips, Parrish, Riggs, Stanley, Sewell Scott, Swain, Anderson, Bishop, Clark, Finley, Morrow, Oldham, Pitts, Smith, Shelton and Tidwell. Central—Adams, Barnes, Brooks, Bell, Beatty, Crump, Devault, Denny, Hill, Harwell, Jopling, Kincaid, Murray, McAlpin, Magill, Sweat, Surratt, Tatum, Walker, Wharton and Carter.

The loss by fire of the minute books of both the circuit and county court, renders it impossible to give the history of them previous to 1858. It is probable that Joshua Haskell was the first circuit judge and Alex B. Bradford was the attorney-general. In 1858 Elijah Walker was circuit judge and Lee M. Bently prosecuting attorney. The usual indictments for "larceny," "A & B," "presentments," etc., followed by "not guilty," nollied, etc., are seen. Henry, slave of J. P. Erwin, was indicted for killing "Diana Erwin, a free, white woman." The offense was committed April 22, 1860, by striking the victim over the head with a billet of wood. The case came before the following jury: Shadrack Maness, John Cannon, Wm. Vertrees, Samuel Irvine, Benjamin New, E. S. Boyington, B. J. Young, G. W. Prewett, J. C. Goodman, F. F. Carroll, Joseph Roark and John Murdock on July 12, 1860, and he was sentenced to hang Tuesday September 7, 1860. The execution was duly carried out on that day. Being the first legal hanging in the county, it drew an immense concourse to witness the scene.

The following will of Lindsey Sanders and wife, written in 1857, seems somewhat prophetic: "Lindsey Sanders and wife, Mary Ann Sanders, who have accumulated their means under the auspices of high Heaven, and the protection of the laws of our county, therefore we covenant and agree that no avowed infidel, atheist, deist, disunionist or secessionist, which is the same thing, shall ever be a beneficiary of our estate. We believe that any rational, intelligent being so low and depraved in morals, so much under the dominion of Satan as to dispute the natural evidence of a Supreme Ruler and Creator and that He has revealed this will to man, or deny our Lord and Savior Jesus Christ, is unworthy of partaking of the good things of this world, with which the good men and women have been blessed. And any American citizen so low and depraved in politics, so wanting in fidelity to our glorious Union as to desire a dissolution or a separation of our State from our sister States, is not only wholly unworthy of enjoying the good things afforded by the National Union but should be driven from the American soil." It further recites that if any of the children should forget themselves as to marry a disunionist or secessionist or any person excluded by this will, that one is no longer a beneficiary of it. It further excludes any one from its benefits if they resort to law for settlement of the estate. The desires of Mr. Sanders were never fully carried out.

A very exciting case was that of M. J. Braden against John W. Stump. This originated on the question of the removal of the county seat. This question has overshadowed every other legal question. Politics, social ties, and too often religion, are forgotten and overshadowed by the question of "removal or no removal." This first came up in 1870, and a vote was had but it was defeated on constitutional grounds. The points for which votes have been had are Falcon and Bethel Springs. On August 23, 1884, an election was held on the question of removal from Purdy to Falcon. There were cast for "removal" 1,921, and "no removal" 560 votes and a few scattering votes for other places. On October 6, 1884, the county court met and canvassed the vote and declared that the measure had carried and that more than two-thirds of the legal voters—the constitutional number required—had voted for removal. The court appointed J. L. Smith and several others to procure a suitable place of deposit and to remove the records thither. This was done promptly and hastily. In October an injunction was filed in the chancery court against the proceedings of the county court on the ground that two-thirds of the qualified voters had not voted for the change. Depositions of over 500 witnesses were taken, and the case was brought before Chancellor George Nixon, who decided against the action of the county court and ordered the records returned to Purdy. An appeal was taken to the supreme court at Jackson when the decision of the lower court was sustained. After a disturbance of seventeen years and an expenditure of from $7,000 to $10,000, the case stands *in statu quo ante bellum*. The attorneys for complainant were Pitts & Hays and for defendant were A. W. Campbell and Wm. M. Inge. Some very able men have been in practice before the McNairy bar. Many of these have gone to wider fields. The oldest member of the present bar is I. W. Huddleston. The younger members are J. D. Christopher and McDougal & Braden.

I. P. Bateman, circuit judge, and Geo. H. Nixon, chancellor, are best known of the later judges owing to their long term of service. During a period of sixteen years the latter never missed a single court. He determined 402 cases and heard 1,506 prayers.

McNairy County, like all other counties in the State, was organized under the militia law. As it was first organized it was Regiment No. 107. The colonels of this regiment named in order were J. T. Burtwell, N. C. Riggs, R. D. Wilson and James Johnson. The lieutenant-colonels were Thomas Hamrick, Thomas Patterson and F. M. Massengill. On the organization of Regiment No. 108 Samuel Graham became colonel. The other colonels to the breaking out of the war were John Campbell, John H. Meeks, O. L. Meeks, J. M. Kirk and W. W. Jeanes. The lieutenant-colonels in order were John Deberry, J. L. Henderson, J. N. Barnhill, J. D. Young and Isaac Booth. The brigadier-generals of the militia were — Graham, R. P. Neely, J. H. Meeks and W. D. Jepling. The regimental and field officers as they stood on the roll August 10, 1861, were W. G. McKay, J. W. Beard, W. J. Massengill, R. W. P. Pool, S. J. Cheney, P. S. Wisdom, P. W. Martin and Daniel Barry. Aside from a few isolated [individual] volunteers no regular troops were mustered in the county till 1861. The county voted 1,318 votes for "separation" and 586 for "no separation." The first company raised in the county was the "Wright Boys," who became F of the Thirteenth Regiment. This company was organized Tuesday, May 21, 1861, at Purdy, by electing J. V. Wright, captain; D. M. Wisdom, first lieutenant; S. W. Henry, second lieutenant; H. S. Pinkston, third lieutenant. John P. Johnson, first; W. S. Raney, second; Jas. Wiley, third; Jas. Houston, fourth, and Rufus Stinnett, fifth sergeants. J. F. Smith, first; A. J. Thomasson, second; E. W. Vail, third, and Leroy Hill, fourth corporals. On the organization of the regiment J. V. Wright became colonel and D. M. Wisdom, captain. Other promotions followed. This company consisted at this time of seventy-three men, rank and file, and on May 28, 1861, it left for Jackson. The second company was the McNairy Guards. This company organized by electing Alphonso Cross, captain; A. M. Covey, first lieutenant; J. B. Cross, second lieutenant; T. D. Moore, third lieutenant. E. L. Sanders, first; J. D. Page, second; J. P. Smith, third; J. K. Byrn, fourth; R. E. Stewart, fifth sergeants. R. C. Wilkinson, first; D. P. McKinzie, second; J. W. Howell, third, and M. R. Haly, fourth corporals. This company consisted of seventy-seven men besides the officers. This company became a part of the One Hundred and Fifty-fourth, which was organized at Memphis. The recruiting was not so rapid after this time and it

M'NAIRY COUNTY.

took more work to recruit troops than before as the realities of war began to present themselves. The next company of infantry recruited in the county was the Washingtonians. This body was recruited in the summer of 1862. The officers of this company were Alva S. Johnson, captain; Samuel Anderson, T. C. Wilkinson and J. L. Morphis, lieutenants. These men were attached to the Twenty-seventh Regiment. Three companies from this county were sent to the Thirty-first Tennessee (Confederate, West Tennessee) Regiment. These were the companies of Capts. W. Y. Baker, Caleb McNight and W. B. Clayton. The regiment was organized by electing A. H. Bradford, colonel; C. H. Cason, lieutenant-colonel, and John Smith, major; the two last named were from McNairy County. These were organized in the summer of 1862.

The Thirty-second Cavalry contained two companies from McNairy, E and F. The officers of E were Albert Cross and John Michie, captains; Albert Casey and M. Whorton, first lieutenants; E. R. Turner, second lieutenant; J. R. Adams, third lieutenant. The officers of F were Robt. Dameron, captain; John Meeks, first lieutenant; John Veal, second lieutenant; Alex Winningham, third lieutenant. The operations of these men were mainly through West Tennessee, northern Mississippi and Alabama under Gen. Forrest. In addition to these there was also a battalion of cavalry under Col. A. N. Wilson. It has been found impossible to get the list of companies belonging to this body, as well as a part of a company belonging to Smith's battery.

There was a very large per cent of the people of the county who adhered to the Union. It became impossible to live in the county without taking sides. The advance of the Federals after the capture of Fort Donelson left the State in possession of the Union forces. Fielding Hurst, who had been imprisoned by the Confederate authorities, was now free and was commissioned by Gen. Johnson to raise a regiment of troops for the Federal service. By October, 1862, Companies A, B, C, D and G had been raised on the west side of the river. This became the Sixth Union Tennessee Cavalry. The following were the regimental and field officers: Fielding Hurst, colonel; W. K. M. Breckenridge, lieutenant-colonel; E. S. Tidwell, R. M. Thompson, majors; Thomas Williams, surgeon; Joe E. Morvin, assistant surgeon; W. J. Smith, regimental quartermaster; T. M. Clayton, regimental commissary; J. J. Smith, chaplain; S. L. Warren, adjutant; B. S. Walker, sergeant-major; J. F. Tidwell, hospital steward; J. R. Ray, regimental quartermaster sergeant; J. A. Lockey, regimental commissary sergeant. Numerous changes occurred during the war. The following was the organization at the close of the war: W. J. Smith, colonel; O. H. Scheorer, lieutenant-colonel; M. J. Liening, S. L. Warren, majors; L. O. Summers, assistant surgeon; J. H. Thorington, adjutant; R. W. Eskredge, regimental commissary sergeant; W. A. Newsom, regimental quartermaster. The officers of Company A were A. M. Thompson, B. J. Riggs and Samuel Lewis, captains; James J. Smith and C. H. Deford, first lieutenants; Thos. Craugh and Wm. H. Swain, second lieutenants. The officers of B were Harry Hodges and Elijah J. Hodges, captains; Francis M. Tucker, first lieutenant; Samuel D. Hanna, Wm. W. Kirby and John Huddleston, second lieutenants. The officers of Company C were Nathan M. D. Kemp, captain; W. T. Smith and Thomas Craugh, first lieutenants; James M. Sanders, second lieutenant. Company D, L. Hurst and James L. W. Boatman, captains; Zach. Norcott, James R. Norcott and John P. Gibbs. first lieutenants; James L. Hardwick, second lieutenant. The officers of Company G* were Elijah Roberts, Wm. Chandler and Wm. C. Webb, captains; J. L. W. Boatman, first lieutenant; Wm. F. Balright and Isaac J. Shull, second lieutenants. The organization of the remaining companies may be seen under the history of Hardin County. These men being acquainted with the roads and peculiarities of the people of Tennessee, they were mainly used in piloting other parties, picking up stragglers of the enemy, and in preventing their recruiting within the lines. A sketch of the Sixth may be seen on page 507 of the State history of this volume.

The act creating McNairy County passed the General Assembly November 8, 1823, and was entitled, "An act to establish a new county west of Hardin County." "Beginning at the southwest corner of Hardin County, running thence north with the west

*Company G was mainly from Decatur County.

boundary of the same twenty-seven and one-half miles, thence west passing the southeast corner of Madison County to a point three miles west of the first range line in the Ninth District; thence south parallel with said range line to the south boundary of this State; thence east on said boundary to the beginning." It was named in honor of Judge John McNairy, and at that time contained 645 square miles or 412,800 acres. These numbers do not allow for the change made in the southern boundary lines by the several surveys. The formation of Chester County robbed McNairy of about 40,000 acres of her territory. It belonged to the western district and was under control of Stewart County till separated as above stated. The present county seat was chosen for the county by James Fentress, Benjamin Reynolds, James Martin and Robert Jetton. Fifty acres, the usual amount required for a county seat, was obtained from John Yount and originally entered by John Phillips. The courts met at the "house of Abel V. Murray, near the center of said county, until otherwise provided by law." This house stood about four miles southwest of Purdy.

The courthouse built in Purdy was a log house about 18x20 feet with clapboard roof and puncheon floor. A more substantial house of brick was built in 1830. This was a brick building and stood until 1881, when it was destroyed by fire, and up to the present time has not been rebuilt. In 1884 $15,000 was appropriated for building a new courthouse, but this was afterward reduced to $8,000. Plans and specifications were drawn and the contract was let for the erection of the new building at Purdy. A restraining order was issued, settlement was made with the contractor and the building committee discharged. The matter thus stands. The builders of the first courthouse are not remembered, but the one built in 1830 was erected by James Reed (Uncle Biddle) and Reuben Walker, with Henry Kirkland as brick-mason.

The first jail was built about the time of the building of the brick courthouse. This was an improvised affair and was replaced by a better one soon after. The present jail and sheriff's residence was built about 1850. It is a substantial brick building with ample accommodations.

The poor were cared for by individuals in different parts of the county, and allowances made by the county court, until 1849, when 120 acres of land was purchased from William S. Wisdom for $350, and deeded to Laney Moore, Maclin Cross and A. A. Sanders as commissioners of the poor. All county charges were then required to go to the poorhouse for care. This was used as the poorhouse until 1884, when, the timber on the land having became exhausted, and other difficulties arising, it was deemed best to sell the lands. These were sold to James Warren for $355. The keeping of the paupers was then let to D. M. Baker, who prepared buildings and contracted to keep the inmates for $72 per capita per annum for a term of three years.

A great spirit of internal improvement pervaded the county from 1833 to 1850. The General Assembly of 1837-38 chartered the Chambers & Purdy Turnpike leading from Purdy to the State line, fifteen miles south of Purdy. By the act one half the stock was taken by the State and the other half was taken by individual stockholders. Wm. H. Beaves, who was a member of the Assembly, returned home, organized a company and secured a subscription for half the stock, and organized directors and officers. The governor appointed an equal number of directors. The road was put under contract to Beaves and upon certificate. State bonds, five in number, of $1,000 at 5 per cent were issued to Beaves, who instead of investing the money in labor on the road, discounted his bonds and bought a stock of goods. The road has never been built and the contractor soon after moved to Texas.

The Memphis & Charleston Railroad was the first built that touched McNairy County. This was chartered in February, 1846, but was not completed till 1857. To aid this the State gave $1,700,000 in bonds. It extends eleven miles through the southern part of the county. The next was the Mobile & Ohio, which was chartered in 1848 and completed in 1859. The State of Tennessee issued to this road $1,296,000 in bonds. The road extends through the county from north to south almost dividing the county in two equal parts. On failure to raise $100,000 in tax and in subscriptions Purdy failed to be a point on the road. At the time of its inception it was the most gigantic railroad scheme on either continent. This road by its charter rights is exempt from taxation. Thus the twenty-eight miles of this road is exempt from taxation, while the Memphis & Charleston Road pays taxes on $179,517.70 for eleven miles of Road, and the Western Union Telegraph Company pays on $2,881.81 for its lines.

Sheriffs—Henry S. Wilson, 1824-28; Laney Moore, 1828-32; Willey B. Terry, 1832-36; James Boyd, 1836-38; James Warren, 1838-44; N. C. Riggs, 1844-50; Andrew McKee, 1850-56; Wm. D. Jopling, 1856-62; Samuel Lewis, 1865-66; J. H. Mitchell, 1866-68; J. L. W. Boatman, 1868-70; W. D. Jopling, 1870-76; J. R. Stovall, 1876-82; W. D. Jopling, 1882-86; W. M. Brown, 1887. County court clerks—Joseph Barrett, 1824-28; Benjamin Jones, 1828-32; William S. Wisdom, 1832-36; J. R. Adams, 1836-44; A. A. Saunders, 1844-56; Joseph Walker, 1856-64; R. M. Thompson, 1866-70; Calvin Shull, 1870-78; Job Bell, 1878-82; J. R. Adams, 1882, term expires 1890. Circuit clerks—Maclin Cross, 1824-36; Peter E. Shull (died); Laney Moore, 1837-40; Lindsey Saunders, 1840-48; A. J. Kincaid, 1848-52; Lindsey Saunders, 1852-56; Milton H. Johnson, 1856-64; D. N. Huddleston, 1865-70; G. E. Meeks and G. M. Moore, 1870-76; W. D. Jopling, 1876-78; T. F. Dalbey, 1878, term expires 1890. Registers—William and A. V. Murray, 1824-36; A. W. Murray, 1836-40; R. S. Harwell, 1840-44; A. M. McKee, 1844-48; Benjamin Wright, 1848-60; Alfred Moore and Asa Bell, 1860-64; George M. Moore, 1866-70; E. R. Turner, 1870-78; James H. Curry, 1878, term expires 1890. Surveyors—Benjamin Wright, Thomas H. Bell, John M. Bell, Fielding Hurst, C. H. Moore, Miles Moore, Fielding Hurst, R. W. Michie and others. Representatives—John M. Johnson, 1835-37; William H. Reaves, 1837-39; John M. Johnson, 1839-41; M. A. Trice, 1841-45; James Warren, 1845-49; John H. Meeks, 1849-53; William F. Brown, 1853-55; J. B. Smith, 1855-57; J. W. Estes, 1857-59; J. L. Morphis, 1859-61; William D. Jopling, 1861-63; S. L. Warren, 1865-67; E. J. Hodges, 1867-69; S. L. Warren, 1869-70; R. S. Houston, 1870-72; E. M. Tillman, 1872-74; Dr. James Mitchell, 1874-76; B. M. Tillman, 1876-78; A. W. Stovall, 1878-80; James Warren, 1880-82; T. J. Barnhill, 1884-85; Job Bell, 1886-87. Trustees—Robert M. Owens, Reuben Hill, John Wharton, David McKinzie, Jacob Lawrence, John A. Moore, David Horn, J. A. Miller, J. L. Littlefield, term expires 1888. Chancellors—S. C. Pavatt, ——; R. H. Rose, 1867; James W. Doherty, 1868-70; G. H. Nixon, 1870-86; A. G. Hawkins, 1887. Clerk and masters—Alphonso Cross, ——; E. C. Hunt, 1867; W. C. Rigg, 1868-70; T. R. Beck, 1870-79; Robert E. McKinney, 1879.

Doubtless the oldest Presbyterian Church in the county is the one at Bethel, which was organized on September 7, 1828, by Rev. John Gillespie, with the following members: Alexander McCullar, George Kidd, W. B. Wilson, Ann Kidd, John Gilliam, Alex M. Brown, Nancy Brown, Rosanna Gilliam, Lydia Wilson, Jane McCullar and Mary Houdon. Alexander McCullar, George Kidd, W. B. Wilson, John Gilliam and A. M. Brown were chosen ruling elders. Rev. Gillespie preached to this flock for a time, and was followed by Rev. John L. Sloan, who remained till 1836. In 1840 Rev. H. M. Kerr was installed as pastor of this church. It is the only Presbyterian Church in the county.

Perhaps the first church of the Baptist denomination was organized in the Hill settlement, north of Purdy, in 1830, by the Rev. Franklin Beard, who became its pastor. This church is called Macedonia. Another church of this denomination is at Gravel Hill. In 1878 forty-eight acres of land were purchased by N. L. Thomas for $450, for a parsonage for the churches at Macedonia, Cool Springs (Hardin County), and Gravel Hill.

The Purdy Cumberland Presbyterian Church was organized by the Rev. Wm. M. Dunaway August 19, 1851. John H. Black, A. Jeff Moore, W. D. McKinney and S. J. Cheney were chosen elders. There were in all sixty-nine members. The most of these were received by confession made in 1832 at Mt. Zion, Mt. Vernon and other places, and others by transfer from other churches in the county. W. D. McKinney was elected clerk of the session and served till his death in May, 1857, when C. F. Sawyer was elected clerk, who served till 1860, when he was succeeded by F. M. Bell. The church was reorganized July 15, 1872, owing to disturbances caused by the war, by the election of Simpson Kernodle and Isaac W. Nash as ruling elders. The latter was also elected clerk, a position which he still holds. The membership at Purdy is now fifty-three. The house of worship was erected about the time of the organization conjointly with Purdy Lodge, No. 132, F. & A. M. The church at Mt. Vernon, near Ramer, is probably the oldest Cumberland Church in the county. This was organized about 1832, and is still the strongest congregation within the bounds of the Madison presbytery, having by report 119 members. Mt. Zion with a membership of now sixteen was in existence in 1833, and how much earlier is unknown to the writer. Other congregations with their members are Mud Creek Valley with thirty-six; New Bethel, thirty-seven; New Salem, seventy-one; Pleasant Hill No. 2, twenty-seven; Pleasant Ridge, fifty-one; Ramer, fifty-one; Sharon, thirty-four; Union Grove, twenty-one, and Adamsville, fifty-four. Several old churches, such as Green Bay, New Providence, have become extinct.

The origin of the Missionary Baptists as a separate organization from what is termed the Primitive Baptists dates about 1817, and points to Elder Reuben Ross as its founder. While this church claims to be the "Regular" Baptists, the public usually designates them as the Missionary Baptists and the other branch as "anti-Missionary" or "Regular Baptists." The first association was formed in October, 1825, and was known as the "Bethel Association," having eight churches, and in a short time five additional ones. Churches were generally organized in West Tennessee till 1833, and the first convention was held in 1835. Some of the pioneer ministers were Jerry Burns, Thomas Owen, P. S. Gayle, C. G. Conner, N. G. Smith, George N. Young, J. M. Hart and David Haliburton. Among the pioneer ministers of this county may be mentioned A. A. Sanders, Reuben Day, A. S. Dorris, W. H. Hodges, E. Washburn and Lewis Savage. Perhaps the first church of this denomination was Pleasant Sight, near ———, in 1828. This church has a membership of forty at present.

The first church edifice built in Purdy was erected by the Methodists. This was on a lot deeded by Austin Miller to S. D. Pace, John Brooks and one other party in 1832. This was a log building and stood across the run north of Purdy. Later a frame church was erected, but this was blown down and was never rebuilt. The churches of this county belong to the Falcon, ——— and Adamsville Circuits; the former of these has six churches, the second four, and the last five churches, having membership of between 800 and 900. Some of these individual churches, however, are not in this county. In addition to the Methodist Episcopal Churches there are also one or two Protestant Methodist Churches and quite a number of colored churches.

Until after the close of the war and the reorganization, the public schools of the county were without system. Good isolated schools were to be found in many neighborhoods and villages almost from the organization of the county. Among the early teachers may be mentioned F. M. Prince, 1825; Wilson McMahan, 1827; Mrs. M. B. Chaney, 1828; Miss Delia Swann, 1844; Miss Loraine Hall, 1848; Miss Maria Bomar, 1850; Miss Rachel D. Halpin, 1851; Miss Hattie Barbee, 1854; R. D. Miller, Mrs. Eudora Miller, James M. Miller, 1848. Others were Barrett Lock, James Comer, Andrew McKee, David A. Street, Isaac Self and Alva Johnson. Under the law for establishing county seminaries a lot was purchased in the west part of Purdy from John Reese, upon which was erected the male and female academy. This was done in 1840 and Wm. S. Wisdom, Maclin Cross, S. O. Pace, Alfred Moore and A. A. Sanders were made trustees. A brick building was erected on this lot and the schools taught at the place till 1857. Desiring to enlarge the usefulness of this school, in 1855 W. A. Kindle, Pleasant Coats, J. F. McKinnie, C. C. Lawler, F. P. Duke, David McKenzie, J. N. Barnhill and J. M. McAlpin had the Purdy University incorporated. Stock was limited to $10 per share. Out of the proceeds of this stock was the present college building erected, and was carried successfully till suspended on account of the war. After the war the stock was bought up and the school put under control of the Methodist Episcopal Church South with Alva Johnson as president. Next it passed to the Wesleyan Methodists under R. M. Thompson, then to the Methodist Episcopal under Prof. Wright, but he failed. It then became the Bolivar District High School. The school is now under control of M. R. Abernathy, whom the stockholders allow the use of the building. An excellent school has been maintained by Mr. Abernathy for the last two years with growing interest. The school is now maintained for ten months in the year. Good schools are usually maintained at Adamsville and other villages of the county. The superintendent's report shows that there were expended last year $9,726.99 in teachers' salaries and that the total expense of the schools was $11,505.32. The white scholastic population of the county is 4,891; colored, 712, or a total of 5,609. There are 82 white teachers and 14 colored teachers. The number of white children enrolled in the school was 4,520, and the number of colored was 320. The average salary of teachers is $32.50. The average length of school term is forty days.

Purdy, the county seat of McNairy County, stands on grounds deeded by John Yount to George W. Barnett, A. V. Murray, William S. Wisdom, Robert Rankins and Thompson M. Price, town commissioners. The land embraces fifty acres of a 214-acre tract, entered by Joseph Phillips. The deed was made to the commissioners on August 24, 1825, the consideration being Lot No. 26 of the original plat. The town was laid off by Col. John Purdy of Henderson County, for whom the town was named, and Mayor Benjamin Wright. The auction sales of lots were made in September, 1825, by William S. Wisdom. The first purchasers of the lots were P. E. Shull, Thomas McAlpin, George W. Barnett, James Reed, J. F. Cloud, Atwood & Murray, Maclin Cross, W. S. Wisdom, James Boyd, J. T. Burtwell, A. E. Griffith, John Chamles, Elisha Hodges, H. B. Mitchell, Austin Miller, William Hopkins, S. N. Pryor, T. G. Hudspeth, J. P. Yount, William Ruleman, Wisdom & Dickens. The first store in Purdy was opened soon after the sale of lots, by John Chambers and Nat Griffith. Their stock consisted of a little tinware, some domestics, a few groceries and other necessaries, and in all probability some "spirituous liquors." The most profitable trade at this time was with the Indians, who were better supplied with money and peltries than their white brethren. From an inscription on the monument of Mayor Wright it is learned that he built the first cabin in the place. He was county surveyor and on the establishment of a postoffice, became the first postmaster. Other early residents of the place were the Adamses, Barneses, Brookses, Bells, Beatys, Crumps, Devaults, Dennys, Hills, Harwells, Joplings, Kincaids, Magills, Sweats, Suratts, Tatums, Walkers, Whartons and Carters. The progress of the place was not rapid, but its growth was constant and substantial, and at the outbreak of the war Purdy was a thriving village with business houses extending around the square. Since that time a multiplicity of causes have militated against it, fires and the question of removal of the county seat being the principal. The principal business men of the past have been John Chambers & Nathaniel Griffith, R. I. Chester & W. S. Wisdom, John T. Burtwell, H. B. Michell, Garrett & Kirkland, Reuben Moore, John Brooks, Moore & Tally, Wisdom & Shull, I. P. Young; Miller, Moore & Wisdom, Terry & Wisdom, Maclin Cross, Cross & Moore, Kincaid & Harwell, A. B. McLaughlin, Charles Teas, L. Saunders & Bro., A. A. Saunders, Hall & Bro., Wisdom & Walsh, Harwell & Shull, Bell & Wisdom, J. K. Duke, Cross & Cates. The principal business of Purdy is now done by W. H. Braden, W. S. McIntire and J. P. Prince. There are also several good boarding-houses.

Purdy Lodge, No. 132, F. & A. M. was chartered October 8, 1847. The charter members were Fielding Hurst, W. M.; Laney Moore, S. W.; Thomas Combs, J. W. Other members were B. R. Harris, Samuel Pace, James F. McKinney, James Warren, James Lane, James Richards, James L. Kindle, James Denny and P. H. Braden. The lodge was set to work under the auspices of Savannah Lodge. The officers now are T. F. Dalbey, W. M.; T. A. Hippe, S. W.; W. C. Chaness, J. W.; T. H. Curry, Sec.; Asa Bell, Treas.; D. W. Cobb, S. D.; Miles Needham, J. D. and W. Case, Tyler. The membership is thirty-four.

The first paper ever published in Purdy was the *West Tennessee Argus*, the first number of which was issued in August, 1856, by I. W. Nash and S. L. Warner. Mr. Nash was identified with the paper from its inception to its close. In April, 1859, its name was changed or it was consolidated with, and became the *Whig Banner*. This was continued until the spring of 1862, when it suspended on account of the war.

The McNairy *Independent* is just completing Volume VIII, and is owned and edited by M. R. Abernathy. The *Independent* is a good home paper with a good circulation and has a good advertising patronage. It is independent in politics.

The *Democrat* is a small Democratic paper published by Dr. Barry & Son. It is a new candidate for public favor, having had but about one year's existence.

The professional men of Purdy are Drs. Bell and Barry; attorneys, I. F. Huddleston, J. D. Christopher and McDougal & Braden.

Adamsville was named in honor of Geo. G. Adams, one of the most distinguished men of the county. It is eight miles east from Purdy and about four miles west of Crump's Landing, on the Tennessee River, and is within one mile of the Hardin County line. It is the best business point in the county. By the last census Adamsville had eighty town lots, valued at $26,565. In February, 1870, the place was incorporated for a term of ninety-nine years. The town limits included one mile square. The town contains an excellent school, churches and the following business men: W. Y. Bell, L. F. Adams, James Adams, T. N. Cheatham, G. W. Sipes, G. A. Sipes, W. E. Parrish, F. M. Freeman, J. B. Newell, J. S. Perkins, J. C. Dodd and Perkins & Atkins.

McNairy Station is ten miles northwest of Purdy on the Mobile & Ohio Railroad. Being near the county line it took the name of the county. It was laid out about the time of the completion of the railroad. It contains fifty-three town lots and about 150 inhabitants. The business-men of the place are J. P. & E. F. Rodgers, G. W. Brown and J. G. Crow.

Bethel Springs is four and a half miles west of Purdy and is also on the Mobile & Ohio Railroad. It was so named from the large spring which rises there and from the old Presbyterian Church or Bethel which was established there in 1828. The town was not laid out till after the completion of the railroad. It was laid out on the lands of J. H. Bell, in January, 1860. The village was occupied first by the Confederate and afterward by the Federal troops. By the latter it was occupied as a permanent post till the close of the war. The population now is about 200 of which one-fourth is negroes. Bethel is second only to Adamsville in point of business. The business men of Bethel are Tatum, O'Neal & Co., J. R. Stovall, J. P. Epps, Pigott & Bro., Hendrix & Bro., J. J. Prince and J. W. Wilson. There are two hotels: the Sanders House and the Ammon House; also two churches—Presbyterian and Methodist.

The village of Falcon contains about 150 inhabitants. It is on the Mobile & Ohio Railroad six miles southwest of Purdy. It has been built up since the war. The village embraces an area of fifty-two lots. In 1884 this became the seat of justice for the county, but it was soon moved back to Purdy. The business men of the place are R. H. Freeman, W. E. Tedford, W. F. P. Browder and J. W. Prather & J. W. Simper. Hotel, L. M. Leech. Professional men: Drs. Smith and Atkinson; J. W. Pace, attorney. The *Falcon Review* is a sprightly little paper published by W. E. Grimes. It is independent in politics.

A short distance below Falcon on the same road is Ramer. This was named from the family of that name who live in the village and vicinity. It took its origin about the time other villages sprang up on the Mobile & Ohio Railroad. The population of the place is about 100. The business men of the place are B. F. Potts, Z. T. Potts and A. B. Hamm.

The population of the village of Chewalla, on the Memphis & Charleston Railroad, is about fifty. The village sprang up on the railroad about the time of its completion, and the name is of Indian origin. J. C. Resser does the business of the place.

Gravel Hill, fourteen miles south of Purdy, and Stantonville eight miles southeast of the same place, have business houses: J. J. Huggins and L. H. Roberson at the former, and J. R. Hurley and Wesly McDaniel at the latter. L. T. Smith and W. P. Pitts do business at Milledgeville, near the northeast corner of the county. Other business places are New South, O'Neal's Mill, Mississippi State Line and one or two other places.

HARDIN COUNTY.

HARDIN COUNTY is divided into two nearly equal divisions by the Tennessee River, which enters about midway on the south side and passes out near the northeast corner. The river forms an irregular bow from where it enters the county to Point Pleasant, whence it bends abruptly almost due east to the limit of the county. The basin of the Tennessee extends to the water-shed between the Tennessee and the Hatchie and Forked Deer on the west and considerably beyond the limits of the county on the east. The principal points on the river are Pyburn's Bluff, so named from an early settler, Crump's Landing and Coffee Landing, both of which are explained elsewhere. Swallow Bluff, below Point Pleasant, is so named from the birds hovering there. The principal islands are Diamond Island, so named from its shape; Wolf Island, so named from an early settler; Delaney, from Jacob Delaney, and Eagle Nest Island, formerly James Island, but took the former name on the sinking of the Eagle off that island. The principal streams on the east side of this river have a northwesterly course. Beginning at the north and on the east side the first stream emptying is Short Creek. This is a small stream, as its name indicates. The next is Hardin Creek, which flows in almost a direct line. The next large stream is Indian Creek, so named from the natives. The principal tributaries of this are Flat Gap, Duncan and Smith Fork. The two latter were named from early settlers. Almost parallel with Indian Creek is Horse Creek, named, it is said, from the early resort of horse thieves. Its tributaries are Gooden, Steele, Turkey and Holland Creeks. These were named from pioneer settlers, except Turkey, and which took its name from the abundance of that game on its banks. A small stream called Mud Creek enters into the Tennessee near Savannah, and another one near Walnut Grove called Dry Creek. The name of each is its own explanation. On the west side is first seen Yellow Creek, then Chambers Creek, named from John Chambers. Next comes Lick Creek and Snake Creek, with its two tributaries, Owl and Clear. These streams are rendered historic from the battle of Shiloh fought near them. Entering the Tennessee near Coffee is Reason Creek. The principal stream, however, on the west side is White Oak River, which enters the Tennessee just above Saltillo. The tributaries of White Oak from the south are Chalk, Crooked and Mud Creeks. Those from the north are Middleton, Hurricane, Delaney, Alexander and Miles Creeks. A small stream also enters the Tennessee near Point Pleasant called Doe Creek. The most of these streams afford excellent mill sites. Nearly all of them have their source in some one of the numerous large springs in which the county abounds. These are more numerous on the east side of the river. The first known of these is Altum Spring, near Hardin Creek. Big Spring, near the Southern part of the county, is formed by the sinking and rising again of Dry Creek. On the west side of the river, not far from the Big Springs, are the White and the Red Sulphur Springs. Gan, or Davy Spring, near Saltillo, is one of the largest in the county. In 1835 a well was begun near Saltillo, prospecting for salt. A depth of 800 feet was obtained, when the work was abandoned. A flow of sulphur water (water impregnated with hydrogen?) was the result, and it has since been known as the Sulphur Well. The Red Sulphur Springs are doubtless the result of iron oxides and a little hydrogen. The former of these elements is abundant in the soil of the eastern part, and the latter is also found in the west in the form of light carbonetted hydrogen, resulting from the decay of the vast amount of vegetable matter under water. The water obtained by boring or digging varies as the deposit in which it is found. About 140 square miles of the county lies in the Tennessee River bottom proper. This, of course, is mainly of alluvial formation, and the mutable habits of the river has left its marks in the old river beds that are now nearly filled up, but have left their distinct outline. Some of these are filled with water and thus become swamps, lakes or ponds. Logs, sticks and all forms of vegetable matter in various stages of decay are found in this deposit by digging. The geological formations are those mentioned, and the Helderberg, and its various grades, the limestone shales, sandstone, orange or green sand, Coffee sand seen at Coffee Landing, Pittsburg Landing and elsewhere, loess or silt. Portions show lacustrine, flusatile, fluno-marine and marine formation. It seems that an arm of the Mexican Gulf once extended over a large portion of this county. This is evident from the numerous oyster and other salt water shells found in the deposits. Little limestone is met with west of the river; the only place where it is found is in the southern part, while some gravel beds are found in the northern parts. The highlands west of the river are mainly composed of orange sand. The main portion east of the river contains limestone and some portions large gravel beds. This gravel predominates to such a degree in the northeastern corner of the county as to render portions of it destitute of vegetation. Various sea shells are found in this gravel. Hydraulic rock is found on the east side of the river. A mill was erected near the mouth of Indian Creek, before the war, for the manufacture of hydraulic cement. Good marble is found on the river below Savannah and on Hardin Creek, also plenty of good building stone in the eastern part, but neither of these have been extensively used. The valley of the large stream on the east side of the river is well suited for the cereals, while the uplands and poorer soil produce good crops of peanuts. The low lands on the west side grow fine corn and cotton. The whole of White Oak Valley is excellent farming land. Valuable timber grows in the greater portion of the county. Among the many kinds of timber may be mentioned pine, cedar, chestnut, maple, poplar, walnut, birch, beech, ash, cypress, hickory and the various varieties of oak. Lumber is shipped extensively to the Evansville, St. Louis and other markets. Large quantities of iron ore are found in various parts of the county, which it is hoped will at no distant day yield a valuable income.

One of the first white man to press the soil of Hardin County was Col. Joseph Hardin and his crew, who came to the county in 1815 from Roane County, Tenn., to locate a land warrant of Col. Hardin amounting to 2,000 acres. This was located a little above Cerro Gordo on the east side of the river. After the survey had been made Col. Hardin cut his name in the bark of a birch tree at the mouth of Swift Creek and returned home. In the spring of 1816 a colony of twenty-six persons consisting of men, women and children began making preparations for removal from the uninviting regions of East Tennessee to the more inviting fields of Hardin County. The company was divided into two parties, one of which was to pass down the river by boat and the other was to travel overland. There were twenty-six in all, twenty-two of whom came by land and four by boat. The party traveling by land consisted of John Brazelton and family, except two who came by boat; Joseph Hardin, Jr., and family; James Hardin and family and Mrs. Elender Tucker and family. These left Roane County sometime about the last of May, driving their stock along and carrying their light plunder with them. They camped out at night and journeyed by day over an almost roadless waste. On July 15 they reached what is now called Crowder's spring on Hardin Creek about seven miles from the river. This party had been delayed in Warren County and were later in their arrival than was anticipated. By previous arrangement the two parties were to meet at the place marked. Soon after their arrival they heard the signal bugle of the party who came by water. On the following day the two parties met near the Altum Springs on Hardin Creek, named in honor of the founder of the county. Here was built a log cabin, the first house in the county. The party in the boat started early in June—it consisted of Solomon Brazelton, Miss Sally Brazelton, Joseph Gooden and wife. Thus for three weeks, this small party floated on the quiet but tractless waters around the tortuous course of the Tennessee. No sound of civilization reached their ears. They missed the mouth of Swift Creek their intended place of landing but passed on till they came to the mouth of Hardin Creek, up the course of which they pushed their boat to a place afterward known as Johnson's Mill where they landed. Miss Brazelton first stepped ashore and was the first white woman to press the soil of Hardin County. The parties in this colony consisted of John Brazelton and wife, Hannah, their sons, Solomon,

Benjamin and William, their daughters, Elizabeth, Sarah, Nancy and Mrs. Elender Thacker, and her sons, William and Shepherd; Col. James Hardin and wife, Nelly, and sons Joseph, Benjamin and James, and daughters, Jane Kizzie, Margaret, Mary Elizabeth and Elender; Joseph Gooden and wife, Hannah, and sons, James and Thomas. The parties soon began to separate to find homes; John Brazelton selected the spot where Clifton now stands to move to but was taken sick on his return home and on September 20, 1816, died. He was buried near Altum Spring, the first in the county. James Hardin and Joseph Gooden settled near Hardin Creek when the first land was cleared by James Hardin. Mrs. Brazelton settled on McCaslan branch, a tributary of Indian Creek. Jonathan Courtney and family, consisting of wife and sons John, James, Benjamin and Stephen, and daughters Melvinie, Nelly and Ona came in from Roane County in 1817 and seetled on Hardin Creek. In the same year the brothers of James Hardin, Gipson, Amos, Benjamin and Robert arrived and settled near Cerro Gordo. In 1820 John Hanna and wife Rebecca and sons, William, James, John, David Alexander, Huel and Thomas, arrived from Union County and settled near Cerro Gordo, between Indian Creek and Smith's Fork. James Barnes, who was the elected register in 1820, was a settler before the organization of the county; also Isham Cherry, the first chairman; Henry Mahan, the first ranger; James McMahon, the first trustee; Daniel Smith, the first sheriff; Hiram Boone, Stephen Roach; Ninean Steele, son-in-law of Col. Joseph Hardin, all members of the first county court. Alex. W. Sweeney obtained the first peddler license and succeeded James Hardin as county court clerk in 1822. Others at this time were David Robinson, John White, John Pickens, Henry Clifton, Henry Reynolds, David Kincannon, Jacob Blacksheer, Wm. Wisdom, Jacob Pyburn, Temple Johnson, Alex. Sloan, Robert Forbes, John and R. M. Dickson, James G. Doren, Jesse Cherry, W. J. Duckworth, Geo. Worley, Robt. Lacefield, Wm. Smith, James English, Richard Ford, Jesse Jones, Thomas Hannum, Robt Steele, James Emerson, Asa Bryant and Isaac Emerson, all of whom were officially connected with the county as early as 1820. The most of the above parties settled on the east side of the river.

About 1819, Simpson Lee settled a short distance northeast of Craven's Landing, and George Orr about the same distance northwest of it. In 1819 William Gann and a man by the name of Massengill built a camp at what was called Gann Springs, since called Davy's Springs, near Saltillo. In the same year a Mr. Barnes settled near Shady Grove Church, about two and a half miles west of the river, and Allen Anderson at Lick Ford, on White Oak Creek; Jacob Delaney on the run near Delaney's Island, and John Chambers on Chambers' Creek, in the southwestern part of the county. The following also settled west of the river about 1820: Thomas Lovelady, George Norwood, Hugh McDonald, John McDonald, Hiram McDonald, Isaac Smith, John and Larkin Lacefield, Samuel and William Kerr, L. Jones, Eli Hudson, Wm. Bradley, Isaac Graham, Robt. King, Joseph Herrod, Stephen Anderson, James Collier and James and Daniel Lacefield. Of these, Norwood and Jones settled on Mud Creek, the Kerrs also on Mud Creek; Graham and King on Chalk Creek, and James English near the head of Chalk Creek. John Middleton on the creek that bears his name. A man by the name of Burnet settled at Crump's Landing, but the place was afterward purchased by Dr. Richard Crump, a distinguished physician of McNairy County, who gave name to the place. Jesse W. Holland settled near Shady Grove Church in 1824, and at the same time Chas. Miles settled on Miles Creek, a tributary of White Oak. In 1825, Jehu Davy bought land at Lick Ford, on White Oak. John Middleton settled about the same time on the creek which bears his name. John and Robert Barham were the first settlers at Coffee Landing, so named from an outcrop of the peculiar sand called coffee sand. Pittsburg Landing, rendered historical from the great battle fought there April 6 and 7, 1862, was named from Pitts Tucker, who once kept a grog-shop there. In 1822 Thomas Shannon moved with his family from Davidson County to near where Saltillo now stands. Himself and others with household effects came by river in a keelboat, the family and flocks came by land. In 1825 a house was erected by Mr. Shannon near the present landing at Saltillo. The first settler at Savannah was James Rudd, who established a ferry at that place in 1821. Pyburn Bluff took its name from its first settler, Jacob Pyburn, who established a ferry there.

The numerous streams in the county and the river required many ferries, and the dense forests required roads through them to allow communication between neighborhoods. In 1821 James F. McMahon was allowed to keep a ferry on his land at Cerro Gordo; James Hardin was allowed one at his place at the mouth of Swift Creek; Thomas James was allowed one at his place; in 1822 J. A. Rawlings was allowed a ferry at his lands on the Tennessee; in 1822 James Rudd, Jacob Pyburn, R. T. Patton and Thomas Shannon were granted ferry licenses at their respective places. The roads usually led from these ferries in the direction of the various county seats in the surrounding counties. In 1820 a road was cut out by Samuel Bruler and others from his ferry crossing Swift Creek to the Wayne County line; Noah Lilly *et al.* were ordered to cut out a road from Errin's ferry to the Natchez trace; Henry Middleton *et al.* were ordered to cut one from White ferry in the direction of Chickasaw Bluffs. All living on Indian Creek and Turkey Creek were ordered in 1822 to open a road from the "Tarkill" to the Wayne County line. In the same year a road was opened from Hardinsville to the Wayne County line, intersecting the Lacefield mill road. In 1823 the road from Rudd's ferry (Savannah) to Hardinsville was opened under direction of Jordan Manny, and James Morrow and Simpson Lee superintended the cutting out of the road from Hardin's ferry in the direction of the McNairy County courthouse in 1824.

Henry Garner built a mill on Indian Creek, a short distance above Clifton ford in 1820. A water mill had been built the year before on Smith Fork by Jesse Lacefield, and another near the same place by John Williams. Charles B. Nelson erected a horse mill on Horse Creek in 1819. A water mill was built near Shady Grove Church by Maj. James Montgomery in 1824, and Jesse W. Holland erected a tanyard near the same place also in 1824. Michael Berry built a mill on his place in 1820, and Samuel Johnson one on Turkey Creek in the same year. John G. Williams built a mill on Indian Creek in 1824, and John Ross one on his land on Beatty's ford on the same stream in 1823, and James Kincannon in 1834. Much meal was made by the hand mills, also by the mortar. Many went as far as Maury County to mill, crossing Duck River at the half-breed Indian, Billy McClish's ford. The abundance of game rendered it unnecessary to raise domestic meats. Deer and turkey were in great abundance, but bear were not so numerous. Smaller game was to be had for the killing. A premium was allowed for the scalps of wolves and wildcats, owing to their destructive natures. The most valuable fur-bearing animal was the beaver, which was found plentiful. The Indians had had possession of this county from time immemorial, till their title was extinguished on October 19, 1818, though they had not generally lived here as permanent dwellers. They frequently passed through the county and traded and hunted with the whites, and their intercourse was very agreeable. The only difficulty that ever occurred was the killing of a man named Blackwell, by an Indian. Blackwell, while hunting on White Oak had stolen the Indian's pony. The offense was repeated, and the Indian, failing to recover his property, deliberately shot his victim and took his pony. Blackwell was buried near Garner's mill in 1820. This was the first killing in the county.

The works of Mound Builders are seen on both sides of the river. The most prominent ones on the west side are on the east side of Middleton Creek, near Baker's mill. These consist of an embankment between 1,300 and 1,400 feet long and fifteen feet high at its maximum. This, with the bend in itself and the creek, incloses about four acres of ground. Inside the wall and parallel with the creek is a trench apparently from which the earth was taken. Near the center of the enclosure is a mound about eighteen feet high, and covering about half an acre of ground. These works were evidently built for fortification. Human remains are numerous in these mounds. Other works are found in the northwest corner of the county, and along the river below Savannah. A line of fourteen mounds is found on the east side of the river, the city of Savannah being near the center. Some of these are of immense size. The largest of these is from twenty to thirty feet above the common level and covers from a quarter to a half an acre of ground. One or two of these mounds are double. It is said a copper wedge and eight small pulleys were recently found in one of these mounds. These are not the work of modern handicraft and evidently came from the Mexicans as they worked these metals. These mounds when examined have yielded the usual charred remains. They were evidently of a sepulchral, templar, sacred, memorial, or military nature, or sometimes a union of these. The fact that numerous Indian relics are found about these mounds is not evidence that there was any relation between the Indian and the Mound Builder. That instinct, if instinct it may be called, which led the Mound Builder to select these places for a habitation also led the Indian to do the same thing. Each depended upon nature mainly for his support; springs for drinking water, streams for fish, woods for game, and natural fortifications for defense were the things sought. The place that furnished these for the one was as provident to the other; hence the identity of these homes—but not of the races. The group of mounds where Savannah stands, it should be stated, is also surrounded by a moat, which, with the river, makes a complete enclosure. This ditch is yet distinctly visible and is easily traced.

The county was formed by an act of the Legislature in 1819 but the courts of the county were not organized till the beginning of the year 1820. The justices appointed met at the house of James Hardin. They proceeded to organize by the election of Isham Cherry chairman. The other officers chosen were James Hardin, county court clerk; Daniel Smith, sheriff; Henry Mahan, ranger; James McMahon, trustee; James Barnes, register; and Stephen Roach, coroner. Walter Wood, Lewis Fortner, Elisha Smith, James H. Steele and J. G. Williams were appointed constables. The next quorum court of pleas and quarter sessions was to be composed of Joe McMahan, Isham Cherry, James Barnes, Samuel Harbour and David Kincannon. It was ordered that "no officer shall be appointed without a majority of the court agrees." The first *venire* consisted of John White, Joe Pickens, S. Ward, Henry Clofton, Jeff. Farrar, Henry Reynolds, Geo. Worley, Robert Lacefield, Wm. Smith, John Martin, John Boyd, James Reynolds, Sr., James English, Richard Ford, Jesse Jones, James Williams, John Dollins, Henry Jones, Thomas White, Thomas Hannum, Robt. Steele, Noah Lilly, James Emerson, Asa Bryant and Isaac Emerson. The usual tax levy of 18¾ cents on each 100 acres of land, 37½ cents on each town lot, 12½ cents on each white poll, 25 cents on black poll, $5 on each retail storekeeper or peddler and $5 on each tavern-keeper was made. The tax listers, each for his respective neighborhood, appointed for 1820 were Samuel White, Isham Cherry, David Kincannon, E. W. Gee, James Huddleston, Joseph McMahon, J. W. Martin and Ninean Steele. Soon after the militia of the State was organized and listers were then chosen for captains of companies rather than for neighborhoods. The first militia captains were William Warnal, Mahan Jones, English and Paine. The will of Michael Berry was offered for probate April 3, 1820. The court allowed Francis Kincannon, J. W. Martin and Ninean Steele pay for two wolf scalps each. Chelton Smith was allowed $31.25 for carrying an Indian to the Columbia jail, and Ebel Smith was allowed $5.25 as guard for the same. This was the Indian mentioned in the killing of John Blackwell. Daniel Smith was fined $20 for failing to attend court "at the present time." Robt. Lacefield was fined 6¼ cents and Alex. M. Sweeney $1 for State offenses. J. R. McMeans resigned as attorney-general on July 4, 1820, and was allowed $30 for *ex officio* services. Ordinary licenses were granted to Harrison Simpson, October 21, 1820; to Isaac Jones, January, 1821; to James Garner, April, 1821; to Samuel Bruton and John Kindle, October, 1821; to Wiley J. Duckworth and T. M. Duckworth, in 1822; and to James Hardin, 1824. These licenses allowed liquors to be sold and drank on the premises, provided no more were sold on the Sabbath "than were necessary." On January 1, 1821, C. B. Nielson, James Boyd, James Boyd, Sr., John Boyd, John Shoat and James Ashrott gave notice that "Stock keepers that allow there stock to range on our possessions may expect to suffer the extreme rigor of the law." J. Watkins was allowed $3 for a county seal, and Daniel Smith was allowed $25 for *ex officio* services as sheriff of the county for the year 1820. The circuit court was organized soon after the county court by Judge Joshua Haskell, of Jackson, Tenn. He appointed J. W. Judkins as circuit clerk. Isaac S. W. Cook and J. W. Combs were sworn in as attorneys on January 2, 1821, and Joseph Casey on January 8, 1822.

In an election for sheriff on January 8, 1822, J. W. Judkins resigned his office that day and ran for sheriff, and was elected over John Huddleson. The court decided that Judkins was ineligible as he held the office of circuit clerk. The court then chose Huddleson. Judkins then offered to prove that his resignation was in the hands of Judge Haskell at the time of election. He was cited to appear at the April term and produce proof. In the meantime Huddleston was to be considered sheriff, but one Reed was to act till that time. To this Huddleston protested but had to yield. At the time of trial both agreed to resign their claims and go into a new election. This resulted in the election of Judkins. James Hardin was declared defaulter as to certain moneys belonging to the office of county court clerk and removed from office January 9, 1822, and Alex. W. Sweeney placed in office *pro tem*. Whereupon Hardin appealed to the circuit court in the nature of a writ of error and was restored to his office till the April term, when he was declared ousted and Sweeney was elected in his place. A similar fate overtook Sweeney in July, 1824. He was removed by the court for producing false certificates for moneys turned over to him. A *mandamus* failed to compel the court to restore him to office. In July J. R. McMeans resigned his office as solicitor and James Scott was elected in his place; at the same date James Taylor was sworn in as an attorney. James Scott was allowed $40 for *ex officio* services as solicitor for 1822. J. W. Judkins took the oath as an attorney July 1, 1822. The election precincts for 1823 were Thomas Robinson's, Noah Lilly's, John Gillespie's and Wm. Boyd's. A small poor-tax was first levied this year. Thomas F. Edwards was admitted as an attorney March 22, 1825. Joel Casey, James Barnes, David Robinson, John G. Williams and J. B. Gantt were appointed school commissioners June 23, 1825. On December 19, of this year, Elison White was admitted to the bar as an attorney. Thos. Wells was put under bond of $500 for his appearance at court for stealing Chickasaw Indian horses. A loss of the minutes of the county court from 1826 to 1834, and all the minutes of the circuit court till 1840 makes it impossible to note many interesting cases. Lewis N. Falkner was sent to jail fourteen hours for contempt in 1834, and John Shannon two hours June 16, 1835, for a similar offense. Hugh Talbot was allowed $120 for transcribing the county records in 1837. In this year occurred the execution of Mrs. Hughes for the murder of her husband. Being the first criminal execution, and that a woman, it naturally attracted an immense crowd of people. The execution took place at the river bank near where the Kendall House now stands. The prisoner was seated in a cart and the rope adjusted by Jesse Jones, deputy sheriff. The cart was driven from under the prisoner and she was thus left hanging. Thomas Gray, who was sheriff, resigned his office June 5, 1837, for fear, it is said, he would have to officiate at another hanging. Some very notable cases occurred between 1835 and 1840. Among these were the cases of the State against Pickett, also the same against Mrs. Coats. Such counsel as James K. Polk, Terry H. Cahal and Felix Grundy were employed. These parties were indicted for murder in the first degree but finally escaped death punishment. A little later came the cases of the State against J. H. Calhoun, and on August 19, 1843, the State against Marion Brooks. Both these cases were for murder in the first degree, but neither was hung. Nelson, a slave of James Elliott, was indicted for the murder of David Sellars on November 11, 1845. The case resulted in the sentence of death on June 8, 1846. By an act of the Legislature of this year J. J. Williams, J. B. Gantt, Daniel Smith, B. Davy and J. W. Cantrell were ordered to survey and make a map of the county. The usual cases, interesting and uninteresting, occurred from time to time till after the close of the war, when some very bitter cases arose from difficulties growing out of that unhappy period. In 1867 "Tobe" Thornton was hung for the murder of Broyles, a well known and highly respected citizen of Savannah. This was the last execution that has occurred; however, several have been tried since for murder but none convicted. Savannah has had her share of distinguished judges and lawyers. Joshua Haskell, of Jackson, was circuit judge from the organization till possibly 1820 to 1832, when he was followed by Austin Miller, who served till about 1838 when B. C. Totten put on the judicial robes and served till 1856, when he was succeeded by James Scott, of Savannah, who served till his death in 1852. Elijah Walker, also of Savannah, came upon the bench and served till the courts were closed by the war. The courts were re-organized by Fielding Hurst, of Purdy, who remained on the bench till 1869, when Judge Walker again served till his death in 1873. T. P. Bateman was then chosen and held the position with credit and honor till 1886, when E. D. Patterson was chosen judge. Of the attorneys A. G. McDougal has been prominent before the bar since 1840. Others are D. W. Broyles, J. A. Cunningham, J. M. Watson, W. J. Watson and H. J. Hefner.

On the question of Union or Secession Hardin County was largely for the Union and on the vote of "separation" or "no separation" the latter was emphatically voted, 1,052 to 498 votes, but when the clash of arms came the county was in majority for the South. The militia was put into active training and all able-bodied men were enrolled. The place for general muster on the east side of the river was Old Town; on the west side it was at the Perkins' place on the road from Savannah to Purdy. The first company of troops raised was at Shady Grove Church, near Saltillo, where a great barbecue and war meeting was held. War speeches were made and volunteers were called for, yet not in vain. A full company of cavalry was soon raised of which C. S. Robinson was captain, J. W. Irvin first lieutenant; Arthur Hardin second lieutenant; and R. W. Reynolds third lieutenant. The operations of these men were mainly under Gen. Wheeler. The second body of men was recruited by L. B. Irvin; this consisted of fourteen men. They were taken to Nashville and became a part of the First Tennessee (Confederate). The regiment was organized in April, 1861. George Maney (general) was elected colonel. (See State history, page 562.) The first full infantry company was raised in the vicinity of Hamburg. Of this company J. O. Tarkington was elected captain. This company was raised in the summer of 1861, and was attached to the Thirty-fourth Tennessee (Confederate) under Col. William Churchwell. This regiment did duty at Cumberland Gap, and other points in East Tennessee, till the invasion of Kentucky by Gen. Bragg in the summer of 1862. (See page 584 of the State history.) After the fall of Fort Donelson and the capture of Nashville, Gov. Harris ordered out all the available forces of the State. Those who did not volunteer were conscripted. Five companies of this character of men were raised in Hardin County under Capts. Flatt, Sawyer, Powers, Bradley and Sneed. They were posted at Savannah, where they were disciplined by Col Crews of Memphis, till February 7, 1862, when the approach of the Federal gunboats "Tyler," "Lexington" and "Conestoga," caused them to leave rather hastily. They were started for Nashville, but on concentration of the Confederate Army at Corinth they were hastened thither. So many of these men were soldiers from force rather than choice that almost complete disorganization followed the battle of Shiloh; from 125 to 150 men only remained. These were consolidated into two companies and attached to the Ninth, improperly called the Fifth Kentucky. The officers of the larger of these were B. A. F. Fitzgerald, captain; W. T. Powers, W. C. Sawyer and Sol Flatt. Numerous changes occurred by death and resignation so that T. J. Powers became captain and so remained till the surrender. After one year's service these men were attached to the Forty-fifth Tennessee, with which they served till the close of the war. Numerous other bodies were sent to the service, among them Capt. J. A. Russell's company and a large number to Capt. J. W. Eldridge's battery.

Companies E, F and H (Federal troops), were recruited in Hardin, Wayne and Perry, for the Sixth Tennessee Cavalry. These were recruited by W. K. M. Breckenridge of Perry County. The officers of Company E were J. D. Poston, captain; F. A. Smith and William Cleary, lieutenants. The officers of F were D. J. Dickenson, captain; E. L. Hardin, R. O. F. Roswell and J. W. Youngblood, lieutenants. The officers of H were J. G. Berry and R. D. DeFord, captains; Colvin Hanna, Nicholas Pitts and W. A. Newsom, lieutenants. The other companies belonged to the regiment were K, L, and M. These were recruited mainly through the influence of Thomas H. Boswell. The officers of K were T. H. Boswell and Albert Cook, captains; J. W. Barham and James E. McNair, lieutenants; Company L, John W. Moore and John H. Edwards, captains; T. B. Waggoner, G. T. Wann and James N. Julin, lieutenants; Company M, Wm. C. Holt and T. C. McMahon, captains; H. L. Neely and James A. Mangum, lieutenants.

The Tenth Tennessee Infantry received Capt. C. W. Shipman's company from Hardin County. The history of both the Sixth and Tenth is given under the head of these regiments in the State history. Besides the trouble and devastation caused by the regular troops of the respective armies, the people were terribly scourged by the guerrilla bands of Burt Hays (Confederate) and Doc Mangum (Federal).

The first absolute proof of war to the county was the approach of the Federal gunboats on February 7, 1862. Before these had gone most of the transports in the Tennessee River. The gunboats reached Savannah on the 8th. Many arms belonging to the citizens which had been collected by order of the Government were captured.

It was March before Grant's army began to move up the Tennessee and it was not till near the 1st of April before the main body arrived at Savannah and Crump's Landing. The objective point of the Federals was Corinth, Miss. The army moved to Pittsburg Landing and was there awaiting the arrival of Buel for concentration before advancing upon Corinth. Gen. A. S. Johnston, anticipating their movements, took the initiative by moving out and attacking the Federals before the arrival of Buell's forces. The battle was fought in the Fifteenth District at Shiloh near Pittsburg Landing on the 6th and 7th of April, 1862. The Federal generals were taken by surprise and were unprepared, their statement to the contrary notwithstanding. The attack was made by the Confederates with that impetuosity peculiar to the Southern soldier and was met by the peculiar stubbornness of the Northern soldier. What might have been the result had not the Confederate chieftain been killed is a matter of dispute, but this much is true, the battle raged with awful fury for two days and the arrival of Buell's forces at the end of the first day saved Grant's army from possible destruction and compelled the retreat of the Confederates. The tongue of man nor the angels in Heaven nor the demons down under the sea could ever portray the sacrifices made here to the great war god. The official reports show the loss of the Confederates of 1,728 killed, 8,012 wounded and 959 missing. The loss of the Federals was 1,700 killed, 7,495 wounded and 3,022 missing.

The Government after the close of war had all the bodies of those who fell at Shiloh and who died in hospitals in the surrounding country disinterred and reburied in the National Cemetery at the old battle ground. The grounds cover about fifteen acres, which are enclosed by a stone wall. The enclosure contains the graves of about 3,000 soldiers. These, as far as known, are marked in divisions according to State and by regiments, which is indicated by a small plain head stone. The others are marked "unknown." Just beyond the cemetery lie the remains of about 2,000 Confederate dead. The contrast between the two burial places is very striking. The former is well kept and furnished with everything attractive; the latter is marked by decay, and is a sad picture to the friends of the fallen.

Hardin County was named in honor of Col. James Hardin, who was a subaltern officer in the Revolutionary war, and laid his claim of 2,000 acres of land in this county. It was the first county carved out of the Western District. This was in 1819 and embraced the territory as far as the Mississippi River. It was placed under control of Stewart and Wayne Counties. Notwithstanding its ample bounds at first, the county has been reduced from time to time, till it now embraces but 610 square miles. Its length from north to south is thirty miles, and its width from east to west is twenty-one miles. It is bounded on the north by Henderson and Decatur Counties; on the east by Wayne; on the south by Lauderdale County, Ala., and Tishamingo County, Miss., and on the west by McNairy and Chester Counties. It is divided into sixteen civil districts, which are determined more by the topography than population of the county. Numbers 9, 10, 11, 12, 13, 15 and 16 are west of the river, the remaining ones are east of it. The courts first met at the residence of Col. James Hardin in January, 1820, near the present town of Cerro Gordo, where they continued to meet till October of that year. On April 3, Hiram Boon, James Barnes, Stephen Roach, Ninean Steele and Hardin Williams were made a committee to contract for the erection of a temporary courthouse. This was early in October of 1820, and the committee were allowed $30 for building the same. In January, 1822, the court appointed Alexander W. Sweeney, Hiram Boon, John Kindle, J. S. Williams and James Barnes a committee to select a permanent seat of justice for the county. The committee failed in its work, and Noah Lilly, Daniel Smith and the ones already on the committee, were instructed to proceed with the location. On July 1, 1822, the committee reported they had purchased fifty acres of land on Turkey Creek for the town of Hardinsville. The court adjourned to meet the next day at 10 o'clock, July 2, to meet at the place selected. The committee on county seat became the first town board of Hardinsville—now known as Old Town. Dissatisfaction arose as to the location of Hardinsville. On December 5, 1825, the Legislature appointed Col. William Bradley, Col. M. McClannahan and Col. A. B. Shelby to select another site of fifty acres for a new town to be called Hardinsville, on the Tennessee River. On the removal of the county seat the owners of lots were to be paid first cost on their lots. The permanent seat was, however, not selected till in December, 1826, and then by James ———, James Chissum and Alfred M. Harris. A fifty-acre tract was obtained from James Irvin at the present site of Savannah. The consideration for this tract was one choice lot.

The first courthouse was built by J. G. Williams. It was a small log building, 16x20 feet, with a dirt floor and clapboard roof. The new courthouse at Hardinsville on the selection of that place by James Barnes was a good brick building. On the removal of the seat of justice to Savannah in 1830, a temporary log house of round logs was built. This stood a little east of the present courthouse. This house was replaced by a good brick building in 1832, which stood till it was destroyed by fire during the late war. The present courthouse was begun in 1867. A tax of 20 cents on each $100, and 15 cents on each poll was levied in 1867 for the purpose of erecting the house. This is a good, substantial brick building, which was built at a cost of about $10,000.

It is said on good authority that the first place of confinement of prisoners was a large hollow tree near James Hardin's. A new brick jail was completed by the commissioners of Hardinville, and received by the county on March 20, 1825. The commissioners received $2,000 for the building. A new log jail was built at Savannah on the removal of the courts to that place but this was replaced by a brick jail about 1837. This house stood two blocks above the present jail on Water Street. This was burned and a new jail was completed in 1860 at a cost of about $2,000. This was destroyed with other public buildings within the period of the war. On the reorganization a new log jail was built, which stood for some time when the present jail was erected, which was built at a cost of about $3,000.

The first official recognition of the poor, " whom we always have with us," was the allowance of $100 to Christopher for keeping Mrs. Choat in 1823. That year a small poor tax was levied. From that time till after the constitution of 1834–35, the poor were farmed out to the lowest and best bidder. A poor-farm was purchased on Steele Creek, which was kept up for some time, but was abandoned for a time, but was re-established again in 1859. The commissioners at this time were Alex. Doran, J. Jones and R. I. Williams. Owing to lack of timber and other causes the poor-house and farm was sold in 1873; the purchasers were A. W. Blevins and B. R. Freeman. The sum realized was $800. M. M. Dickson, N. W. Covey and R. W. Reynolds were appointed a committee to select and purchase a new poor-farm, which was soon afterward done.

The grounds of the Agricultural & Mechanical Association of Hardin County were purchased of T. A. Kerr in March, 1872, but the first fair was not held till 1873. The grounds are about five acres in extent, and lie immediately south of Savannah, on an elevation overlooking the town. An amphitheater forms nearly three-fourths of a circle, and is capable of seating from 6,000 to 8,000 people. On the grounds is a large floral hall, capable of accommodating not only exhibitors but spectators as well. Departments are set apart for mechanical display, also the farm, garden, kitchen and works of art. The association has held fourteen annual fairs without a single failure. The officers of the association are John A. Dodds, president; T. M. Brown, vice-president, and L. F. DeFord, secretary. The directors are J. D. Martin, E. P. Blount, J. C. Walker, J. K. Barlow, R. W. Reynolds, William Barnhill and J. A. Harbert.

Sheriffs. Daniel Smith was sheriff to 1822; J. W. Judkins (John Huddleston from January to April) 1824; Louis Falkner, 1828; James Robinson, 1834; Thomas Gray, 1837; John

O. Barnett from January 6 to September 4; Alexander Nevill, 1840; Daniel Smith, 1844. John Kirby, 1846; S. M. Hargrove, 1848; Robt. Forbes, 1852; J. G. Hamilton, 1856; R. I. Porter, 1860; J. G. Cunningham, 1862; E. D. M. Perkins, 1865–66; C. W. Shipman, 1870; W. J. Thomas, 1872; I. W. Ross, 1878; R. E. Bennett; W. C. Story, 1886; J. A. Counce, 1887. County court clerks: James Hardin to 1822; Alex. M. Sweeney, 1824; David Robinson *pro tem.*; John Houston, 1832; W. J. Duckworth, 1836; C. C. Gibbs, 1837; A. B. Campbell, 1840; Wesley Corey, 1848; W. H. Cherry; D. T. Street, 1866–68; N. T. McDaniel, 1872; W. R. Henkle, 1882; J. C. Mitchell, 1886; W. J. Watkins, 1887. Circuit clerks: J. W. Judkins, 1822; W. J. Duckworth, 1841; Hugh Tarbet, 1846; J. J. Irvin, 1854; G. A. Duckworth, 1865; J. S. Winborn, 1869; J. C. Street, 1877; T. M. Hurst, 1879; J. H. Skinner, 1882; G. W. Harbert, 1886; A. B. Mitchell, 1887. Chancellors: P. M. Miller from 1836 to 1837; Milton Brown, 1841; Andrew McCampbell, 1848; Calvin Jones, 1854; Stephen C. Pavatt, 1862; R. H. Rose, 1866–68; J. W. Doherty, 1870; G. H. Nixon, 1886; Abernathy, 1887; Clerks and masters: Hugh Tarbet, 1838; Geo. F. Benton, 1842; Hugh Tarbet, 1848; Geo. F. Benton, 1854; G. W. Hamilton, 1870; E. P. Patterson, 1886; McDougal, 1887. Representatives in the Legislature: Joel Walker, 1820–23; James Barnes, 1823–25; Benjamin Hardin, 1825–27; ———— 1827–31; Bradley Halford, 1831–33; John Rayburn, 1833–35; John M. Johnson, 1835–37; C. C. Gibbs, 1837–39; C. H. McGinnis, 1839–47; Daniel Smith, 1847–51; G. M. Hamilton, 1851–53; C Broyles, 1853–55; B. G. Brazelton, 1855–57; J. T. Carter, 1857–59; D. A. Roberts, 1859–61; Thomas Maxwell, 1865–67; Alfred Pitts, 1867–69; W. F. Hinkle, 1869–73; S. W. Riggs, 1873–75; D. W. Herring, 1875–77; G. W. Haynes, 1877–79; E. G. Yancy, 1879–81; H. B. Neel, 1881–82; J. D. Martin, 1882–85; J. A. Hanna, 1885–87. Senator from the district of which Hardin County is a part: Joel Walker, 1821–22; Thomas Williamson, 1823–24; Joel Walker, 1825–30; Wm. Davis, 1831–32; John Rayburn, 1833–34; H. H. Brown, 1835–40; Hezekiah Bradley, 1841–42; B. Gordon, 1843–44; A. G. McDougal, 1845–50; E. Polk, 1853–55; A. G. McDougal, 1857–58; Geo. B. Peters, 1859–60; John Aldredge, 1867–70; A. D. Bryant, 1870–7–; S. L. Warren, 1873–74; S. L. Ross, 1875–76; W. P. Morris, 1879–80; P. M. Tilman, 1881–82; Warren Smith, 1885–86.

The first church built in the county was by the Primitive Baptists. This house was erected about the time of the organization of the county. The house stood near Indian Creek, nearly on a line east of Cerro Gordo. Here the Hardins, Brazeltons, Goodens, and Smiths attended church. Rev. Charles Riddle was the first pastor of this church. This denomination was quite numerous in the early history of the county, but on the separation of the church into the two branches, Primitive and Missionary Baptist, this church has been greatly weakened. However, good congregations are found at Cool Springs and elsewhere in the county.

The organization of the Missionary Baptist Church in the county first appeared about 1833. Its membership now is quite numerous. There are churches of this denomination at Bruton Branch, with twenty-eight members; one at Enon with forty-eight members; one at Fairview with thirty members; one at Harmony with thirty-three members; one at Hopewell with seventy-seven members; one at Mt. Carmel with twenty-one members; one at Shady Grove with forty-three, and one at Turkey Creek with twenty-eight members; also an organization of ten members at Savannah, but no house.

The congregation of the Cumberland Presbyterian Church at Savannah was organized December 9, 1860, by Rev. C. D. Hudson, with twenty members. A house was built in connection with the Masons. Meetings were not held from August 6, 1862, till August 29, 1868, owing to the war, at which time the congregation was re-organized by Rev. G. C. Stockard, with twenty members. Since that time the pastors have been W. C. Walker, W. M. Neeley, T. J. Nixon, G. C. Stockard and J. R. Alexander. The ruling elders are E. T. Basye, R. A. Shaw, W. U. Ross and A. F. Franks. The present membership is thirty-one. Ross Chapel, about four miles south of Savannah, is the oldest organization of the church in this county, and numbers seventy members. Mt. Tabor is another old organization, but its membership is small. Good congregations are found at Willoughby, Alder Grove, Union, Harmony, Bethlehem, Indian Creek and Liberty. There are also congregations at Loweryville and Oak Grove.

The first organization of the Methodist Church was at what is called Watson Church, in the northeastern part of the county. This was by the Rev. John Watson, in 1830, who was from South Carolina. The date of the organization at Savannah cannot be learned, as all of the early records have been lost or destroyed. Mrs. Francis Irvin's name is found as early as 1826. The following have been pastors within the date mentioned: Wilson McAllister, 1826(?); Charles Harris, 1842; J. M. McCracken, 1852; W. H. Browning, 1854; —— Nance, 1865; W. G. Davis, 1867; A. S. McBride, W. W. Graves, 1870; G. W. Martin, 1871; A. G. Dinwiddie, 1873; P. A. Sowell, R. R. Jones, 1876; S. L. Lain, 1881; L. Powell, 1884; J. T. Curry, 1886. This class now has an excellent brick church edifice and a membership of about 200. There are also churches of this denomination in almost every neighborhood in the county, besides quite a number of Methodist Episcopal Churches.

A fine new church has just been completed by the Christian Church denomination at Savannah. It is a frame structure of commodious size and of modern architecture. Its construction was largely due to Reuben East, of Savannah. As yet no regular services are held.

The first schoolhouse built in the county was erected near the Clifton ford on Indian Creek. This was a small log house without seats, floor or chimney. This was in 1824 and Thomas Stockton was the first teacher. At this school attended the Hardins, Brazeltons, McMahons, McConnells, and others. Similar schools were to be found in the various neighborhoods of the county. The first official act of the county looking to the public schools was the appointment of Joel Casey, James Barnes, David Robinson, John G. Williams and Jesse B. Gantt as school commissioners in June, 1825. No system of schools was adopted by the county till after the adoption of the new constitution of 1834–35, and then under an act of the General Assembly of 1839–40. The new law provided that schools should be taught three months in the year in each district or forfeit their share of the public funds. The enumeration for the year above named showed a scholastic population of 2,374, twelve districts, and funds on hand to the amount of $1,453.89. Under the provisions of the session act of North Carolina, Hardin County established an academy. This was done in 1832. The first trustees were James Irwin, David Robinson, and three others. This building stood near where Dr. Barlow's residence now stands. In this old academy nearly all the children of Savannah were educated. This was the only school building in Savannah until 1853, when the funds had so accumulated and children increased that a division of the school was deemed best. A lot was purchased where the college building now stands and the female academy erected thereon. The first trustees of this were Jas. Irvin, G. D. Morrow, W. H. Cherry, A. S. McDougal and G. M. Hamilton. In 1859 the present college building was erected by a stock company, but this stock has since been sold out.

The college buildings are owned by the principals, Profs. H. P. Wood and H. J. Cox. Two years' management have placed the school in an enviable light. The attendance now is about one hundred. The managers promise to do and do do the work thoroughly between the common school and the university. The course is liberal and practical and sufficiently thorough for all the necessities and purposes in life. The healthful surroundings, the excellent society, and the exceptionable moral influence about Savannah, make it a good place for the success of such a school as Hardin College affords.

Ross Academy is a graded school of two departments. It stands about four miles southeast of Savannah. It is owned by stockholders. The principal of this school is J. M. Watson. The school has been in successful operation for six or seven years. The enrollment is about 100, and the school term lasts about ten months in the year.

Bell Academy is a graded school of ten departments. It stands about eight miles south of Savannah. It has been in successful operation for about four years. J. A. Steele is principal.

Saltillo Academy was incorporated in 1879 by J. H. Hanna, S. J. Stockard, T. J. McGill, J. M. Alexander and W. P. Alexander. The people of Saltillo have been singularly unfortunate in regard to their school building, having had two burned within the last decade. The school has four teachers and a school term of ten months in the year. The principal is H. E. Watson.

840   HISTORY OF TENNESSEE.

The common school superintendent's last report shows eighty white and twenty-five colored licensed teachers in the county besides thirty-one in private schools, and a total of thirty-six schoolhouses. The length of school term is sixty days. The total receipts for the year were $11,200, and the amount expended was $5,920. The white scholastic population was 5,918, colored 978, or a total of 6,896. The white enrollment was 3,520; colored 901. The daily attendance was, white, 2,345; colored, 639. The average monthly compensation for teachers was $28. The most of the schools are incorporated under the "four mile law," this being sufficient to drive the sale of whisky entirely from the county —something few counties can boast of.

Savannah, the county seat of Hardin County, lies on the east side of the Tennessee River, near the center of the county, 480 feet above the sea level, and in latitude 35° 20' north, and 11° 11' west of Washington. It was selected as the county seat in 1826, and became the formal seat in 1830. The first settler in the vicinity of the place was James Rudd, who settled at what was called Rudd's Ferry. He settled at that place about 1818 and built a dwelling, and opened a ferry in 1821. The name Savannah is doubtless derived from the savannas which lie across the river from the place. The town site was given to the commissioner by James Irvin, who was long identified with the business interest of Savannah. The original plat of the town covered fifty acres. Among the first town commissioners were James Irvin, J. J. Williams and David Robinson. These men composed the first town commissioners. In 1837 the limits of the town were defined as "beginning at the branch below Joe N. Baker, thence east to include David Robinson's house; thence south on the Florence road by the mile post; thence west to the river; thence down the same with its meanders to the beginning. In 1850 the place was incorporated on petition of L. H. Broyles, W. L. Pool and twenty-seven others. The first hotel in the place was kept by John Kendall. This was a hewed log house. L. H. Broyles and James Irvin became a business firm in 1830. The first brick house was built by Col. Stephens north of the public square. David Robinson, who was identified with the early court and business of the town, built the Cherry mansion. The removal of the court to Savannah caused a rapid change, and the thick growth of timber soon gave way to a thriving village and one of the most healthful in the State. While the growth has not been marvelous, it has been regular and healthful. The place contains three churches, an excellent school, the Hardin College and no drinking places. The following were the leading business men before the war: L. H. Broyles, Broyles & Irvin, Beuler & Webb, Cherry & Benton and Porter & Shield.

The business men of Savannah of to-day are general stores—J. J. Williams & Bro., Baker & Bro., Barlow & Hughes, Benton & Bro., D. A. & T. J. Welch, W. H. Carrington, W. H. Seaman, W. E. Hughes and DeFord & Morris. Groceries—J. W. Carender, W. T. Story, Powers & Haynes and E. C. Kendall. Drugs—J. K. Barlow and J. W. Akin. Millinery stores—Mrs. H. E. Akin and Mrs. Fanny Morrison.

Savannah has had a newspaper most of the time since about 1843, but it has been rather changeable in its nature. The Savannah *Courier* is now in its third volume. This is a clean sheet, and is owned and edited by C. L. Hefner. The paper is strictly a non-political sheet, and has good advertising patronage and circulation.

The Savannah *Times* is a new newspaper venture. It is in its first volume. It is Democratic in politics, and is a sprightly paper owned by Barlow & Cooper.

Savannah Lodge, No. 102, F. & A. M., was chartered October 4, 1843, on petition of G. D. Morrow, G. F. Benton and L. H. Wells. These brethren were elected to office in the order named. The lodge was suspended a short period during the war. The present officers are W. B. Smith, W. M.; E. P. Blount, S. W.; J. R. Abernathy, J. W.; J. H. Benton, Treas.; J. W. Carender, Sec.; W. T. Powers, S. D.; D. M. Jones, J. D.; L. E. Owen; Chap.; and R. L. Clark, Tyler. The membership is forty-four.

Farragut Post, No. 6, G. A. R., was organized some years ago. The post numbers about sixty members.

The first settlement in what is now Saltillo was made by Thomas Shannon in the fall of 1822. The family consisted of himself, wife and eight children. A log house was built near the landing by William and Nathan Shannon, sons of Thomas Shannon, in 1825. A stock of goods was shipped to the place in 1825, and sold by Nathan Shannon in a log store-house. The place was then called Hawkins' Landing. A store-house was soon afterward built by the Hawkins brothers near Gann Spring, a short distance from Saltillo. It took its present name about 1849, from the Mexican city of that name. The place was incorporated in 1870. Its growth has not been rapid but healthful. The population now is about 300. It contains a Presbyterian Church, a Masonic hall, an academy and the following business houses: J. M. Alexander, Mitchell & Hinkle, Craven & Wilkinson, White & Craven, J. L. Broyles & Co., E. A. Barham and J. S. Holland. The trade of the place consists largely of cotton and lumber.

The vicinity of Cerro Gordo is the most historic ground in the county. James F. McMahon settled on the west side of the river opposite Cerro Gordo, and in 1821 took out license to keep a ferry at that point. In 1830 John White and Elisha Bryant settled at the present site of the place and started a ferry and business house there. From White it was called White's Landing till 1849, when it was changed to its present name from a city made historic by the Mexican war. The business men of the place now are E. B. Harbour and W. S. Hawkins. Other places of business in the county are Pickwick, where Sanders & Atkins, S. B. Burk, M. L. Crow and M. V. Thornton have stores; Hamburg, where M. F. Fraley, R. L. Milligan and M. H. Pratt sell goods. At Pittsburg Landing are J. P. Atkins & Bro. and W. C. Meek & Co.; J. S. Warrington and W. J. & J. S. Phillips, near Adamsville; W. E. Morris & Co., at Boyd's Landing; McKelvey & Paulk and J. H. Seaton, at Walnut Grove; S. J. Kendall, at Loweryville; G. W. Grisham and W. E. Hughes, at Nixon; T. J. Hurley, near Stantonville; A. L. McKinzie & Son and E. Dodd & Co., at Coffee Landing; J. T. Lewter, at Crump's Landing; E. Mulry & Co., Olive Hill; Bradley & Co., Sibley; S. J. Moffet, at Morris Chapel, and John Pitts, near Milledgeville.

HENDERSON COUNTY.

Hon. Jackson Anderson, a well known agriculturist of the Seventeenth District, was born in 1831, in Edgecombe County, N. C., a son of John and Nancy (Taylor) Anderson. The parents were born in same State and county as our subject; the father in 1801, and the mother in 1800. John Anderson resided in his native State until after his marriage. In 1837 he immigrated to Henderson County; purchased property where he now resides. He was one of the earliest settlers and is the oldest person in the county; he is well known and highly respected. His wife was of Dutch descent; was the mother of five children. Jackson was the only one who lived to be grown. Mrs. Anderson lived to a ripe old age, honored and beloved by all. She departed this life in 1883. The subject of this sketch was about six years old when his parents came to Henderson County; he remained with them until after his majority; in 1853 he married Miss Harriet E. Jackson, daughter of Wm. P. and Martha Jackson. Mrs. Anderson was born in 1837 and died in 1866. She bore four children: Emily Melvina, wife of Jesse Holmes; William H., deceased; John Slater and James Y. After marriage Mr. Anderson located where he now resides, near the old homestead. He owns about 300 acres of valuable land, and has a desirable home. He is one of the most enterprising and influential men of the county; and by honor and integrity has won the confidence and esteem of the entire community. In 1859 he was elected magistrate of the Nineteenth Division, adjusting all cases brought before him with satisfaction for twenty-three years. In 1882 he was elected to represent Henderson County in the State Legislature. He served with so much credit and distinction that he was re-elected in 1884. He is a stanch and leading Republican; he was a Whig previous to the war; cast his first vote for Gen. Scott in 1852. He is a Mason, belongs to Juno Lodge, No. 64, and is a devout member of the Methodist Episcopal Church.

William V. Barry, the able editor and publisher of the Lexington *Progress*, was born in McNairy County, Tenn., in 1858, and is the second of a family of eight children born to Dr. Daniel and Eliza J. (Moore) Barry. The father is a native of Tennessee, born in 1830, and a physician and surgeon by profession. He graduated at Memphis in 1852, and the same year married and located at Purdy. He has since that time made Purdy his home, with the exception of from 1874 to 1878, when he resided in Wayne County. In connection with his practice he has at various times edited papers, and at present is editor of the *Democrat* at Purdy. Mrs. Eliza J. (Moore) Barry died in 1876 at the age of forty-six years. The following year Dr. Barry married Miss Georgia Treadwell. Dr. Barry is one of the oldest, most respected, and most influential men in McNairy County. Our subject was educated in the schools of Purdy and remained at home until his majority, after which he taught school for one term. In 1880 C. D. Barry, brother of William, established at Decaturville a paper called the Decatur *Beacon*, the first newspaper ever published in Decatur County. William was his assistant, and in 1881 he assumed the entire control and continued the publication until 1884, when he moved to his present location and began the Lexington *Progress*, which has for its motto "We speak of men as we find them, and of things as they are unfolded to us." It is a newsy, interesting paper, and has an extensive circulation. Mr. Barry ranks among the leading journalists of West Tennessee. January, 1883, he married Mollie A., daughter of C. P. and Nancy J. Dennison. Mrs. Barry was born in Henderson County, 1868, and is the mother of three children: Charles L., Henry D. and one other. Mr. Barry is an earnest Catholic and Democrat. His first presidential vote was cast for Hancock. He is a pleasant, courteous gentleman, and very popular.

G. W. Beacham, an enterprising farmer of the Twelfth District, was born in Henderson County, in 1834, and is one of a family of three children born to Daniel S. and Vina (Shepard) Beacham. The father was born in 1810, in Anson County, N. C. He immigrated to Henderson County when a youth, where he lived at time of his marriage. About 1837 he moved to Wilcox County, Ala., remaining there ten years, going to Clark County, Miss., where he died in 1886. He was twice married and the father of seven children. The first wife was Martha Piles. The second wife, and mother of G. W., was born in Henderson County; died in 1836. The subject of this sketch was raised without a mother's love or care, but remained with his father until the outbreak of the war, when he became one of the valiant "boys in gray." He enlisted in Company A, Eighth Tennessee Infantry; was engaged in the battles of Shiloh, Murfreesboro, Chickamauga, Missionary Ridge, Atlanta and Nashville, also in several other skirmishes. At the battle of Murfreesboro he was wounded in the thigh by a ball and disabled for six months. He served until the surrender. November 14, 1866, he married Miss A. Neislar, who was born in 1826, a daughter of David Neislar, of Henderson County. To this union three children were born: Josephene, Levina Jane and Nancy Ann. Mrs. Beacham died September 28, 1874. November 14, 1875, Mr. B. married the second time to Miss Nancy Jane Hodgins, born in Henderson County in 1853, a daughter of David M. Hodgins. To this last marriage seven children were born: Mary Ellen, Sallie, William E., George H., John W., Mahala and Lucinda. Mr. Beacham owns about 500 acres of valuable land in the Twelfth District, where he has been living for several years. He has made a decided success in farming, and is known as one of the county's most flourishing and prosperous agriculturists, and a worthy citizen. He is a Republican, casting his first vote for A. Lincoln in 1864. He is a Mason of good standing, belongs to Lodge No. 440. Mrs. Beacham is an estimable lady, and a devoted member of the Methodist Church South.

Felix R. Bray, merchant at Lone Elm and member of the firm of Bray & Co., was born in Henderson County in 1847, a son of John and Minerva Ann (Walker) Bray. The father is of English descent, born in Randolph County, N. C., in 1820. He immigrated to Decatur County, Tenn., in 1837. After his marriage, which occurred in 1842, came to Henderson County to the Tenth District, engaging in agricultural pursuits for a number of years. In 1882 he became a citizen of Lone Elm, since which time he has been hotel keeping. His wife was born in North Carolina, 1827, and has borne six children: William M.; Nancy J., wife of C. P. Dennison; Felix R., Curry, and Askew and Alice, twins. The subject of this sketch received his education in his native county. December, 1867, he married Miss Kittie Fuller, daughter of James H. and Eleanor Fuller. Mrs. Bray was born in the county in 1849, and by this union has nine children: Demonia, Sidney M., Eleanor, Millie, Katie, Lizzie, Artie, James H. and an infant son. In 1872 Mr. Bray established a general store at Lone Elm, in which business he has since been engaged, carrying a first-class and large stock of goods. By his attention to business, courtesy to patrons, and ability he has succeeded in establishing an extensive and profitable trade. He is a Republican, gave his first vote for U. S. Grant in 1868; is a Mason, belonging to Lodge No. 467, Chapter and Council Mason of Lexington. He and Mrs. Bray are devoted members of the Primitive Baptist Church.

W. F. Brooks, clerk and master of the chancery court of Henderson County, was born in the town where he now resides, in 1842; he is the youngest and only living one of a family of four children born to William and Margaret (McCauley) Brooks. The father was born in Newtonlavady, Ireland, in 1805. He emigrated from his native land in 1827 to Hardinsville, Middle Tenn., and began merchandising; in 1832 he moved to Lexington, continuing the sale of goods. In 1835 he visited the Emerald Isle and married Miss McCauley, who was born in Londonderry in 1811. They at once came to America. In 1860 they went on a visit to the scenes of their youth. After a mercantile life of thirty-four years in Henderson County, and one which was replete with success, Mr. Brooks in 1865 turned his business over into the hands of the son, W. F., and December 31, of same year, died. His good wife's death occurred six weeks previous to his own. The subject of this sketch received an excellent education in the academy at Lexington, Andrew College, Trenton and West Tennessee College, Jackson. In 1860 he departed for Europe, making an extended visit of two years, seeing all the principal cities and curiosities of that country. He returned to America in 1862 and during the war remained in the Northern States; coming home in 1865, he assumed charge of his father's business, the next year entering into partnership with Saml. Howard and A. H. Rhodes in merchandising. Mr. Brooks was manager. He continued mercantile life until 1875, having different partners at various times, when he engaged in farming. Mr. Brooks has always affiliated with the Democratic party, casting his first vote for George B. McClellan; although the county has a Republican majority of over 300, Mr. Brooks is so highly regarded, popular and efficient, that he has held public offices for a period of fifteen years. In 1871 he was appointed deputy sheriff, serving two years; in 1876 he became deputy county court clerk, and served twenty-one months; in 1877 he was elected county superintendent of public instruction for two years; in 1879 he was appointed by Judge G. H. Nixon, clerk and master of chancery court, and in 1885 was reappointed to the same position. December 25, 1867, he married Miss M. E. Covey, who was born in Henderson County, in 1847, and a daughter of A. K. Covey. Mr. and Mrs. Brooks are devoted members of the Cumberland Presbyterian Church, in which Mr. Brooks has been an elder for six years. He is also a member of the A. O. U. W. Lodge, No. 82, of Lexington, and K. of H., Lodge No. 199, of Jackson.

Prof. J. L. Cochran, of Sardis, Tenn., was born in Mississippi in 1847, son of S. M. and Nancy (Talley) Cochran. The father was of Irish descent, born in 1808 in Marion County, N. C. He came to Middle Tennessee in 1829, and located in Marshall, where he lived at the time of his marriage to Miss Talley, by whom he had a family of nine sons and five daughters. Mr. Cochran was a skillful cabinet-maker. In 1841 he moved to Pontotoc County, Miss., where he engaged in agricultural pursuits. After the death of his first wife he married Miss Mary Ann Orman, of Alabama, who bore him six children. She still resides in Mississippi, where [her husband died in 1868. Our subject remained with his parents until he reached his majority. He had very limited educational advantages, as his time was employed in earning a livelihood. He left home the possessor of two suits of clothes, $30 in his pocket and little or no learning, but feeling keenly the need of knowledge he at once determined to obtain an education and began making efforts for accomplishing this end. He applied himself closely and diligently, without the aid of an instructor, to gain sufficient information that he might earn money to pay his tuition and board at school. He returned to Tennessee, entered the Union Academy which he was enabled to attend for four years. In 1871 he began teaching, and taught the first six sessions in the same district of Bedford County, thus favorably illustrating his success as a teacher. At one time he had ninety pupils enrolled. In 1879 he became principal of McClure's Institute, holding that position for three years; then taught seven months in Thomasville, Ga.; came back to Tennessee, and since that time has been a resident of Sardis, where he organized the high schools and conducted them for three years in a highly commendable manner. He is universally spoken of as an efficient teacher and a most excellent disciplinarian. He also instructs in all the dead languages: Latin, Greek, etc. July, 1873, he married Miss Ophelia Hardin, a native of Marshall County, and the daughter of Rev. Robert Hardin, D. D. Mrs. Cochran presented her husband with two bright children: Amy Bemis (named after the daughter of Dr. Bemis, of New Orleans), and Thomas A. Prof. Cochran is a Democrat and cast his first presidential vote for Seymour and Blair. He is a member of the Masonic Lodge, No. 137, of Farmington, Tenn., being a Master Mason. The past summer he spent in looking after the interests of his valuable farm which contains about 592 acres. Prof. Cochran is, in every sense of the word, a self-made man. By his own efforts and force of character he has risen from poverty and obscurity, to be acknowledged by all as one of the most cultivated, respected and substantial men in the entire community. He and wife are members of the Presbyterian Church. He taught school at Sulphur Springs, Lincoln Co., Tenn., from 1886 to June, 1887, and then at Spring Place, Marshall Co., Tenn., from 1887 until he was elected principal of McClure's Institute.

A. B. Cunningham, an enterprising farmer of the Seventh District, was born December, 1829, in Henderson County, a son of Ransom and Sarah (Rice) Cunningham. The father was born in Virginia in 1797. When an infant his parents moved to Granville County, N. C., where he remained until after the time of his marriage. He came to Henderson County in 1825, and settled in the Eighteenth District, and lived there until 1844, when he went to the Tenth District, making that his home for about five years. The last year of his life was spent in the Seventh District. At one time he owned 400 acres of fine land; he was one of the oldest settlers and best known men in the section. His death occurred in 1875. His wife was born in North Carolina in 1804; was the mother of eight children, of whom A. B. is the fourth and only surviving one. Mrs. Cunningham departed this life in 1862. The subject of this sketch received a fair education in the schools of his native county, and made his home with his parents until about the age of twenty-five. In 1855 he was united in marriage to a daughter of B. J. Young, Miss Mary Elizabeth, who was born in Henderson County in 1838. To this union four children were born: John, Josella, Martha (wife of John Gardner) and Walter. After his marriage, Mr. Cunningham settled in the Seventh District, where he now resides; he has been unusually successful in all his undertakings, owning about 1,000 acres of fine land; has been operating a grist-mill for a considerable length of time, and for six years a cotton-gin, making about 125 bales per season. In politics he is very conservative, voting strictly for principle, not for party. His first vote was given Gen. Scott (1852). He is a Mason of good standing; belongs to Juno Lodge, No. 43. He and his estimable wife are both members of the Methodist Episcopal Church South.

Dr. R. A. Davidson, a well known and skillful physician, of Lexington, is a native of Lawrence County, Tenn., and the fourth child of a family of eight, born to John D. and Mary (Wasson) Davidson. The father is of Irish descent, born in North Carolina in 1813. He came with his father, John D., Sr., to Tennessee in 1827, and located in Bedford County. After a few years they moved to Lawrence County, where John D., Sr., died. John D., Jr., remained at the same place several years and was married in 1865. He became a resident of Henderson County, Fourth District, where he purchased a large tract of land, about 370 acres, where he now resides. His wife was born in 1823, in Lawrence County. Our subject received his literary education at Lawrenceburg; came to Henderson County when about thirteen years of age, and in 1870 entered into a clerkship in a grocery store for Caraway & Stegall, of Lexington. In 1874 he embarked in the same business for himself, continuing for three years and meeting with success. Much of his leisure time, during the year 1875, had been devoted to the study of medicine. Following the advice of Dr. John Howard, in 1876-77, he attended the medical department of Louisville University, where he graduated in March, 1877. He then returned to Lexington and began to practice. He is now recognized as one of the eminent and leading physicians of the county, where he has an extensive and lucrative practice. The Doctor is a Democrat, casting his first presidential vote for Hancock in 1880. He is also a Mason, member of Lodge No. 67, Lexington. He has many friends by whom he is held in high esteem.

P. J. Dennison, a member of the well known dry goods firm of Dennison & McCall, of Lexington, was born in 1851 in Henderson County; is the eleventh of a family of sixteen children (of whom eight are living), born to Robert R. and Nancy D. (Walker) Dennison. The father was of Irish origin, born in 1814, in Virginia. When a small boy he left his native State with his father, Stephen Dennison. After a few years they located in Decatur County, W. Tenn. About 1857 he became a resident of Henderson County, where he resided until his death in 1866. Robert R. was quite a young man when he came to the county where he lived at the time of his marriage. He settled in the Sixteenth District, which has since been his home. His wife was born in 1820 in North Carolina. She is still living, greatly respected. The subject of this sketch received his education in the Henderson County schools, and remained at home with his parents until about twenty-one; was a salesman in his father's dry goods store for three years previous to that time. In 1872 he opened a store at Lone Elm; remained there until 1881, with the exception of one year spent at Moore's Hill. He established a grocery store at Lexington and one year later, 1882, formed a partnership with Mr. G. W. McCall. By their good management, attention to business, and courtesy, have gained a liberal patronage, and have one of the leading stores of the place. August, 1872, Mr. Dennison married Miss Clemmie McKelvy, of South Carolina, born in 1849. They are members of the Missionary Baptist Church.

Clark Diffee, a prosperous farmer and well known resident of the Second District, was born in Henderson County in 1832; is the second of a family of six children born to Moses and Mary (Lollar) Diffee. The father was born in Randolph County, N. C., in 1806; was of English descent. In 1828 he immigrated to Henderson County, with his father, John Diffee. After his marriage he settled in the Seventh District on the old home place; the last few years of his life were spent with his son Clark; his death occurred in 1876. He was one of the earliest settlers, most substantial farmers and respected citizens of the county. His wife was born in the same State and county as himself, in 1807, and died in 1873. Clark Diffee remained with his parents until the war between the North and South broke out. He entered the Confederate service in May, 1861, enlisting in Company I, Thirteenth Regiment Tennessee Infantry. He participated in the engagements at Belmont, Shiloh, Perryville, Murfreesboro, Chickamauga, Missionary Ridge, Atlanta, Nashville, Franklin and many skirmishes. He was on active duty until December 24, 1864, when he returned home. During the entire time of his gallant service, he was fortunate enough to have never received a severe wound, nor to have been made a prisoner. August 29, 1867, he married Miss Mary B., daughter of Dr. John Parsons. Mrs. Diffee was born in Decatur County, in 1848; is the mother of six children: Robert L., John T., Dora B., Bettie May, Charles V. and Johnnie. In 1868 Mr. Diffee purchased 338 acres of land in the Second District where he located and has since resided. He has all modern improvements and best of buildings on his place, and owns in all, about 954 acres. For the past ten years he has been running a cotton-gin, ginning, on an average, about forty bales a season. He is one of the most enterprising and successful farmers in the county, where he is universally esteemed. He is a stanch Democrat; gave his first vote in 1856 for Filmore. His wife is a devoted and respected member of the Missionary Baptist Church.

James C. Dodds, a well known farmer of the Fifth District, was born in Henderson County, 1837, the oldest of a family of five boys and eleven girls born to Thomas M. and

Mary G. (Crook) Dodds. The father was of English descent, born in 1810. When a youth he came to Henderson County with his father, James Dodds; they located in the Third District, a portion of the county which was then called Chester County; they were among the pioneer settlers. Thomas M. after his marriage moved to the Fifth District, residing there until 1848, when he sold out, and bought property in the Fifth District of Chester County and resided there until his death in 1874. His wife was also of English origin, born in South Carolina in 1820; since Mr. Dodd's death she has been living on the home place with her youngest son, Robert B. James C. received his education in the Henderson County schools, remaining at home until his majority. In November, 1860, he married a daughter of Henry and Catherine Anderson, Miss Mary E., who was born in the county in 1839. To this union nine children were born: Annie L., wife of C. M. Keys; James W.; John S.; Mamie C.; Oscar L.; Lura E.; Carrie E.; Maggie May, and Robert E. Soon after his marriage the late war broke out and Mr. Dodds donned the gray, enlisting in July, 1863, in Company D, Twenty-first Regiment, Tennessee Cavalry. He took active part in many engagements, was at Okalona, Fort Pillow, Nashville and at Brice's Cross-roads, where he received a severe wound in the right shoulder, which disabled him for five months. On December, 1864, he was captured and made prisoner, was taken to Johnson's Island and retained until restoration of peace; on May, 1865, he went to Mississippi, remaining there until 1871, and then returned to his native county. In 1874 he purchased 337 acres in the Fifth District, where he now resides. He has bought a considerable amount of real estate; is one of the most enterprising and prosperous farmers in the section, where he is well known and universally respected. In 1882 he was elected magistrate of his district, and since that time, has adjusted all difficulties brought before him, with judicial fairness and satisfaction to all. He is a Democrat, casting his first vote for John Bell in 1860. Mrs. Dodds is an estimable lady, a consistent member of the Methodist Episcopal Church South.

William Elkins, a popular citizen of Lexington and a member of the firm of Galloway & Elkins, was born in Henderson County in 1853 and is the eldest of a family of four children born to Scion and Mary (Galloway) Elkins, both native Tennesseans. The father was born in 1826 of Irish extraction. While a resident of Henderson County he was married and afterward settled in the Second Civil District. About 1858 he moved to Benton County. He was a farmer and died in 1862. His wife was born in 1823. After Mr. Elkins' death she married Samuel Whitney, by whom she had two children. William Elkins, our subject, received his education in Henderson County. He began merchandising in 1875 with his uncle, M. S. Galloway, and has remained with him since that time. In 1877 they established a livery stable in connection with their store. It was destroyed by fire in 1878 and the following year they again built, and have one of the best stables in this section, well stocked with fine horses, buggies, double vehicles and all fixtures necessary to the equipment of such a trade. The firm is recognized as one of the most substantial in the county, its members being men of ability, accommodation and honor. In 1878 Mr. Elkins married Miss Nannie Ross, of Henderson County, a daughter of James Ross, an old and respected resident. To this union two children have been born: Bessie and Willie. Mr. Elkins is a Democrat and cast his first vote for S. J. Tilden in 1876.

Euphrates Flake, a successful farmer of the Seventeenth District, was born in Henderson County in 1847, a son of William B. and Nancy (Howard) Flake. The father was of Irish origin, born about 1803 in North Carolina; about 1820, with his father, Samuel Flake, immigrated to Henderson County, settling in the Seventeenth District, which at that time contained very few residents. William B. soon after his marriage located near the homestead; he was a prosperous farmer and merchant; had a general store on the farm; he owned about 540 acres of fine productive soil. His death occurred in 1856. His wife was born in North Carolina in 1809, and died in 1859; they had eight children, only two of whom are now living; our subject was the sixth child. After the death of his parents he made his home with his uncle, Dudley L. Flake, who died in 1862. Euphrates then went to live with an uncle in Mississippi, James House, but in 1866 returned to his native county, accepted a position as salesman with P. E. Parker at Wildersville, where he remained four years. In 1873 he established a retail liquor store in Lexington, but only continued there a year. The following three years he was engaged in the same business in Huntingdon. In May, 1878, he married a daughter of Samuel Howard, Miss Bina, a native of Henderson County, born in 1856. To this union two children have been born: Howard and Bettie. In 1882 Mr. Flake purchased 640 acres of land, and located where he now resides. He erected a cotton-gin the same year, which he operates in connection with his farm; he makes on an average, thirty bales per season. He is an enterprising, industrious and prosperous farmer, and good citizen. He is a life-long Democrat, casting his first vote for Seymour and Blair in 1868. He is an old member of the I. O. O. F. Lodge No. 150. Mrs. Flake is an estimable lady, and a consistent member of the Methodist Episcopal Church.

G. W. Florence, a prominent merchant of Lexington, was born in Caswell County, N. C., in 1840, a son of J. T. and Alvis (Simmons) Florence, both of whom were of Turkish-French descent, natives of North Carolina. The father was born in 1812 and while a resident of his native State married. In 1842 he immigrated to Benton County, W. Tenn., where for many years he taught school, being one of the pioneer professors of that section. The latter portion of his life he devoted to agricultural pursuits; he departed this life in 1883. The mother was born in 1814, and is still living, beloved by all. Of a family of nine children born to them, eight are still living, the subject of this sketch being the eldest; he was but two years of age when the family came to Tennessee. His education, which is thorough and liberal, was received in Benton County. At the age of eighteen he became salesman in the store of C. K. Wyly at Camden, Tenn., remaining there three years. When the late civil war broke out he donned the gray, and in 1861 enlisted in Company G, Fifty-fifth Regiment, Tennessee Infantry. He took active part in the battles of Island No. 10, Chickamauga, Knoxville and numerous other minor engagements. He was twice captured, the first time was exchanged immediately, but the next time was taken to Fort Donelson and retained about eleven months. He returned home in May, 1865, after the restoration of peace. He resumed work in Mr. Wyly's store; two years later came to Lexington, accepted a position as clerk in the house of A. R. Hall; in 1879 they became partners; in 1882 Mr. Florence bought the entire stock, and from that time has conducted the business. He now carries an extensive general stock, including dry goods, clothing, boots and shoes, furniture, wooden-ware, and various other commodities. He is an industrious, energetic and intelligent man; by his integrity and ability has met with unusual success in life. Mr. Florence is a Democrat, casting his first vote for H. Greeley, in 1872; he is a Mason, belonging to Lodge No. 67, of Camden.

H. W. Foster, farmer of the Sixth District, was born in Halifax County, Va., 1833; he is one of the three living children of a family of ten, born to Joshua and Susan (Adams) Foster. The father was of English extraction, born in 1788, in Nottaway County, Va. While a resident of his native State, he married a lady of Halifax County, who was also of English descent, born in 1801, and departed this life 1867. In 1835 Mr. Foster emigrated from the "Old Dominion" to Henderson County, locating in the Sixth District, where he purchased 300 acres of land and engaged in farming; in 1857 he moved to Yell County, Ark., and in 1868 to Kaufman County, Tex., where he continued his agricultural pursuits. He was an unusually hale and robust man during the greater portion of his life; he died in 1883 at the advanced age of ninety-five years. H. W. Foster was a small child when his parents came to Henderson County, where he received his education, attending school only about five months. He remained at home until about twenty-three years of age; two years previous to that time he began teaching; he taught about twelve sessions in the Sixth, Tenth and Eleventh Districts. December 20, 1857, he married a daughter of Benjamin and Easter Smith, Miss Nancy, who was born in the county in 1833. To this union ten children were born: Fannie W., wife of N. C. Patterson; Leora D., wife of G. W. Priddy; Mollie A., wife of C. W. Johnson; Joshua B.; Nancy S.; Josephine L.; Samuel H.; George; Phillip T. and James H. When hostilities broke out, Mr. Foster's sympathies were with his people, and September, 1861, he enlisted in Company I, Twenty-seventh Regiment, Tennessee Infantry. He participated in the battles at Perryville,

Shiloh and Clifton; after the battle of Shiloh he was commissioned as first lieutenant of his company and remained as such until the reorganization of the army in 1863, when he returned home. In 1873 Mr. Foster purchased 190 acres of land and located where he now resides. For the past twenty-five years he has run a cotton-gin; in 1878 built another one, since which time he has been ginning, on an average, 200 bales per year. He is one of the most flourishing farmers in the county, a man of ability and determination and by his good management and economy has accumulated about 1,250 acres of good land. He is a stanch Democrat, casting his first presidential vote for Filmore in 1856. He belongs to the I. O. O. F. Lodge, No. 154, Lexington.

James H. Fuller, of Lone Elm, was born in 1823, in the portion of Humphreys County now called Benton County, a son of Ephraim B. and Mary (Conyers) Fuller, both natives of North Carolina. The father was of English origin, born 1787, in Granville County. At an early date, and after his marriage, he immigrated to Humphreys County; in 1832 became a resident of Henderson County, locating four miles north of Lexington; about 1839 moved to the Twentieth District, remaining there until his death in 1871. His wife was born in 1790, departed this life in 1865; was the mother of nine children, five of whom are still living. James H. was but nine years of age when his parents moved to Henderson County. He remained with them until after his majority, giving them the proceeds of his labor. September 9, 1845, he married Miss Eleanor McCall, a native of the county, born August 21. 1824, a daughter of Andrew and Jane McCall. Mrs. Fuller died January 22, 1874, being the mother of eight children: Harriet F., Martha J., Tallitha C., Mary I., Patrick F., James H.; Joseph W. and William, deceased. Mr. Fuller settled in the Twentieth District and began farming. He commenced a poor man, but by his industry, energy and judicious management, accumulated considerable means and property. He owned 1,000 acres of good land, which he disposed of in 1881, and moved to Lone Elm, where he leads a quiet and retired life. November 23, 1876, he united in marriage with Mrs. Elizabeth Marsh, nee White. Mr. Fuller has always been a Republican, and one of the leading men of his party; gave his first vote for Henry Clay in 1844; in 1846 he was elected magistrate for his district, serving until the war; after peace was restored he was appointed by Gov. Brownlow, and afterward elected and re-elected, holding the office until 1880. The last fourteen years of his official life he was chairman of the county court. He is one of Henderson County's most substantial, honored and popular residents, a consistent member of the Primitive Baptist Church, a true, Christian gentleman.

M. L. Galloway, a well known member of the firm of Galloway & Elkins, was born in Henderson County, March 2, 1835, and is the sixth of a family of seven children born to M. J. and Martha (Norris) Galloway. The father was born in Chatham County, N. C., in 1800, and was of Scotch-Irish descent. He married a native of his State, who was born in 1798. They immigrated to Middle Tennessee in 1824, and a year later located in the Second District of Henderson County. They lived in different parts of the county, and the father was one of its most respected and influential citizens. He was a teacher for several years, also twice a representative of Henderson County in the State Legislature. He died in 1874, two years previous to the death of his widow. Our subject was reared at home and educated in the county schools. He began farming at an early age, continuing until 1875, when he entered the mercantile business in Lexington. Two years later he and Mr. Elkins established a livery and feed stable, but were burned out in 1878. The next year they rebuilt and have now a fine stable, in connection with which they manage a first-class grocery. In 1858 Mr. Galloway married Miss Helen M. Bartholomew, a native of Henderson County, born in 1835. She died in 1864, leaving one child, Amanda W., wife of E. E. Muse. In 1872 Mr. Galloway married Miss P. A. Reed, of Henderson County, and a daughter of W. A. Reed. Mr. Galloway is one of Lexington's worthiest and most substantial citizens. He is a Democrat, and his first presidential vote was given to James Buchanan. He is a member of the Masonic fraternity, Lodge No. 64, Chapter No. 87.

J. N. Hall, a leading druggist of Lexington, was born in 1844, near his present place of residence. He is the son of Robert W. and Martha (Thomas) Hall. The father is of Scotch-Irish descent, born in Huntsville, Ala., in 1813. When a youth he commenced clerking in the dry goods store of Mr. Bradley, where he continued in the same capacity for about fifteen years. When about twenty-six years of age he went to Reynoldsburg, Tenn. The following four years he was engaged as clerk, captain or overseer on the Tennessee and Mississippi Rivers. In 1843 he came to Lexington and established a mercantile house, where he displayed marked business qualifications, and met with success. In 1860 he moved two and a half miles out of the town; in 1866 went to Jackson and resumed merchandising; in 1883 he sold out, and has since lived a retired life. He has the confidence and esteem of all. His marriage with Martha Thomas occurred in 1843, at Paris, Tenn., an estimable lady of Henry County, born in 1826, of French-Scotch descent. To them eleven children were born, nine of whom are living, the subject of our sketch being the eldest. He received his education in the academy at Lexington. When quite young he entered his father's store as clerk, and remained there until 1873, when he came to Lexington and opened a first-class drug store, in which business he is still engaged, carrying a large stock of drugs, paints, oils, brushes, perfumes, etc. He is a man of ability and integrity, inheriting largely many of his father's noble traits of character. He is a member of the Methodist Episcopal Church South, and a Mason, belonging to St. John's Lodge, No. 139, of Jackson. He is also a Democrat, and his first presidential vote was given Horatio Seymour in 1868. Mr. Hall was married November 13, 1879, to Lyda Fielder, a native of Lexington and daughter of John S. and Mary P. (McHenry) Fielder. The father is a well known druggist. Mrs. Hall is the mother of three children: Robert W., John F. and Lyda. Mrs. Hall is a true Christian woman, a member of the Missionary Baptist Church.

Isaac W. Hassell, the popular hotel proprietor and farmer of Sardis, was born October 19, 1838, in Perry, now Decatur County, and is a son of Nathaniel G. and Pena A. (Raphael) Hassell, both natives of North Carolina. The father was born in 1800, and immigrated to Tennessee in 1836. The following year he married. He was a tanner by trade, and his death occurred in 1858, in Hardin County. His wife, who was born in 1818, married the second time, to Mr. A. B. Craig, who is also deceased. Mrs. Craig resides in Sardis. Isaac W. remained at home until his majority. He then began teaching school, which he continued for ten years in Henderson and Hardin Counties. October 7, 1866, he married Miss Miranda Hanna, a native of Henderson Co., born Jan. 10, 1843, and the daughter of Capt. James Hanna, a well known and prominent man. To Mr. and Mrs. Hassell seven children have been born: James A., Emma D., Mary E., John W., Minnie A., Nellie and Isaac W. Nellie died August 5, 1879, at four years of age. In 1871 Mr. Hassell moved to his present place of residence. He built the first house and was the first postmaster in Sardis. He sold goods at that place for three years, after which he gave his attention to agriculture, and now owns 200 acres of good land. He operated a cotton-gin from 1874 until 1884. The past four years have been devoted to hotel-keeping in Sardis, and he does all in his power for the pleasure and accommodation of his guests and consequently receives a liberal patronage. He was a strong Union man and is now a Republican, casting his first presidential vote for John C. Breckenridge in 1860. He is a Mason of good standing, belonging to Lodge No. 267, Saltillo, Tenn. He and wife are members of the Methodist Episcopal Church. Mr. Hassell is a man of strong character and independent nature, advocating a principle if he believes it to be right, regardless of the opinions of others. He is enterprising and genial and is held in high regard.

Samuel Howard, ex trustee of Henderson County, and one of its old citizens and farmers, was born in 1823 in North Carolina, son of William and Ursley (Henson) Howard, both of English descent, and both natives of North Carolina. The father was an agriculturist and came to Henderson County in 1825, where he remained until his death. He was one of the first white settlers and most successful farmers, owning about 1,000 acres of land. He died in 1868 and his wife two years later. To them were born twelve children, Samuel being the fifth. He received his education in the common schools of Henderson County, remaining at home until he was twenty-four years of age. In 1847 he married Mary, daughter of Richard and Mary Timberlake. She was born in Henderson County in 1831, and died in 1864. She became the mother of six children, four of whom are living: Richard W., Charles F., James N., and Melvina, wife of E. Flake. Mr. Howard married the second time, in 1870, to Bettie H. Hinkle, a lady of Kentucky. Mr. Howard is a Democrat, previous to the war a Whig, and cast his first presidential vote for Henry Clay in 1844. In 1850 he was elected constable and served two years. In 1853 he was made justice of the peace of the Tenth District, and for three years adjusted all difficulties brought before him with judicial fairness, but resigned after that length of time. In 1877 he was elected trustee of Henderson County, by the county court to fill the unexpired term of B. A. Priddy, who resigned. In 1878-80-82-84 he was re-elected by a large majority, thus illustrating his popularity and the satisfaction he had given the people. His successor, Mr. A. G. Douglass, took possession of the office Monday, September, 1886. Mr. Howard is one of the most prosperous farmers in this section, owning about 1,700 acres of valuable land. He is a member of the Masonic Fraternity, Blue Lodge, No. 64, and Chapter No———. His wife is a member of the Methodist Episcopal Church South.

J. W. H. Knowles, a prominent resident and well known farmer of the Sixth District, was born in Rutherford County, Tenn., in 1829, a son of Edmond and Elizabeth (Matthews) Knowles. The father was of English extraction, born in Sumter District, S. C., in 1799; he immigrated to Rutherford County about 1824, and moved to Henderson County about 1831, locating in the Sixth District, where the remainder of his life was spent; his death occurred in 1882. He was one of the most prosperous farmers in the county, owning at one time 3,000 acres of land; he was also one of the earliest settlers, best known and respected men. His wife was of Irish origin, born in South Carolina in 1801; is still living and in her eighty-seventh year. The subject of this sketch was only one-and-a-half years old when his parents came to Henderson County; he made his home with them until his majority. May 10, 1856, he married Miss Elizabeth Darden, a native of North Carolina, born in 1827, and a daughter of Miles Darden, who was one of the largest men in the United States, weighing upward of 800 pounds at the time of his death. Mr. and Mrs. Knowles have eight living children: Mary F.; Robert E. and Martha are twins (Martha is the wife of Wm. Webb); James D., Susan A., John M., Hubert F., Lura V. After marriage Mr. Knowles located on a portion of the estate given him by his father, which contained nearly 500 acres, and has resided there since that time. He is an extensive landholder; besides his home and other real estate, he owns eleven fine lots in Henderson, Chester County. He is one of the most enterprising and energetic farmers; has always met with success in all his undertakings; he is well known and universally liked; is a stanch Republican; voted the first time for Gen. Scott, in 1852. He is a Mason, belongs to Lodge No. 64, of Lexington. He and Mrs. Knowles are esteemed members of the Missionary Baptist Church.

Dr. G. L. Laws, one of the most eminent, respected and substantial physicians and surgeons of the county, is a resident of the Seventeenth District, eight miles north of Lexington. He was born in Russell County, Ala., in 1836, a son of Hiram and O. A. (Sims) Laws. The father was of English-French origin, born in 1803, in Orange County, N. C., where he resided at the time of his marriage, in 1826, immediately after which he immigrated to Carroll County, Tenn., engaging in agricultural pursuits. In 1834 or 1835, he moved to Russell County, Ala., during the Creek and Indian war. The latter part of 1835 or 1837, with his family, he fled from the State to escape the treachery and ferocity of the Indians. He returned to Carroll County, locating near Clarksburg, where he owned 290 acres of land. He died in 1879. His wife was of English descent, born in 1807, in Orange County, N. C. She was the mother of six children, four of whom are living. Her death occurred in 1872. Our subject, Dr. G. L. Laws, was the fifth child; he received his literary education in the common schools of Carroll County, and the academy at Huntingdon, Tenn. When quite a young man he worked as a farm hand; at the age of twenty began teaching school, which he followed for four years, during vacation attending school. When about twenty-three years of age, he began the study of medicine under guidance of Dr. Henry McCall of Clarksburg; in 1860 he entered the medical department of Nashville University, and the following year located at Macedonia, Carroll County, where he began the practice of his profession; a year later he came to Henderson County, settling where he now resides. In November, 1863, he married a daughter of Peter and Mary Ann Pearson, Miss Mary Pearson, who was born in Henderson County in 1843, and who bore him one child, William D. Mrs. Laws died in 1867, and in 1869 he married his sister-in-law, Jemima M. Pearson, a native of the county, born in 1852; they have one child living: Joseph H. The Doctor has an extensive and lucrative practice, and is considered one of the most able physicians and surgeons in the county. He is also one of the most prosperous and successful business men; he owns 1,400 acres of valuable land, and attends to all of his real estate interests. Previous to the war the Doctor was a Whig, and is now a Republican; he cast his first vote for U. S. Grant in 1868. The Doctor and Mrs. Laws are esteemed and earnest members of the Christian Church.

John C. Lockhead, one of the most enterprising young farmers of the Tenth District, was born in Marshall County, Ky., November 12, 1862, a son of John W. and Helen (Ellis) Lackhead. The father was born in 1840 in Scotland; when quite young immigrated to the United States with his parents, locating at Eddyville, Ky. Mr. Lockhead was a firm supporter of the Union, and in 1861 crossed the Mason and Dixon line, going to Illinois. In the fall of 1862, he enlisted in the Fifteenth Kentucky Regiment Cavalry; was elected orderly sergeant. At the end of first year the regiment disbanded; he at once enlisted in the Forty-eighth Regiment, Kentucky Infantry, and was appointed adjutant, having the rank of lieutenant. At Princeton, Ky., he was taken sick with erysipelas and died December 7, 1863. August 15, 1861, he was united in marriage to Miss Helen Ellis, a daughter of Dr. Jonathan and Lucy A. (Gould) Ellis. Mrs. Lockhead was born July 22, 1842, in Jefferson County, N. Y. In April, 1866, she married at Birmingham, Ky., George W. Council, a resident of Lexington, Tenn., and where they immediately made their home. Their union was not a happy one, and in March, 1884, Mrs. Council obtained a divorce, moving the same year to her farm one mile east of Lexington, where she now resides with her son. They had 670 acres of valuable, productive land. John C. is a young man of sterling qualities, industrious, energetic and a good manager, has the respect and goodwill of all who know him. He is a stanch Republican, casting his first presidential vote for James G. Blaine. The mother is a devoted member of the Christian Church, and universally liked.

Hon. W. T. Logan, a prominent attorney at law of Lexington, was born at Saltillo, Hardin Co., Tenn., in 1857, a son of Dr. John H. and Sarah (Davey) Logan. The father is of Irish descent, and was born in Marion Co., Ala., in 1820. The grandfather, John Logan, Sr., was a native of Ireland; he participated in the Irish rebellion in 1798, made his escape and came to America, taking up his abode in North Carolina; in 1809 he moved to Marion County, Ala., where he died at the age of fifty-six. John, Jr., when a youth immigrated to Hardin County, Tenn., settling at Saltillo, and commenced practicing medicine, having graduated in 1843 in the medical department of the University of Louisville, Ky. He is still actively engaged in his profession, and for many years has been recognized as one of the leading and most popular physicians in the section in which he lives. His wife is also of Irish extraction, born in 1822; she is the mother of four children, of whom our subject is the third. He received his academic education in his native town; at the age of twenty-two began to read law, his preceptor being Judge Levi S. Woods of Lexington. In June, 1880, he graduated in the law department of Cumberland University at Lebanon, Tenn., immediately afterward locating in Lexington and entering upon the practice of his chosen profession; he is a man of wonderful talent, brilliancy and depth; one of the most eminent lawyers of the county. In 1884 he was nominated by the Democratic party as the representative of his county in the Legislature. His competitor was the Hon. John E. McCall, a young man of fine ability. They canvassed the county jointly, in which Mr. Logan won the reputation of being an able, logical debater and forcible speaker. In August, for attorney-general, Mr. McCall received over 400 majority, and for Representative Mr. Logan was defeated by the small number of 116. April 25, 1883, he married a daughter of John S. and Mary P. Fielder, Miss Celestia A., who was born in Henderson County in 1862. To this union one child has been born, John F. Mr. Logan is an exemplary Christian, and an earnest member of the Missionary Baptist Church.

William B. Long was born in Henderson County, Tenn., May 7, 1848, of poor but respectable parentage. His father, Jefferson Long, dying when William was very young, left him in almost destitute circumstances. He was reared by his mother and step-father, "who was also in moderate circumstances," up to the age of seventeen years, after which he started out penniless, with nothing but his unflinching determination to succeed in life. He worked incessantly, almost day and night, until he by dint of hard labor earned a sufficiency to set himself up in business, which he commenced in the village of Middleburg (Long) in 1880. He was elected justice of the peace over his opponents by a handsome majority in 1882. He has made rapid strides in the way of fame and wealth, and at this early date is worth between $10,000 and $15,000, and now stands as one of the leading and most enterprising men of his county. Mr. Long is a man of smooth temperament, unassuming, accommodating, and well liked by all unbiased minds who have dealings with him.

G. W. McCall, a member of the dry goods firm of Dennison & McCall, of Lexington, is a son of Andrew and Jane (Dennison) McCall. The father is of Scotch-Irish extraction, born in South Carolina in 1827; when but three years of age left the Palmetto State with his father, Andrew Dennison, Sr., immigrating to Henderson County, Tenn., and located in the Twentieth Dist., where the latter bought about 300 acres of land and began cultivation. He was one of the pioneer settlers and best known men in the county; departed this life in 1841 at the age of fifty-one years. Andrew, Jr., was married in 1849, to a lady who was born in Decatur County in 1833, and who bore him eight children, of whom our subject is the third. Mr. and Mrs. McCall are living on the old homestead, where they own 320 acres of valuable soil. G. W. McCall received a good education in the Henderson County schools, and attended two sessions at McKenzie, Carroll County. In 1873 he accepted a situation in a general store at Fulton, Ky., where he remained two years; he continued clerking for some time in different localities and in 1882 entered into a partnership with Mr. P. J. Dennison, establishing a first-class dry goods house in Lexington. They are both men of energy and ability, and have met with great success in their undertaking. Mr. McCall is a Republican; cast his first vote for the late James A. Garfield in 1880. He is a genial man and worthy citizen, having a large circle of friends and acquaintances.

Hon. John E. McCall, attorney at law, of Lexington, was born at Clarksburg, Carroll Co., Tenn., in 1859, a son of Dr. Henry and Frances (Bowlin) McCall. The father was of Scotch-Irish descent, born in South Carolina in 1817; when seventeen years of age came with his father, Andrew McCall, to Henderson County, settling in the Twentieth District. Andrew died in 1841. When about twenty Henry commenced the study of medicine; he graduated as an M. D. at Nashville University. He resided in Madison County at the time of his marriage; about 1850 he moved to Clarksburg, where he remained until his death, in 1880. Dr. McCall was for many years one of the leading and most skillful physicians and surgeons of Carroll County. His wife was of English origin, born in Alabama in 1827. She was the mother of seven children: Caledonia I., wife of L. F. Williams; George T., an attorney of Huntingdon; M. Jennie, wife of J. W. Scott; Patrick H., a dentist at Clarksburg; James C. R., county court clerk of Carroll County; Ella, and John E., whose literary education was received at the University of Tennessee at Knoxville, which he attended for three years; in 1881 he began to read law under direction of Judge Joe Hawkins; in 1883 he located at Lexington, where he commenced his practice. Mr. McCall is an ardent Republican, casting his first vote for Jas. A. Garfield in 1880. In 1884 he was elector on the Blaine and Logan ticket for the Eighth Congressional District. In August, 1886, he was a candidate for attorney-general of the Eleventh Judicial Circuit; the Democratic majority is about 1,000, but Mr. McCall brought it down to 265, thus illustrating his popularity among his people. In November, 1886, he was elected Representative of Henderson County in the State Legislature; his opponent was the Hon. W. T. Logan, a gifted and able lawyer and eloquent speaker; they canvassed the county jointly, which resulted as above mentioned. Mr. McCall is one of the bright and shining lights of the profession, possessing unusual intellect and keen discernment, and is a courteous, genial gentleman. October 14, 1885, he married a daughter of Edward J. and Lula Timberlake, Miss Addie, who was born in Henderson County in 1864. They have one child, Addie. Mrs. McCall is a most estimable lady and member of the Methodist Episcopal Church South.

Dr. D. E. McCallum, a prominent physician and surgeon of Wildersville, was born in Madison County, Tenn., in 1858, a son of Peter and Roxy (Estis) McCallum. The father was of Scotch descent, born in 1828 in Madison County, where, with the exception of ten years spent in Henderson County, he passed his entire life. He was one of the most prosperous farmers and successful speculators in the section. He owned about 1,000 acres of fine land. He was magistrate of the Thirteenth District for many years. His death occurred in 1880. The mother, who is still living, was also born in Madison County in 1830. She has five children living: John R., who resides at Claybrook, is a farmer and speculator; Duncan E. (our subject); Francis P. lives at his mother's home; of the twins, Annie is at home and Joseph is a student in the literary department of Cumberland University at Lebanon, Tenn.; Peter L. (deceased). Our subject, Dr. D. E., received his literary education in the University of Tennessee, at Knoxville, which he attended three and a half years. In 1880 he began the study of medicine under the tuition of Dr. Savage, of Jackson, who is now a professor in the Vanderbilt University at Nashville, and from which institution Dr. McCallum graduated in the medical department in March, 1884. Immediately afterward he located at his present place of residence, and entered upon the exercise of his profession. By his thorough knowledge, skill and courtesy to patrons, he has now an extensive and lucrative practice and is recognized as one of the leading and most popular physicians in the county. He owns about 250 acres of land and a half interest in a cotton-gin, his partners being the Rosser Bros. They made 100 bales in 1886. The Doctor is a Democrat, voting the first time for Cleveland.

W. C. McHaney, a retired merchant and respected old resident of Lexington, was born in Pittsylvania County, Va., in 1818, and is the son of Cornelius and Patience (Hurt) McHaney. The father was also born in Pittsylvania County, Va., in 1780. He was of Irish extraction and a farmer by occupation. In 1835 he immigrated to Henderson County, Second Civil District, where he became possessed of 1,000 acres of land. He was one of the early settlers of West Tennessee, and died August 19, 1842. The mother was of Scotch descent, born in Charlotte County, Va., in 1796, and died in 1836. They had a family of ten children—seven sons and three daughters—only three of the family now living. Our subject was the fourth child and came to Henderson County when seventeen years of age, having clerked for two years previous to that time. In 1836 he was employed by Gladden, Gorin & Co., of Lexington, in a general merchandise store, where he remained two years. In 1840 he embarked in the grocery business for himself, sold out three years later and established a dry goods house but sold out in 1847. He then moved to the Third District and gave his attention to farming. From 1865 he was interested in a general store at Crucifer, and in 1872 re-opened a dry goods store, which he turned over to his two sons, in 1878, Cornelius F. and John C., and two sons-in-law, Hon. John M. Taylor and Judge Levi Wood. He has, since that time, led a retired life. In 1841 he married Miss Louisa Henry, a native of Smith County, Tenn., born in 1821, the daughter of Felix and Caroline Henry, and a member of the Methodist Episcopal Church South. To this union were born twelve children, seven of whom are living: Cornelius F.; Amanda J., wife of Hon. John M. Taylor, present congressman from the Eighth Congressional District; Mary S., wife of Hon. Levi S. Wood, present circuit judge of the Eleventh Judicial District; John C.; Elizabeth, wife of William T. Lawler; Nannie L. and Henry A. Mr. McHaney was for forty years one of the solid business men of Henderson County, possessing ability and other characteristics which have enabled him to succeed in all he has ever undertaken. The welfare of the community was always dear to him and he extended a helping hand to all beneficial enterprises. In 1840 he cast his first presidential vote for

Harrison but has since been a stanch Democrat. He was elected by the county court in 1842 to fill the unexpired term of S. M. Orton, county register in 1846–47; served as deputy sheriff for two years. He was also one of the commissioners who supervised the building of the courthouse.

Hon. La Fayette F. McHaney, one of the influential and best known residents of the Second District, was born in Pittsylvania County, Va., in 1825. He is the seventh of a family of ten children born to Cornelius and Patience (Hurt) McHaney. The father was born in above mentioned State and county, in 1780, of Irish descent, a farmer by occupation. He came to Henderson County, Tenn.; in 1835, being one of the early settlers, and was an extensive land owner, having 1,000 acres. He died August 19, 1842. The mother was of Scotch origin; born in Charlotte County, Va., 1796, departed this life in July, 1836. Our subject was ten years old when his parents came to Tennessee; received his education in Lexington; at the age of seventeen he became salesman in a general store, working for Bradford & Cobb, of Mifflin; remained with them one year, following two years clerked for his brother, W. C., and Isaac Lollor; in Lexington. In 1848, with his two brothers, W. C. and C. D., he established a store in Mifflin; at the end of four years sold his interests. and began farming; in 1865, with his brother, W. C., again engaged in merchandise, opening a store at Crucifer, where they met with great success. In 1876 W. C. sold his interest to La Fayette, who carried on the business two years, and since that time has devoted himself to agriculture and politics. He is an ardent and earnest Democrat, one of the strong and leading members of the party. In 1858 he was elected deputy sheriff of the county, serving until 1862; he was elected to the State Legislature in 1880, and two years later elected as joint representative from Madison and Henderson Counties, thus demonstrating the high regard in which he is held by his people. He was one of the committee on claim and agriculture interests. He is one of Henderson County's most able and enterprising men. He owns about 800 acres of valuable land and has a delightful home. In 1849 Mr. McHaney married a daughter of Felix and Caroline Henry, Miss Samantha A., a native of the county, born in 1829. She died in 1860, leaving two children—Robert, and Ida, wife of Dr. J. T. Raines. In 1863 Mr. McHaney married Miss Minerva M. Jones, who was born in Madison County, in 1845. Their union has been blessed with four children: Caroline, Bessie May, William and Guy. Mr. and Mrs. McHaney are devoted members of the Methodist Episcopal Church South.

Prof. S. A. Mynders, principal of the Lexington Academy, was born in Northfield, Minn., in 1861; son of A. and S. M. (Simmons) Mynders. The father was born in New York in 1827, and was a carriage manufacturer by trade. At the time of his marriage he was living in Troy, N. Y., where his wife was born in 1831. They moved to Minnesota in 1855; from there to Knoxville, Tenn., in 1866, where he died in 1882, and where his wife now resides. To their union eight children were born, five of whom are still living, the fourth being our subject. He received a very thorough academic and collegiate education at the University of Tennessee, graduating in June, 1880, taking the degree of A. B. The same year he was elected professor of mathematics in the I. O. O. F. College, at Humboldt, Tenn. The following year he became president of that institution, remaining in the chair for three years. He has been instructor in the State Normal Institutes of this State for the past three summers. In January, 1885, he was elected principal of the academy at Lexington, which position he now holds, giving universal satisfaction. He is recognized as one of the most able and proficient instructors, also one of the finest disciplinarians, in West Tennessee. He is a man of high moral character, having the esteem of patrons, pupils and faculty. He is a Democrat; a member of the I. O. O. F., K. of H., of Humboldt, and F. & A. M., Lexington, Tenn. In August, 1884, he married Miss Pobrecitta Richerson, who was born in Buenos Ayres, Argentine Republic, South America, in 1865, and is a daughter of Capt. Alfred and Bettie Richerson, of Humboldt, Tenn. Prof. and Mrs. Mynders have two interesting children—Clarence and Hamon. Both parents are members of the Cumberland Presbyterian Church.

Hon. Peter Pearson, an old and respected citizen of the Eighth District, was born in Anson County, N. C., in 1814, a son of John and Penelope (Taylor) Pearson. The father was of French-Welsh descent, born in Perquimans County, N. C. In 1836 he immigrated to Henderson County, Tenn., where he died at the age of sixty-eight. His wife was of Irish descent, a native of Edgecombe County, N. C. She lived to the age of ninety years, was the mother of four children, only two of whom are living. Nathan, who is about two years older than Peter, is also a resident of Henderson County. The subject of this sketch came to Tennessee about one year earlier than his father, and December 22, 1835, married a daughter of Scion and Hannah Prichard, Miss Mary, who was born in North Carolina and died January 26, 1866, at the age of forty-six years. She left seven children: James N., John D., Peter S., Jemima, wife of Dr. G. W. Laws, and Martha, wife of William Milam. In July, 1873, Mr. Pearson married, the second time, Harriet McMurray, born in Maury County, Tenn. Mr. Pearson is a stanch Democrat, an influential man in his party. Previous to the war he was magistrate for four years; in 1865 was elected on a general ticket as representative, and for three terms represented his people in a manner highly creditable and satisfactory. He is an old and honored member of the I. O. O. F., head officer at the lodge at Wilderville. Mr. Pearson commenced life as a poor man, and the property he accumulated was all destroyed during the war, but by industry, courage and judicious management he is now the possessor of a fine farm containing 808 acres of valuable land, well cultivated, stocked and improved. He is a man of sound judgment, a good adviser, whose council is often sought. He is highly esteemed wherever he is known.

John Pearson, a prosperous farmer and old resident of the Tenth District of Henderson County, was born in 1834, in Anson County, N. C., a son of Shadrach and Betsy (Cox) Pearson, both natives of North Carolina. The father was born about 1810, was a farmer by occupation. After his marriage he moved to Henderson County in 1836, locating in the Eighth District, and purchased a plantation containing about 200 acres of land. About 1848 he moved to Carroll County, where he resided until his death in 1875. The mother of John died about 1846. Mr. Pearson was twice married afterward, and the father of twenty-four children, eight of whom are now living, the subject of this sketch being among the eldest. He was but two years of age when his parents came to Tennessee, and went with them to Carroll County. In 1853 he married Miss Elizabeth Williams, who was born in Henderson County in 1838. To them one child was born, William Dudley. Mrs. Pearson died in 1864. Soon after his marriage Mr. Pearson returned to Henderson County and settled on his father's old place. In 1866 he united with Eveline Parker, of Carroll County. To this union seven children were born: Sidney A., Lou Emma, wife of John Jones; Melvina E., Walter C., Priestly, Ethel and L. In 1870 Mr. Pearson bought 200 acres of fine land in the Tenth District, four miles north of Lexington, where he now resides, making altogether about 610 acres. In 1876 he erected a cotton-gin, and in 1886 another one. He gins on an average about 140 bales per year. He is one of the most successful and enterprising agriculturalists in the entire section, well known and universally liked. He is a stanch Democrat, and is a member of the I. O. O. F. in best standing.

Stephen Powers, one of the prosperous farmers of the Fourteenth District, was born in 1843 in Henderson County. He is the son of John S. and Elizabeth (Grice) Powers. The father was born in 1809, in Marion District, South Carolina. At the age of sixteen he came to Henderson County, and in 1830 married. Mrs. Powers departed this life in 1863. The following year he married Miss Nancy Moody, who died in 1885. In 1882 Mr. Powers located where he now resides. He is one of the oldest and best known men in the county. For the past ten years his eyesight has been very dim. He feels the disadvantage greatly. Of his fourteen children four only are living. Stephen Powers received his education in his native county, and resided under the paternal roof until the outbreak of the war. He enlisted August, 1862, in Company A, Seventh Tennessee Cavalry, remaining in service until the surrender; was mustered out in 1865. He is a Republican; gave his first presidential vote for U. S. Grant. November, 1861, Mr. Powers married a native of his county, Miss Mary Ann Bartholomew, who was born in 1842. Of the eleven children who blessed their union nine are now living: John H., William R., Frank W., Andrew, Joel W., Adore A., Nancy L., Tennessee C. and Stephen L. Mr. Powers moved to his present place of residence in 1866, owning 435 acres, which he was enabled to purchase by his economy, industry and good management. He is a man of integrity, greatly respected by all who know him. He and his wife are members of the Missionary Baptist Church.

Moses Segraves, a well known farmer of the Ninth District, was born in Wilkes County, N. C., in 1832, the only child of Sherrod and Martha (Laws) Segraves. The father was born May 22, 1811, in Wake County, N. C. His parents died when he was a small child, and he was bound to James Jones. He married in his native State in 1833; he left his family, going to Davidson County, Tenn., where for some unknown reason he married a native of that county, Miss Margaret Neely, who was born in 1808. In 1842 he moved to Dyer County, where he has since resided. He has been very prosperous. The first wife, Miss Laws, was born in Wilkes County, N. C., in October, 1816; with her son came to Henderson County in 1845, settling in the Seventeenth District. The same year she married Benjamin Philips, by whom she had two children. Her death occurred February 26, 1879. Moses remained with his mother during his single life. August 22, 1852, he married Miss Susan P. Crabb, a native of Benton County, born October 29, 1834. They have four children living: Mary H., wife of James D. Smith; John H., Nancy C., wife of Lem Smith, and Sidney J. In 1864 and 1865 Mr. Segraves made his home in Massac County, Ill. In 1866 he returned to Tennessee, purchased some property in the Ninth District where he has since resided. He is quite an extensive landholder, owning about 500 acres, which he was enabled to buy through his energy, ability and judicious management. He is a man of enterprise and integrity and has the respect of all who know him. Politically he is conservative, voting from principles not for party. His first vote was cast for Fillmore in 1856. Mr. and Mrs. Segraves are exemplary members of the Missionary Baptist Church.

Maj. T. A. Smith, register of Henderson County, was born in Randolph County, N. C., July 6, 1817. He was the oldest son of Benjamin and Easter (Argo) Smith. The father was of Dutch origin, born in Richland County, S. C., in 1790; was married in North Carolina to a native of that State, who was born in Anson County in 1792 and died in 1861. Benjamin came to Tennessee in 1827, located in the Sixth District of Henderson County, where he purchased some property and engaged in agricultural pursuits. The last twenty years of his life were spent in the Eleventh District. His death occurred in the same year as that of his wife, 1861. They had a family of four sons and four daughters. The subject of this sketch was about ten years old when his parents came to Tennessee. He remained with them until his twenty-ninth year, and for seven years kept "bachelor's hall." March 3, 1858, he married Miss Mary J. Campbell, who was born in Henderson County in 1841. They have seven children living: Mary E., wife of John White; Thomas B., Grant, Jennie O., Elizabeth, Lettie May and James H. When the war between the North and South was declared, Mr. Smith became one of the "boys in blue." He organized for the United States Army, Company A, Seventh Regiment, Tennessee Cavalry, and was elected captain of the company serving two months in that capacity, after which he was promoted to rank of major for his brave and meritorious conduct. He was twice captured, the first time at Trenton, and taken to Camp Chase, Ohio, where he was very sick and consequently sent home. He was captured the second time at Union City, and taken to several different prisons in the South, being retained about nine months, being paroled December, 1864, and mustered out at Washington, D. C., the winter of 1865. He is a stanch Republican and one of the leading and influential men of that party. From 1840 to 1848 was constable of the Eleventh District; was elected magistrate in 1849, serving two years; was census taker in 1870, for the county. In 1884 he was elected county register, and again called to the same office two years later, holding the position at the present time. He has been a faithful and conscientious public servant for many years, always giving satisfaction. The greatest portion of his life has been spent in Henderson County, where he has won the esteem of the people. Since 1878 he has resided in the Tenth District, owning 464 acres of valuable land.

John A. Smith, a prominent farmer and old resident of the Sixth District, was born March 6, 1819, in Randolph County, N. C., the second child of a family of four sons and four daughters born to Benjamin and Easter (Argo) Smith. The father was of Dutch origin, born 1790, in Richland County, S. C.; when an infant was taken to North Carolina, where he remained several years and was married; in 1827 immigrated to Henderson County in the Sixth District, bought some property and carried on farming. The last twenty years of his life were spent in the Eleventh District. He died in 1861. His wife was born in Anson County, N. C., in 1792; departed this life the same year as her husband, 1861. John A. was but eight years of age when his parents came to Tennessee. He remained with them until twenty-two years of age. March 4, 1841, he married a daughter of C. and Mary Robertson. Miss Mary Ann, who was born in Halifax County, Va., in 1825. To them eleven children were born: James F., William T., Joseph N., Zachariah T., Benjamin O., John P., George W., Mary C., Martha J., Christopher C. and Nancy A. After marriage, Mr. Smith bought 200 acres of land in the Eleventh District, and gave his attention to agricultural pursuits. In 1866 he purchased 700 acres in the Sixth District and settled where he has since resided. He has given 200 acres to his sons, and still has a fine tract left. He has always been an enterprising and successful farmer, and a worthy, respected citizen. He is a Republican; gave his first vote for Harrison in 1840. Mr. and Mrs. Smith and five children are exemplary members of the Missionary Baptist Church.

L. A. Stanford, a well known and respected farmer of Lexington, was born in Henderson County, in 1837; he is the eighth and only living child of a family of nine born to Thomas and Clarissia (Ross) Stanford. The father was born in Greenville District, South Carolina, in 1797; he married a native of same State and district, who was born in 1801, and in 1834 immigrated to Henderson County, in the Ninth District; after living there two years moved to the Seventeenth District, purchased a plantation, and followed agricultural pursuits. He died in Lexington in 1880, at the advanced age of eighty-three years, an old settler, a prosperous and esteemed man. The mother is still living, making her home with L. A., who was raised and educated in his native county. At an early age he began farming, since which time he has continued the same business, having met with great success, and now owns 800 acres of valuable land; in 1882 he established a cotton-gin in Lexington in connection with his farming interests, and gins on an average 100 bales of cotton per year. When the late civil war broke out he was among the first to serve his country; in 1861 enlisted in the Confederate Army, Company H, Twenty-seventh Regiment Tennessee Infantry, and did gallant service at the battle of Shiloh, also in other engagements and skirmishes of less note, remaining in the army over twelve months, April, 1863, he married Miss Margaret Whyte, of Henderson County, who was born in 1843, a daughter of Joseph and Mary Whyte. To their union several children were born. Thomas, Lizzie, Lemuel, George W., Arcadius, James, Ruby and Johnnie. In 1873 Mr. Stanford was elected town marshal, and served about seven years; in 1879–80 was constable of the Tenth District. He is a life-long Democrat, casting his first vote for John C. Breckenridge. Mr. Stanford is one of the solid, enterprising and best known men in the county; his wife is a consistent member of the Missionary Baptist Church.

T. M. Stubblefield, an old and well known resident of the Fourth District, was born in 1813, in Wilkes County, Ga.; is one of the two living children of a family of ten born to Peter and Sallie (Harris) Stubblefield. The father was born in Virginia in 1777; he left the "Old Dominion" when quite a young man, moving to Georgia, where he remained until after his marriage in 1824; came to Tennessee, locating in Maury County; in 1835 went to Wayne County, where the remainder of his life was spent; his death occurred in 1839; his wife was born in Wilkes County, Ga., in 1786, and died in 1830. The subject of this sketch was raised at home, receiving his education in his native county, being about ten years of age when his parents came to Tennessee. August, 1835, he married Miss Sarah Lipscomb, daughter of John and Judith Lipscomb; she (Mrs. Stubblefield) was born in Maury County in 1812, and became the mother of ten children: Sarah E., wife of R. J. Dyer; Amanda C., wife of C. G. Hardeman; Bevelry M., Charles H., Martha J., widow of Augustas Helms; Mary E., wife of M. A. Maines; Margaret E., wife of L. D. Horton; Wm. F., Nancy N., wife of Charles A. Helms, and Thomas F. The year after marriage Mr. Stubblefield moved to Wayne County, and in 1846 came to Henderson

County; located in the Fourth District, where he purchased 122 acres, mostly dense woods his nearest neighbor being three-quarters of a mile distant. He has been a hard working, industrious man; by good management and perseverance, has added acre to acre, until he is now the possessor of about 1,000 acres. He has a fine farm, operated on the modern plan, cultivating and fertilizing according to the latest improvements. In 1885 Mr. and Mrs. Stubblefield celebrated their golden wedding, a pleasure but rarely enjoyed. Previous to the war, Mr. Stubblefield was a Whig, since that time has been a Democrat, casting his first vote for Hugh L. White in 1836. In 1874 he was elected county surveyor of Henderson County, and served four years. He is a Mason, belongs to Lodge No. 441, at Mills Springs; he is a devoted member of the Methodist Episcopal Church South and his wife of the Cumberland Presbyterian.

Hon. John M. Taylor, one of Henderson County's most gifted and popular sons, and congressman of the Eighth Congressional District, was born May 13, 1830, a son of Jesse and Mary (May) Taylor. The father was born in Virginia in 1790, was of English-Irish extraction; when quite a small boy, with his mother, left his native State and moved near Lancaster, Ky. In after years he was cashier of a bank in Shelbyville, Bedford Co., Tenn. At the time of his marriage he was living in Madison County; in 1834 became a resident of Henderson County; the following year was appointed by the court as clerk of the county court, and afterward elected by the people to the same position, which he retained until 1859. His death occurred in 1860, and the county lost one of its worthiest and most esteemed men. Mr. Taylor was twice married; the first time to Miss Lyda Williams, by whom he had four children, all living; the second union was with Miss Mary May, by whom there are two children living, one of whom is the subject of this sketch. The latter was educated in the academy at Lexington and Union University of Murfreesboro; in 1858 he began the study of law, reading with Maj. A. G. Shrewsbery, of Lexington, later attending the law department of the Cumberland University, at Lebanon, Tenn., where he graduated with honor in 1860. Upon his return home he began the practice of his chosen profession, which received an interruption in a short time by the outbreak of the civil war. In 1861 he enlisted in Company K, Seventy-seventh Regiment, Tennessee Infantry, and assisting in its organization, was elected first lieutenant. He took active part in the battles of Shiloh, Perryville, Franklin and Nashville. His thigh bone was broken by a ball, the wound being so severe that he was disabled for a year, during which time he was in the hospital at Harrisburg, Ky. He was taken prisoner at Danville, Ky., and carried to Camp Chase, Ohio; after his release he joined his company at Dalton, Ga., and was immediately elected captain at the re-organization of the company. After the battle of Shiloh he was promoted to the rank of major for his undaunted and gallant service. After the restoration of peace he returned home and resumed the practice of law, meeting with marked success. In 1864 he married Miss Amanda McHaney, an estimable lady of Henderson County, born in 1845, a daughter of W. C. McHaney, one of the best known and most respected residents of the section. Maj. and Mrs. Taylor have three children living: Mary Lou, William and Daisy A. Mrs. Taylor is a true Christian woman and consistent member of the Methodist Episcopal Church South. In 1869 Capt. Taylor was elected mayor of Lexington, serving one year; the same year was made a delegate to the Constitutional Convention, which held its meeting in 1870; the August of 1870 became attorney-general of the Eleventh Judicial District, which place he held for eight years, winning many laurels and much renown. In 1880 was a delegate to the National Convention at Cincinnati; the same year was elected to the Legislature to fill the unexpired term of Dr. Murray; in 1882 was elected congressman of the Eighth Congressional District, receiving a plurality of 2,820—his opponent was S. C. Hawkins. Capt. Taylor was one of the committee on postoffice, post-roads and expenditure in the war department; in 1884 was re-elected and was chairman of the naval department, also one of a committee of five who prepared the appropriations on postal service. He is a Mason, belonging to Lodge No. 64 (a Council Mason); a member of the K. of H., at Jackson; of I. O. O. F., at Lexington, and has taken all of the degrees of that order; and is also one of the A. O. U. W. Mr. Taylor is a man of brilliancy, high mental and moral standing, who has always had the interests of his county and people at heart.

J. A. Teague, clerk of the county court, was born in Henderson County in 1843, a son of J. W. and Alice (Fuller) Teague. The father was of Scotch-Irish origin, born in 1813 in Chatham County, N. C. In 1825 he, with his father, Isaac Teague, immigrated to Middle Tennessee, locating in Warren County, where he remained two years; in 1827 settled in the Seventh District of Henderson County and purchased a plantation and turned his attention to agriculture. J. W. was about fourteen years of age when he came to Tennessee, where he resided at the time of his marriage. He settled in the Tenth District where he lived until 1883 when he returned to the Seventh District. His death occurred in 1885 at the ripe age of seventy-two. The mother was born in Henderson County in 1819. She raised a family of five children; all are now living, our subject being the second; his educational advantages were limited, having attended school only about five months. When hostilities broke out between the North and South, he enlisted in the United States Army, August, 1862, in the Seventh Tennessee Cavalry. He participated in many skirmishes. At Union City, Tenn., he was captured and taken prisoner to Andersonville, afterward to Florence and thence to Charleston; after being retained eleven months he made his escape, February, 1865; made his way to the Federal lines, remaining with them until the surrender, reaching home August, 1865. In 1866 he formed a partnership with L. A. Teague, establishing a large grocery, thus continuing for three years. He was sole proprietor until 1878, in that year was elected circuit court clerk by a majority of 522, showing to a considerable extent his popularity. He has always been a Republican, one of the leading members of that party. For nineteen years he has been a Master Mason, belongs to Blue Lodge No. 64, Chapter 37; he is a K. of H., Lodge No. 199, and a member of A. O. U. W., Lodge No. 32. October 7, 1868, he married Miss N. L. Bird, of Lexington, born in 1851 and is a daughter of W. R. Bird. Mr. and Mrs. Teague have an interesting family of six children: James J., Arthur, Hattie, Ernest E., Wm. R. and Birdie. Mrs. Teague is an estimable lady and an earnest member of the Methodist Episcopal Church.

E. J. Timberlake, a prominent farmer of the Seventeenth District, was born in Henderson County in 1845; was one of a family of five children born to Richard and Tabitha (Trice) Timberlake. The father was of Scotch origin, born in Franklin County, N. C., in 1788, and moved to Henderson County in 1826, settling in the Tenth District, three miles north of Lexington. He was twice married and the father of seven children. His first wife was Mary Neal; the second wife, and mother of E. J., was born in Orange County, N. C., in 1802, and departed this life in 1875. Mr. Timberlake was one of the oldest settlers and substantial men of the county, where he was generally known. At the time of his death, which occurred in 1860, he was the possessor of about 2,000 acres of valuable land. Our subject received a liberal education in the schools of his native county, attending the University of North Carolina during 1859 and 1860. He taught school several months during the war; in 1862 married Miss Louisa H. Small, who was born in Henderson County in 1844, a daughter of Alex. Small. They have seven children: Eddie, wife of John E. McCall; Louanna; Edward; Richard; Charles; Jessie and Kate. Mrs. Timberlake is a member of the Methodist Episcopal Church South. In 1863 Mr. Timberlake located on a 200-acre tract of land given him by his father, which is situated four and a half miles from Lexington; with the exception of seven [years spent in town he has lived on the place since the year after his marriage. He is one of the leading Democrats of the County, he was elected circuit court clerk in 1870 and in 1874 was a member of the Thirty-ninth Legislature. He is a K. of H., belonging to Stonewall Lodge, No. 199, of Jackson; is also a member of the A. O. U. W. Mr. Timberlake is an extensive landholder, a prosperous farmer and worthy citizen.

Dr. William H. Warren, an old and respected physician of Lexington, was born in 1812, in Chesterfield County, Va. The father, Robert Warren, was born in Virginia in 1782, of English descent, a collier by occupation; most of his life was spent in his native State; he served gallantly in the war of 1812, and died in 1834. His wife, Catharine Vivian, was a Virginian of French descent; was the mother of four children, all of whom lived to maturity. She died in the year 1851. William H. was the only son. He was reared in, and received his literary education in, his native State; at about the age of seventeen he began the study of medicine under the tuition of Dr. Barrand of Norfolk, Va. In 1834 he graduated at the medical college at Philadelphia, Penn.; returning home entered upon the practice of his profession; in 1837 he came to Tennessee, locating at Lexington; the following year he resumed his practice, where he has met with extraordinary success, and is recognized as the leading surgeon and physician of Henderson County. For the past fifteen years the Doctor has, to some extent, suspended his active practice and devoted his time to his business and the entertainment of his friends, who are numerous, for no man has more completely won the confidence and esteem of the community. In 1841 he married Miss Adaline A. Harmon who, was born in 1820, and one of the first white female children born in Henderson County. She was a daughter of John Harmon, one of the first white settlers who came to the county in 1819, was born in 1779, and died in 1851. His wife, Elizabeth Harmon, was born in 1786, and departed this life in 1865. Mrs. Warren is a consistent member of the Methodist Episcopal Church. The Doctor is a Democrat, was a Whig previous to the war, and his first vote was cast for Hugh L. White in 1836.

O. P. White, a farmer and influential resident of the Second District, was born in Henderson County in 1825, a son of Stephen Finney and Hannah (Dixon) White. The father was of Irish origin, born in South Carolina in 1781; when a youth he immigrated to the portion of Rutherford County now called Cannon County, Middle Tenn., and remained there until after his marriage. In 1824 he came to Henderson County, settling in the Second District; in 1830 he moved to the Seventh District, where he resided until the time of his death in 1858. He was one of the pioneers of the county, where he was well known and respected. His wife was born in North Carolina in 1792, and departed this life ten years later than her husband. Of the nine children born to them, four only are living: Louisa was born in Rutherford County in 1817, Lucinda was born in the same county in 1822, Bennett G. is a native of Henderson County born in 1827, and our subject. Since 1860 the four have been living together, leading harmonious and peaceful lives, devoted to each other; none of them have ever been married. The sisters are devout members of the Methodist Episcopal Church South. Bennett G. was one of the gallant boys in gray, he enlisted in March, 1862, in Tenth Texas Battery; was in numerous severe skirmishes and engagements, and remained in active service until the surrender. The two brothers are Republicans, each voting the first time in 1848 for Gen. Taylor. They own about 217 acres of valuable land, are industrious, honorable men, having the confidence and esteem of the entire community.

Dr. E. G. Whitehead, an eminent and skillful physician and surgeon, of Moore's Hill, was born in Haywood County, Tenn., March 1, 1840, a son of Richard and Lucinda (Gordon) Whitehead. The father was of Irish origin, born in 1801, in North Carolina. When a young man he immigrated to Sumner County, Tenn., and at an early date moved to Haywood County, where he bought a large tract of land and engaged in agricultural pursuits. His death occurred in 1867. The mother was of Scotch descent, born in Louisiana, in 1806. Of the nine children whom she bore, seven lived to reach maturity; she died in 1868. The subject of this sketch was the youngest of the family. He received his literary education at Brownsville, Redland, Miss. and elsewhere. At the age of twenty-two he began the study of medicine; soon afterward engaged in teaching school, which he continued for several years, devoting his vacations and leisure time to the study of medicine. In 1874 he located at Moore's Hill and entered into the practice of his profession; in 1877 he graduated as an M. D. at the medical department of the University of Nashville. August 27, 1877, he married a daughter of J. D. and Margaret Evans, Miss Vina, who was born in Henderson County in 1860. They have four children living: Ella E., Lela, Lula and Richard. Mrs. Whitehead is a consistent member of the Missionary Baptist Church and a true Christian woman. The Doctor has succeeded in building up an extensive and lucrative practice; he is one of the most popular physicians in the district. He is esteemed and highly regarded both in professional and private life. In 1880 he erected a pretty house of modern style and has continued to add to its improvement since that time. The Doctor is a stanch Democrat.

Richard Williams, a well-to-do and highly respected farmer of the Eighteenth District, was born May 5, 1846, in Decatur County, Tenn. He was the second of a family of twelve children born to Kerney C. and Teressa (Taylor) Williams. The father was born in 1816, in Chatham County, N. C. When a youth he immigrated to Decatur County, West Tenn., where he lived at the time of his marriage with Miss Taylor, who was a native of the county, born in 1826; she departed this life September 1, 1877. In 1855 Mr. Williams moved to Carroll County and in 1864 came to Henderson County, locating in the Eighteenth District, where he purchased some valuable property and resided until his death, February 11, 1886. He was married a second time, the result of the union being one child. The subject of this sketch came to this county when about eighteen years of age, and remained with his parents until about twenty-four. May 10, 1871, he married Miss Elizabeth Morris, a native of the county, born in 1851, who bore him one child, Gecovy. Mrs. Williams died October 15, 1873. Mr. Williams then united in marriage, March 4, 1878, with Miss Frances Frizzell, of Decatur County, born in 1854. They have one child living, Charles. Mr. Williams has lived in the district many years. In 1874 he bought 200 acres of good land, where he now resides. He commenced life a poor man, but by his industry and good management, has accumulated considerable property, owning altogether about 400 acres. He is an enterprising and flourishing farmer, a worthy and esteemed citizen. He is a Democrat, casting his first vote for Seymour and Blair. He is also a Mason of good standing, belongs to Lodge No. 502. Mr. and Mrs. Williams are both members of the Missionary Baptist Church.

J. T. Wilson, an enterprising farmer of the Seventh District, was born in Rockingham County, N. C., in 1829, the fourth of a family of nine children born to J. B. and Sallie (Coffey) Wilson. The father was of Irish descent; born in 1798 in the State of North Carolina, where he married a native, born in 1800; they came to Henderson County in 1832, settling in the Eighth District and buying a home. Mrs. Wilson died in 1846. Mr. Wilson's second marriage was with Miss Mary Pugh. His death occurred in 1878. The subject of this sketch was about three years of age when his parents came to Tennessee; he made his home with them until after attaining his majority. In 1866 he married Miss E. M. Barger, who was born in East Tennessee in 1846. They have seven children living: Sallie, Theodore, Margaret, Emma, Lizzie, Henry Arzo and Lular. At the time of his marriage Mr. Wilson was residing in Carroll County. He moved to Henderson County and bought 269 acres in the Eighth District; in 1886 he located at present place of residence, five miles west of Lexington, where he owns 330 acres of fine land. Mr. Wilson is an energetic, prosperous farmer, a good neighbor, and one of the best known and respected residents in the section. He is a Republican—gave his first vote for Gen. Scott in 1852. He and his wife are members of the Methodist Episcopal Church.

Hon. Levi S. Woods, circuit judge of the Eleventh Judicial Circuit, was born in Carroll County, Tenn., November 17, 1848, a son of Levi S. and Arantha Jane (Dinwiddie) Woods. The father was a native of Madison County, Tennessee. His father, John Woods, was a Virginian, and in 1782, with a party of men from his native State, set out to seek a new home in Kentucky. Daniel Boone was one of their number; on their way they were suddenly attacked by Indians. Sixty of the Virginians were killed. The remainder of the party continued their journey and settled in the West. About 1800 John immigrated to Williamson County, Tenn., and in 1819 came to Henderson County, being one of the very first white men who located in the county. Levi S., Sr., settled in Carroll County, where he was married; he was an agriculturist, an honored and esteemed man and departed this life in 1857. His wife was born in Virginia in 1811, a descendant of Robert Dinwiddie, who was governor of Virginia in 1753. Mrs. Woods was the mother of thirteen children; her death occurred in 1853. Our subject was the twelfth child; his academic education was received at Trenton and Jackson; at the age of twenty he began to study law under instructions of Hon. L. M. Jones and Judge Cathel, of Trenton. He attended the law department of the Cumberland University at Lebanon, Tenn., in 1869 and 1870, and in the latter year located in Lexington, entering upon the practice of his profession, displaying at once his superior qualities, and being soon in the front ranks of the Lexington bar. He is an eloquent orator, a clear and logical speaker. In 1873 was elected by the county court as superintendent of the county schools and served three years. During Judge Bateman's term Mr. Woods was several times appointed special judge. August, 1886, he was elected to his present position by a majority of more than 1,500, his opponent being the able Judge T. C. Muse, of Jackson. Judge Woods is a Council Mason; also belongs to I. O. O. F., Encampment Lodge. November 3, 1873, he was married to a daughter of W. C. and Louisa McHaney. Mrs. Woods was born in Henderson County in 1849; has been the mother of four children, only one is now living, Georgia A. Two died in infancy, and Myrtle at the interesting age of four years.

CHESTER COUNTY.

John R. Bray was born in North Carolina in 1839, and is one of nine children born to the union of Matthew and Nancy (McDaniel) Bray. The father was born in North Carolina in 1806, was reared in his native State, and received a fair English education. He was married at the age of twenty-one, and in 1837 removed to Middle Tennessee; settled near Lewisburg, where he remained two years. He then came to Henderson County, and followed agricultural pursuits until the time of his death, which occurred in 1848. Mrs. Bray was born in North Carolina in 1812, and died about 1884 in Texas. Both father and mother were devout members of the Missionary Baptist Church. Our subject received a good practical education, and November 18, 1850, was married to Mary C. Bray, a native of North Carolina, born in 1833, and the daughter of Samuel and Mary Bray, both natives of North Carolina. Mr. Bray, our subject, has a fine farm of 379 acres, all under a good state of cultivation, and six miles northeast from Henderson. In 1862 he enlisted in Company A, Twenty-first Tennessee Cavalry, under Capt. W. H. Bray, and remained in service until the final surrender, being engaged in the quartermaster's department. He returned home and resumed his farming, after an absence of over three years. Politically Mr. Bray is a life-long and ardent Democrat, and cast his first presidential vote for Franklin Pierce in 1852. He and wife are active members of the Missionary Baptist Church.

Dr. B. H. Brown, physician and surgeon of Mifflin, is a son of David W. E. and Clarissa (Anthony) Brown, both natives of North Carolina. The father was born in 1803, and reared in his native State, where he received but a limited education. He immigrated to Maury County with his father in the early settlement of that county, and was married there about 1825. He came to Henderson County in 1833 or 1834, and located about ten miles north of Lexington, where he cultivated the soil until 1866. He then removed to Mifflin, and in a few years after removed to Mississippi, where he died in 1874. The mother was born in North Carolina in 1805, and died in 1861. Her father, Philip Anthony, served as a soldier during the Revolutionary war. Our subject was born in Maury County, Tenn., in 1828, was reared at home and educated in the common schools of the county. At the age of eighteen he began the study of medicine, and in 1849 entered the medical department of the University of Louisville, Ky., where he graduated in 1850. He immediately began the practice of his profession at Pleasant Exchange, in Henderson County, and afterward at Red Mound, where he was located at the breaking out of the war. He organized a company of sharpshooters, of which he was made captain, and, at the organization of the Twenty-seventh Tennessee Regiment, was promoted to the rank of lieutenant-colonel. After the battle of Shiloh he was promoted to the rank of colonel for gallantry. In the same engagement he was considered mortally wounded, and was discharged from the service. He did not sufficiently recover to again enter the ranks. Previous to the war in 1851 he married Miss Elizabeth A. Taylor, daughter of A. and F. Taylor, and to this union were born six children, four of whom are living: Cornelia S. (Mrs. C. F.

Howard), Dr. Willis C., Andrew E. and Jessie E. (Mrs. R. C. Cooper). Mrs. Brown was born in North Carolina in 1827, and died in January, 1874. In February, 1875, he married Mrs. Sarah B. Cooper, daughter of Richard W. and Mary E. Hudson. She died in March, 1883. In 1866 the Doctor located at Mifflin, where he has since continued his practice with his usual energy and success, being now one of the leading practitioners of the county. He is a man of good information, and has the confidence and esteem of all his acquaintances. He is a life-long Democrat, and cast his first presidential vote for F. Pierce. He is also an active member of the Methodist Episcopal Church South.

T. J. Butler, farmer, of Mifflin, is a son of Obediah and Nancy (Williams) Butler, both natives of North Carolina, and both born in the year 1806. The father was married at the age of twenty-one and soon after came to Madison County, Tenn., where he followed agricultural pursuits until his death in 1866. The mother died about 1852. They were both consistent members of the Methodist Episcopal Church South. Our subject was born in Madison County in 1830, and was one of seven children, four of whom are living. He received his education in the common schools of Madison County, and in 1861 enlisted in Company A, Thirty-first Tennessee Infantry (Confederate Army), and was in active service during the entire Rebellion. He was twice wounded, once at Murfreesboro, and again at Peachtree Creek. He then returned home, after four years of honorable service, and resumed his agricultural pursuits. In 1866 he married Catherine Swank, who was born in 1841, and who is the daughter of Wilburn and Mary C. Swank, of Madison County. To our subject and wife were born seven children: L. H., John W., Thomas O., Mary E., Hattie P., David R. and Callie. Mr. Butler remained in Henderson County until 1877, when he came to Mifflin and is living there at the present time. He is the owner of about 1,800 acres of land in this and Henderson Counties, and is an extensive and enterprising farmer. He is a Democrat in politics, and cast his first presidential vote for Franklin Pierce. Mrs. Butler is a worthy member of the Methodist Episcopal Church South.

Col. C. M. Cason, present register of Chester County, Tenn., was born near Henderson, Tenn., in 1827, and is one of a family of five children, four of whom are living, born to the union of William and Mary (McKnight) Cason. The father was born in South Carolina in 1804, and came to Middle Tennessee with his parents when but an infant. They located in Wilson County and remained there until 1826 when William came to West Tennessee, and located near Henderson, being one of its first settlers; he was a farmer by occupation and filled the position of constable for many years. He was also deputy sheriff, and is now a resident of Henderson. His wife was born in Wilson County about 1804, and died in February, 1885. Our subject was reared at home and received his education in the district schools. In 1850 he married Mary H. Barbam, a native of Hardin County, born in 1829, and a daughter of John Barbam. By this union they have eight children: W. T., circuit court clerk of this county; John B., hardware merchant and salesman; R. E., wife of Prof. J. B. Inman; Susie, J. R., B. P., D. K. and J. E. In 1848 Mr. Cason engaged in the mercantile business at Montezuma and continued at this until about 1871. He has also been engaged in business at Henderson since 1867. At the organization of the county he was elected register of the same and was re-elected at the last election. He is a Democrat in politics, and he and wife are members of the Methodist Episcopal Church South. In 1861 Mr. Cason enlisted in the Thirty-first Regiment, Tennessee Infantry (Confederate Army), under Col. Bradford of Brownsville, Tenn., and was himself captain of the company. He remained in active duty for some time, but, on account of ill health was obliged to leave the service. He returned home in 1863.

Robert and H. D. Criner, liverymen at Henderson, established their business in 1885. They were born in Henderson County, the former in 1854 and the latter in 1856. Their parents, John A. and Patsey Ann (Stanfield) Criner, are both natives of Tennessee, the father born in Lincoln County about 1817 and the mother in Henderson County about 1820. After marriage they located on the old farm in Henderson County where they reared a family of eleven children, six of whom are now living. Robert Criner began life as a public officer, serving several years as constable, afterward as deputy sheriff of his native county. He then served two years as clerk in a dry goods store at Center Point and also filled the same position in Henderson. In 1882 he was elected to the office of sheriff of Chester County, which position he filled with credit to himself and to the people. He then returned to his father's farm where he remained until he entered the livery business. H. D. Criner remained on the farm until 1885 when he engaged with Robert in their present business. He was married in December, 1882, to Miss Belle Young, daughter of H. H. and Mary Young and a native of Henderson County, born in 1863. She and Mr. Criner are members of the Christian Church and are respected citizens. Both brothers are Democrats and cast their first presidental votes for S. J. Tilden. They are active business men and do a prosperous livery business, giving general satisfaction to their patrons.

John R. Edwards, a well known farmer of the Fifth District of Chester County, was born in Henderson County in 1840, the fourth child of a family of six children born to Samuel T. and Charlotte (Robertson) Edwards. The father was of Welsh descent; born in North Carolina in 1809, he came with his mother in 1830 to Henderson County, where he lived at the time of his marriage; he settled in the Third District, the portion now called Sixth District of Chester County. He lived there until the time of his death, which occurred in 1844. His wife was also of North Carolina, born in 1812, and died in 1870. The subject of this sketch received his education at the schools in Mifflin, Lexington, Bethel College and McLemoresville where he attended for four years; he remained at home with his mother until he was about sixteen years of age. In 1856 he accepted a position as salesman in a general store at Mifflin, where he worked over four years, or until hostilities broke out between the North and South. In May, 1861, he enlisted in the Confederate service, Company I, Thirteenth Regiment, Tennessee Infantry. He took active part in the engagements at Belmont, Shiloh, Murfreesboro, Chickamauga, Atlanta, Franklin and Nashville, also in numerous skirmishes. At the battle of Belmont he was captured and held as prisoner of war, but only for a short length of time. He remained in service until the surrender, was with Gen. Forrest the last six weeks; he returned home April, 1865, after four years of duty. February, 1865, he married Miss C. A. Buckley, of Henderson County, born in 1844, a daughter of John Buckley. To their union six children have been born: Lizzie, Carl, Hubert, Annettie, Helen and an infant son. In 1866 Mr. Edwards established a general store at Princeton, Madison County. In 1868 he abandoned mercantile pursuits and returned to his native county and began farming. In 1875 he bought 222 acres of land in the Third District, now the Fifth District of Chester County, where he settled and now resides. For the past three years he has also owned an interest in a general store in Mifflin, the company being known as Wheeler, Edwards & Co. Mr. Edwards is quite an extensive land holder, all the land being under fine cultivation and improved with buildings. He is a man of great energy, ability and honor; has met with unusual success, and has the respect of the entire community. He is a stanch Democrat, cast his first vote for Jefferson Davis in 1864.

H. D. Franklin, county court clerk of Chester County, Tenn., was born in North Carolina, January 12, 1848, and is one of a family of five children, two of whom are now living. His parents, David J. and Sarah B. (Browder) Franklin, are both natives of Halifax County, Va.; the former born about 1826 and the latter about 1818. The father came to this State about 1848 and located near Henderson. He is a Baptist minister by profession and is also engaged in the mercantile business at McNairy Station. He is an active business man, a zealous Christian worker, and one of the prominent citizens of the county. The mother died in October, 1883. Our subject was reared at home and received his education in the district schools. In 1869 he married A. B. Sherwood, a native of Clark County, Ala., born in 1851, and the daughter of Alonzo and Harriet Sherwood. By this union they have four children: Evie, Etna, Rubie and David. In 1867 Mr. Franklin was appointed postmaster and held that office for about thirteen years; at the same time he was engaged as salesman for a dry goods house, and express agent. He continued the mercantile business until 1882 when he was elected to his present office. He was re-elected and still fills the position. He is a Democrat in politics, a member of the Masonic fraternity, also a member of the A. O. U. W., and he and wife are members of the Baptist Church, of which he is a deacon.

J. A. Fry, farmer and lumberman of the Tenth District, Chester County, was born in East Tennessee in 1825 and is one of a family of five children, two of whom are now living. His parents, Joseph and Catherine Fry, are both natives of North Carolina. The father was born in 1794 and came to Madison County in 1825, being among the early settlers of that region; he was a farmer by occupation and died in 1846. The mother was born in 1798 and died in 1834. Our subject was reared and educated in Madison County. In 1857 Mr. Fry located where he now lives and built a steam saw-mill, which he has operated ever since in connection with farming. He is a Democrat in politics but was formerly an old line Whig, casting his first presidential vote for Henry Clay. He is a good citizen and has the respect of all his acquaintances.

C. G. Hardeman, present trustee of Chester County, was born in Giles County, Tenn., in 1840; son of Benjamin F. and Ellen (Sanders) Hardeman. The father was a native of Middle Tennessee, born in 1815. His educational advantages were very limited, but being a man of great observation and a lover of literature, he, through self study became a well informed man. He was married in Giles County about 1835 and in 1851 removed to Henderson County where he tilled the soil up to the time of his death, which occurred in 1858. He reared a family of ten children—eight sons and two daughters—who are still living. Five of his sons were in the Confederate Army all of whom returned without receiving any serious injury. He served as captain in the Mexican war and was a man of considerable influence. The mother was born about 1817 and is still living on the old homestead in Henderson County. Our subject received his education partly in the common schools and partly by observation and reading. January, 1862, he married Miss Amanda Stubblefield, a native of Wayne County, Tenn., born in 1838 and the daughter of Thomas and Sallie Stubblefield, natives of North Carolina and Virginia respectively. They are still living in Henderson County. To Mr. and Mrs. Hardeman were born nine children, six of whom are now living: Thomas B., Jasper G., Sarah Alice, Elizabeth, Cora and C. Maude. Our subject first located near Centre Point where he remained until 1884 engaged in farming; since then he has resided near Henderson and is the owner of 400 acres of land in the vicinity; he also owns land in Henderson County. He held the position of magistrate from 1872 till 1884 when he was elected to the office of trustee of Chester County and re-elected in 1886. He is an ardent and uncompromising Democrat and cast his first presidential vote for Jeff. Davis in 1861. He is a long-standing and prominent member of the Masonic fraternity and is also a consistent member of the Old School Presbyterian Church. Mrs. Hardeman is a member of the Methodist Episcopal Church South.

Hiram Johnson, an old resident and magistrate of the Sixth District, was born in Moore County, N. C., May 2, 1824, and is one of a family of twelve children, seven of whom are living. His parents, Joseph and Christina (McCollum) Johnson, were both natives of North Carolina. The father was born in 1774 and came to West Tennessee in 1825, locating in Madison County. He was a farmer by occupation, and was a magistrate in the First District of Madison County for some years. After living there twelve years he moved to McNairy County, where he died June 24, 1858. The mother was a few years younger than her husband, and died about 1830. Our subject received his education in the common schools, and August 15, 1855, he married Bettie McCleod, a native of Somerville, Tenn., born January 24, 1834, and a daughter of Dickson C. and Martha M. McCleod. To them were born four children: Joseph D., Hiram H., Maggie and Marvin. Mr. Johnson has always followed agricultural pursuits, and has lived on the farm that he now owns, with the exception of a few years, when he moved to town for the purpose of educating his children. In March, 1853, he was elected magistrate and has performed the duties of that office ever since, to the evident satisfaction of all. He is a Democrat in politics but cast his first presidential vote for Z. Taylor. He is a Mason, a member of the I. O. O. F. and he and Mrs. Johnson are members of the Methodist Episcopal Church.

J. A. Miller, citizen and farmer of the Third District of Chester County, Tenn., was born in McNairy County, Tenn., April, 1847, and is one of a family of ten children. He is a son of R. S. and Elizabeth (Willett) Miller and a grandson of Francis and Margaret

(Skimer) Miller. R. S. Miller was born in South Carolina, in 1816, and came to McNairy County, Tenn., with his parents when a young man. He was a farmer by occupation, a tanner and a prominent citizen of the county. He died July 11, 1874. Elizabeth (Willett) Miller was born in McNairy County, in 1822, and is now living with her son, J. A. Her parents were Edward and Polly (Tedford) Willett, the former born in Virginia about 1790, and moved to Lincoln County when a young man. He was twice married, was a farmer by occupation and was in the "Jackson war" a short time. He died in 1862. His wife, Polly (Tedford) Willett, was born in East Tennessee about 1800, and died in 1836. Our subject was reared at home and received his education in the district schools and at Purdy. In 1879 he was elected magistrate of the Eighth District, McNairy County, and the next year was chosen trustee of the county. He held this position until that part of the county was cut off to help form Chester County, and at the organization of that county he was elected magistrate of his district (No. 3, Chester County), a position he continues to hold. He is engaged in farming, and is operating the same cotton-gin that his father built in 1858. He is a Republican in politics and a member of the Grange order.

Caleb McKnight, a prominent citizen and farmer of the Sixth District of Chester County, was born in Wilson County, Tenn., in 1820, and is one of a family of nine children, three of whom are living. His parents, William and Rhoda (Kissee) McKnight, are both natives of South Carolina. The father was born in September, 1773; was married in his native State and came to Wilson County, Tenn., a few years afterward, where he remained until 1825. He then moved to Madison County. He was a tiller of the soil and died in 1857. The mother was born in March, 1774, and died in 1854. Our subject received his education in the district schools near home, and December 29, 1839, he married Elizabeth Hardage, a native of Middle Tennessee, born in 1818, and the daughter of Zachariah and Margaret Hardage, early settlers of Madison County. Seven children were the result of our subject's marriage, all of whom are deceased. In 1839 Mr. McKnight located where he now resides. He is a Democrat in politics and a member of the Masonic fraternity. He and Mrs. McKnight are members of the Methodist Episcopal Church South. In 1861 he enlisted in Company B, Thirty-first Tennessee Infantry, and was captain of the same, the colonel being R. H. Bradford. He remained out some time and was obliged to return home on account of ill health.

John A. Parrish, farmer and prominent citizen of District No. 4, is a son of Thomas A. and Martha (Stone) Parrish, and was born in Virginia in 1832. The parents were both natives of Virginia and died in 1867 and 1848 respectively. The mother was a worthy and consistent member of the Baptist Church. Our subject was reared at home, and educated in the common schools. He came to Henderson County in 1856, and at the breaking out of the late war enlisted in Company I, Thirteenth Tennessee Infantry, and was in all the engagements in which his command participated. He was wounded at Franklin and rendered unfit for duty the rest of the war. He then returned home after an absence of three and a half years' service. In 1866 he settled on his present farm, which consists of 265 acres of good productive land under a high state of cultivation, all of which he accumulated by his industry and successful management, having started in life without a dollar. January 13, 1885, he married Mollie McGee, a native of this county, born about 1852, and the daughter of A. P. and P. McGee. Our subject is a Democrat in politics and cast his first vote for Fillmore in 1856. Mrs. Parrish is a member of the Christian Church.

William Rush, Esq., a prominent farmer and citizen, of the Tenth District of Chester County, was born in Madison County February 22, 1827, and is the only child born to the union of William and Mary (Tidwell) Rush. The father was born in Pennsylvania, and came to Madison County about 1825. He died in 1827. The mother was born August 31, 1807, and is still living. Our subject received a good practical education at Jackson, and December 21, 1850, married Margaret E. Naylor, a native of North Carolina, born in 1829, and the daughter of George and Martha Naylor. By this union they have six children: John A., Mary E. (Mrs. O. T. Siler), William A., M. B., George T. and Sarah F. In 1849 Mr. Rush located near where he now resides and has since been engaged in farming. He is also a carpenter by occupation, and ran a saw-mill and cotton-gin for many years. In 1850 he was elected magistrate, and held that office until the war. When Chester County was organized he was chairman of the board of commissioners that formed the county, and was first chairman of the county court. He is a Democrat in politics, and he and wife are members of the Methodist Episcopal Church South.

C. R. Scarborough, present chairman of the county court of Chester County, and a prominent citizen of Mifflin, is the son of Edmund and W. (Tarbutton) Scarborough, both natives of North Carolina, the father born in 1800 and the mother in 1802. They were married in 1820 and three years later came to Henderson County, and afterward immigrated from there to Madison County where they were classed among the early settlers. The father has been magistrate of Madison County for a number of years, is a member of the Methodist Episcopal Church, and is still living. The mother was also a member of the Methodist Episcopal Church and died in 1884. Our subject was born in Henderson County in 1825, and received his education in the common schools. He spent a portion of his early life in teaching, and February, 1849, married Mary J. Hodges, a native of Tennessee, born in 1824, and the daughter of Josiah and Mary Hodges, of Henderson County. Nine children were born to this union, six of whom are living: Lorenzo, W. L., William H. of Arkansas, Samuel A., Mary E. (Mrs. J. H. Wheeler), Jessie F. and Fannie L. Mr. Scarborough has been a resident of his present farm since 1857, and is the owner of nearly 400 acres of land. He began life with little or nothing, and has succeeded beyond his most sanguine expectations. In 1870 he was elected to the office of magistrate and has been three times re-elected to the same office, holding that position at the present time. He has for four years been chairman of the county court, the first year in Henderson County, and since then in Chester County. In 1868 he was appointed postmaster of Mifflin, which position he continues to hold to the general satisfaction of all concerned. He is a Democrat in politics and cast his first presidential vote for Gen. Cass. Mr. Scarborough is a Mason and he and wife are members of the Methodist Episcopal Church South, together with nearly all their living children.

Capt. B. M. Tillman, a prominent citizen and farmer residing in the Sixth District, Chester County, was born in Marshall County, Tenn., October 21, 1840, and is one of nine children born to the union of John and Nancy (Edwards) Tillman. Eight of these children are living; one, T. R. died while in the Confederate service. The parents were both natives of North Carolina. The father was born in 1807, came to Tennessee when a young man, located in Marshall County, where he remained until about 1841. He then settled in Henderson County, and was a farmer and mechanic by occupation. He was a prominent citizen and died in 1866. The mother was born in 1818 and died in 1880. Capt. B. M. received his education in the district schools near home and in the Montezuma Academy. In the spring of 1861 he enlisted in Company C, Fifty-second Tennessee Infantry, and occupied the position of orderly sergeant. After the consolidation of the Fifty-first and Fifty-second Regiments he was elected captain and took an active part in the battles of Shiloh, Perryville, Chickamauga, Missionary Ridge and many minor engagements. He received three slight wounds at Chickamauga, and was once captured and held a prisoner for about four months. In the spring of 1864 he was assigned a special department, and July 4, 1865, returned home. In 1866 he married Miss M. A. Newsom, a native of Marshall County, Ala., born in 1849, and the daughter of W. V. and Mahala Newsom. To our subject and wife were born two children: John V. and an infant. After the war Mr. Tillman located near where he now resides, and began farming, which occupation he has continued up to the present time. In 1872-73 he represented the people in the State Legislature, and was elected to the same position in 1876-77. In 1880 he was elected State senator of the Eighteenth Senatorial District, composed of five counties. Capt. Tillman is an active progressive man and one to take the lead in all public enterprises. A short time since he was admitted to the bar. He is a Democrat in politics and a member of the Grange order.

William C. Trice, farmer, was born in Henderson County, in 1833, and is one of four children, two now living: Mrs. F. Hamblett and our subject. Their parents, John C. and

Elizabeth (Crook) Trice, are natives of North Carolina and Kentucky respectively, the father born in 1804 and the mother in 1806. John C. was reared in his native State and received but a limited education. He came to Henderson County about 1822 and in about 1828 was married, after which he settled near Jacks Creek where he still resides. He is one of the county's prominent citizens and is a member of the Primitive Baptist Church. The mother is still living. Harrison Trice, grandfather of our subject, was a native of North Carolina and came to Henderson County about 1827, where he died. The subject of this sketch was educated in the common schools and November 19, 1856, he married Eliza E. Boren, a native of Henderson County, born in 1835, a member of the Christian Church, and the daughter of Elijah and Mary Boren. By this union they became the parents of seven children, six of whom are living: Luke L., Callie R. (Mrs. J. E. Christopher), Lora A., Eva B. (Mrs. M. F. O'Neal), Mattie H. and Lessie. Since his marriage Mr. Trice has resided on his present farm which consists of 1,200 acres of land, the most of which is under a high state of cultivation. He is one of the most extensive landholders in the county and is a practical and ideal farmer. In 1865 he was appointed magistrate and has filled that office in a capable manner ever since. He was a Whig in politics before the war and is now a Republican. He is a member of the Masonic fraternity.

John H. Trice, farmer and citizen of District No. 4, was born in McNairy County, November 7, 1860, and is one of two children, only our subject now living, born to the union of John H. and Susan (Anderson) Trice. The father was born in Henderson County about 1832 and was of Scotch-English ancestry. He was married in 1856, and settled in what is now Chester County, where he was engaged in farming. He was elected to the office of magistrate at the age of twenty-two and was holding this position at the time of his death, which occurred December 8, 1861. The mother was born in McNairy County about 1834, and is now living in Madison County. She is a member of the Cumberland Presbyterian Church. John C. Trice, grandfather of our subject, was a native of North Carolina, born in 1804. He came to Henderson County about 1822 and located near Jacks Creek, in 1824. He is still a resident of that county. John H., our subject, received his early education at Medon, afterward at Jackson College and finished at the University of Tennessee at Knoxville. He spent several years of his early life as clerk in a mercantile house and in January, 1883, he married Lessie Cawthorn, a native of Chester County, born in 1861, and a member of the Missionary Baptist Church. Her parents are John L. and Martha Cawthorn. Mr. Trice owns 300 acres of as fine land as is to be found in the county. He is one of the county's most enterprising citizens and is a Democrat in politics having cast his first presidential vote for Grover Cleveland.

J. M Troutt, leading attorney of Henderson, Tenn., is a native Kentuckian, born in Marshall County, April 8, 1848; son of William and Isabella (Watkins) Troutt, both natives of Marshall County, Tenn. The father was born about 1804, and moved to Kentucky about 1840. He served for many years both as constable and deputy sheriff. He was also engaged in agricultural pursuits in which he was quite successful. He died about 1857. The mother was born about the same year as her husband and is now living with her son, Dr. J. R. Troutt, at Clear Springs, Ky. Our subject was educated at the McKenzie College, and also at Bethel College but subsequently attended Princeton College, Kentucky. In 1871 and 1872 Mr. Troutt read law under Judge McCampbell of Paris, and was admitted to the bar about 1874; after which he practiced at Dresden until 1880. He then came to Henderson where he has since remained. He is an able practitioner and has built up an extensive practice. He was one of the leaders in organizing Chester County, after the act was passed setting it aside as an independent county. In 1874 Mr. Troutt married Emma Travis, a native of Henry County, Tenn., born in 1850, and the daughter of Dr. Joseph Travis. She died in 1876. December, 1877, he married R. Province, a native of McKenzie, Tenn., born in 1852 and the daughter of Andrew and Mary Province. To this union was born one child, James McCord. Mr. Troutt is a Democrat in politics, an excellent citizen and a member of the Methodist Episcopal Church. Mrs. Troutt is a member of the Presbyterian Church. In 1864 he enlisted in Company G, Third Kentucky Mounted Infantry, Confederate Army, and participated in many important battles. He was captured at Selma, Ala., paroled at Montgomery and returned home in 1865.

W. C. Tucker, M. D., farmer and citizen of District No. 5, is a son of W. C. and Mildred H. (Kilber) Tucker, both natives of Virginia, born in the years 1801 and 1802, respectively. The father was reared in his native State and married in 1826. He was a farmer and died in 1827, in the prime of life. The mother died in the year 1878, a consistent member of the Methodist Episcopal Church South. W. C. was born in 1827, and was reared by his mother, his father having died when our subject was but an infant. He was educated at Cedar Forest, Va., and came to Henderson County in January, 1852. He engaged in mercantile pursuits at Mifflin until 1856, when he began the study of medicine under Dr. Cochran of that place. In the fall of 1856 he entered the Eclectic Medical College of Cincinnati, Ohio, took one course, and immediately began practicing at Mifflin, but was soon compelled to abandon it on account of ill health. He once more engaged in the mercantile business at Juno, Henderson County, and continued till his business was destroyed during the late war. In 1860 he was elected to represent Henderson County in the State Legislature, and served a term of two years to the general satisfaction of the public. December, 1862, he married Lucy D. Buckley, daughter of John H. and Mary C. Buckley, natives of Virginia. To Dr. and Mrs. Tucker were born six children: Mary, Mildred A., Alice R., William F., Nathaniel A. and Lucy D. Mrs. Tucker was born in Henderson County in 1840, and died in 1876. The Doctor has since been a resident of his present farm, being now the owner of about 600 acres of good productive land in two tracts, all well improved. In politics he was formerly a Whig, but is now a Democrat. He has been a member of the Masonic fraternity since 1854.

D. M. Tull, farmer of District No. 6, and the son of John and Jane A. (Busick) Tull, was born in what is now Chester County, in 1851. The father was born in North Carolina in 1806, and was of Irish extraction. He was reared at home, received a good English education, served in the Creek war, and came to this county with his parents, March, 1842. He was a mechanic and died in 1865. The mother was born in North Carolina, in 1815, and was of Anglo-Irish, Welsh and Italian extraction. She died in 1873. Both parents were worthy members of the Methodist Episcopal Church South. Nicholas Tull, grandfather of our subject, was also a native of North Carolina. He removed to Davidson County, Tenn., at a very early day and from there to this county in 1823. He died in 1861. Our subject was born on the farm where he is now living, and received his education at the common schools and at the Henderson and Mifflin Academies. January 18, 1877, he married Mrs. Mattie Crook, a native of McNairy County, Tenn., born in 1853, and the daughter of Thomas Robinson. To our subject and wife were born five children: Ernest, Alice, Thomas, Inez and Guy. Mr. Tull owns 150 acres of good land in the home place, 100 acres in another tract and also has property in Henderson. He is an ardent Democrat and cast his first presidential vote for H. Greeley. He is a member of the Masonic fraternity.

F. H. Weir, an enterprising farmer of the Sixth District of Chester County, was born in Madison County, August 20, 1834, and is one of a family of eight children. His parents, S. L. and Mary Weir, were both born in Blount County, Tenn., the father in 1793 and the mother in 1800. They came to Madison County in 1830, where he was engaged in farming until his death, in 1854. The mother died in 1884. Our subject was reared at home and received his education at the district schools and at Bethel College. In 1858 he married Rittie Cain, a native of Madison County, born in 1834, and the daughter of Andrew and Sarah Cain. They have an interesting family of children. Mr. Weir is an active energetic man and has followed agricultural pursuits the principal part of his life. In 1868 he was elected deputy sheriff, and filled that office with credit, occupying that position for about six years, to the satisfaction of all concerned. He was also elected magistrate when Chester County was organized. In the fall of 1861 he entered the Confederate Army, joining an independent company of scouts under Gen. Forrest. He served through the principal part of the war and was a brave and gallant soldier.

McNAIRY COUNTY.

Prof. M. R. Abernathy, principal of the Purdy Male and Female Institute, and superintendent of public instruction of McNairy County, Tenn., was born in Alabama in 1846, and was one of a family of eight children born to Dr. Smith and Elizabeth Abernathy, both natives of North Carolina. The father was born in Franklin County in 1802, was a physician and followed that profession many years. He was a Whig in politics and also a local preacher of the Methodist Episcopal Church. He died in 1876. The mother was born in Chatham County in 1810 and died in 1867. Her maiden name was Ramsey. Our subject received his education almost entirely through his own efforts. He came to McNairy County in 1866 and soon afterward began teaching, which occupation he has followed the principal part of the time since. In 1869 he married Miss Rachel M. Cox, a native of McNairy County, born in 1848, and the daughter of Anderson and Rebecca Cox. The result of this marriage was the birth of nine children: William K., Terry W., Florence W., Bessie L., Mary, Pearl, George M. (deceased), Orpheus and an infant. In 1868 Prof. Abernathy was elected county superintendent of public instruction and occupied this position until 1871. In 1885 he came to Purdy to take charge of the Male and Female Institute at that place. Previous to this he had taught a few years at Adamsville. January, 1885, he was chosen to his present office of county superintendent, and has filled that office to the general satisfaction of the people up to the present. In 1886 he assumed control of the *McNairy Independent* which under his able management will undoubtedly become one of the leading newspapers of West Tennessee. Prof. Abernathy is an independent Republican in politics, and he and wife are members of the Christian Church.

Hon. R. D. Anderson, one of the leading farmers and prominent citizens of the Sixth District, is one of six children born to the union of Thomas and Jane (Gates) Anderson. Two of the sons and two daughters are now living. The father was of Scotch-Irish descent, born in Logan County, Ky., in 1805. After having lived in Middle Tennessee and Alabama, went to Hardeman County, Tenn., where he married in 1834; shortly afterward, moving to Tippah County, Miss., he remained there until 1844; when he came to McNairy County, engaging in farming until his death in 1883. By close study he obtained considerable practical knowledge, and held the office of magistrate for a number of years. The mother was born in Bedford County, Tenn., about 1812, is still living in the Sixth District, is an earnest and esteemed member of the church. Our subject was born in Tippah County, Miss., in 1840, was reared under the paternal roof, and educated in the common schools. He enlisted in the Confederate service in 1861, being of those eager and anxious to don the gray for his country, was in a company of heavy artillery under command of Capt. J. C. B. Jones, of Memphis, served in different artilleries in the Army of Tennessee, until the close of hostilities, taking active part in all engagements in which his company participated. After nearly four years of gallantry for his country, he returned home after the surrender and resumed farming. In December, 1865, he married Miss Eliza A., daughter of Thomas and Mary Kerr, who was born in Maury County, Tenn., in 1841, and came to McNairy County when a child. To Mr. and Mrs. Anderson two children have been born: Wm. R. and Mary Jane. Mr. A. has lived at his present home since 1870, owns 180 acres of the most productive and valuable land in the section; it is under a high state of cultivation, well improved; upon it stands a fine commodious dwelling, four miles east of Falcon. Mr. Anderson is a man of business capacity and ability, in his early life spent years in giving instruction in penmanship, being quite proficient in that art. In 1882 was brought forth as the choice of the people to represent the county in the Legislature; he was elected by a large majority; he served the term with satisfaction to the people and credit to himself. He is a Democrat; his first presidential vote was for Horace Greeley. He is a warm advocate and supporter for any and all enterprises which may be beneficial to his country. He and his wife are active and esteemed members of the Christian Church.

Peyton Atkins, a well known farmer and early settler of McNairy County, and resident of the Ninth District, a son of George and Martha (Martin) Atkins, was born in North Carolina in 1814. His grandfather, Joseph Atkins, was a native of North Carolina and a soldier in the Revolutionary war. The father, George, was of Irish ancestry, born in North Carolina in 1785, and while a resident of his native State, married a lady who was born there in 1790. In 1832 they came to McNairy County, where Mr. Atkins engaged in farming until his death in 1849. Mrs. Atkins' death occurred in 1874; she was a consistent member of the Methodist Episcopal Church South. The subject of this sketch was raised under his father's roof and received a fair education at the common schools. January, 1841, he married Nancy, daughter of William and Martha Donnell. She was born in North Carolina in 1817, and became the mother of nine children—six sons and three daughters: Artimesia, wife of V. A. Sanders, of Corinth, Miss.; George, of Hardin County; Martha, wife of D. W. Babb, of Mississippi; Pinckney C., of Arkansas; James E., of Hardin County; Adolpheus S., of Arkansas; John Peyton, of Hardin County; Nancy, wife of Samuel Chambers, and Robert Tolbert. Mr. Atkins has always led an active and industrious life, and by his own efforts has accumulated considerable valuable property, owning the place upon which he resides, a farm of about 400 acres, well improved.

Hon. J. T. Barnhill, one of the native citizens and prominent farmers of District No. 14, is a son of John N. and Elizabeth (Chambers) Barnhill. He was born in McNairy County in 1848, and is one of ten children, three sons and two daughters now living. The father was born in North Carolina about 1811 and was of Scotch ancestry. His father, William Barnhill, removed to this county from Alabama about 1826, and afterward to Texas, where he died. John N. Barnhill received a good practical education and came to this county about the same time that his father did. He was married when about the age of eighteen or nineteen, and was a life-long tiller of the soil. He was a man of good business capacity and led a public life for a number of years in various capacities; was also one of the pioneers of this county, having settled here when the country was a dense forest and the settlers were few and far between. He died in 1881. The mother was a native of Alabama, born in 1809, and is still living in this county. Her parents were Samuel and Elizabeth Chambers, also early pioneers of McNairy County. Our subject was reared at home on the farm where he was born and where he now resides. His rudimentary education was received at the common schools, but he subsequently graduated in the law department of Cumberland University, at Lebanon, Tenn., in January, 1881. He has quite an extensive law practice in connection with his farming interest. He owns about 1,500 acres of land in the vicinity of Chewalla. His home farm, one mile north of that village, is under a high state of cultivation and is in a desirable locality. Although Mr. Barnhill is comparatively a young man, he is already one of McNairy County's most efficient and promising farmers, active business men and politicians. In 1884 he represented McNairy County in the Lower House of the State Legislature, being elected by a large majority, and served during the term with commendable distinction. He is a Democrat in politics and cast his first presidential vote for H. Greeley. He is an active member of the Masonic fraternity. February 22, 1880, he married Miss Docia Rosson, a native of this county, born in 1859, and a member of the Missionary Baptist Church. She is a refined and much esteemed lady, and is the daughter of Joseph T. and Charlotte Rosson.

John G. Combs, a well known and prosperous farmer of the Seventh District, was born in Virginia in 1827, the only child of Thomas and Catherine (Straton) Combs, both natives of Virginia. The father was born about 1796, came to McNairy County in 1831, was a carpenter by trade, also a farmer, a man very highly respected; he died in 1864. The mother was born in 1804 and died in 1871. The subject of this sketch was raised at home, was educated at Savannah and Purdy. About 1847 he married Margaret, daughter of Peter and Celia Shull, both old residents of the county. Mrs. Combs died in 1864, leaving four children: Peter, Henry, John and Willie. In 1865 he made a second marriage to Mrs. Frances Perry, who was born in Giles County, Tenn., in 1839, a daughter of James and Mary Arnis. This union resulted in the birth of Maggie, James, Archibald, Lee and

Guy. In 1862 Mr. Combs enlisted in the Confederate Army from Arkansas, joined Company E, McCrary's brigade, and was in active service a short time when he returned home. He is an ardent Democrat, and a Mason. He and his wife are members of the Cumberland Presbyterian Church. Mr. Combs has always been engaged in agricultural pursuits, and with the exception of two years, a resident of the county since childhood; he is an industrious and respected man, taking interest in and supporting any enterprise for the improvement of the community.

N. A. Erwin, of the firm of Erwin Bros., merchants of Falcon, Tenn., was born October 20, 1848, and is the son of N. A. and M. E. (McKenzie) Erwin. The father was born in Sumner County, Tenn., about 1818 and came to McNairy County with his parents when about eight years old. At this early period there were very few settlers in the county. He cultivated the soil and was one of the leading citizens of the county. His death occurred February 8, 1885. The mother was a native of McNairy County, born about 1828. She died September, 1862. Our subject was reared under the parental roof and secured his education principally at Pebble Hill, this county. March 5, 1872, he married Miss Josie Kerr, who was born October 14, 1851, in McNairy County. She is the daughter of Thomas and Mary A. Kerr, and by her marriage became the mother of two children: Mary D. and Pearl. In 1880 Mr. Erwin and his brother engaged in mercantile pursuits at Falcon, where they have since remained engaged successfully in this business. He is a Democrat in politics and a good citizen. Mr. Erwin's grandparents were Nathaniel and Mary Erwin, natives respectively of South Carolina and North Carolina. The grandfather moved to Sumner County where he remained some time. He then came to McNairy County and followed agricultural pursuits. His wife was the only daughter in a family of twelve children, and five of the boys were soldiers in the war of 1812.

Dixon Etheridge, a well known farmer of the Seventeenth District, is a son of Kindred and Serena Massingale Etheridge, born in Dixon County, Tenn., about 1838. The father was a native of Edgecombe County, N. C.; immigrated to Dixon County, Tenn., when but a boy, with his father, Willoughby Etheridge; he was raised and married in that section. He moved to McNairy County in 1848. He was an active and industrious man, engaged in farming until time of his death about 1868. Our subject was reared under the paternal roof, his educational advantages were limited. At the age of twenty-five he married Miss Mary Jane, daughter of James and Katie Patterson. To their union eight children were born, seven of whom are living: Nathan Clark, Jackson, Robert D., Mary E., John H., Julia Ann and Winnie. In 1875 Mr. Etheridge settled on Sweet Lips, and moved to where he now resides, two miles south of McNairy, which by his industry, frugality and good management he owns; it consists of about 373 acres. Mr. Etheridge has always been a hardworking, energetic man, is a most worthy citizen and kind neighbor. He is an ardent Democrat, having cast his first presidential vote for John C. Breckenridge. He has been for several years a prominent member of the Masonic fraternity. He and his wife are consistent and faithful members of the Christian Church, and held in respect by all.

F. M. Freeman, hotel proprietor and merchant, is a native of Adamsville, born in 1849. His parents were C. J. and Mahala (Williams) Freeman. The father was born in Mississippi in 1823, came to McNairy County, Tenn., in 1846, returned to Mississippi in 1882, where he now resides; he is a blacksmith. The mother was born in 1828, bore five children; her death occurred in 1872. Our subject was raised at home, received a good education in Hardin County. He married Miss Mollie, daughter of J. S. McWhirter, one of the oldest settlers of the county. Mrs. Freeman was born in Adamsville in 1849; is the mother of five children: Minnie, Hattie, James, Napoleon and Josie. Mr. Freeman immediately after his marriage moved to Texas where he remained four years. In 1880 he located at Adamsville and began the drug business. He has always been an enterprising, industrious man and by his own efforts has accumulated considerable property. He is a warm Republican, taking considerable interest in politics; is a genial and worthy man.

W. A. Gooch, a farmer and highly respected resident of the Fourth District, is a native of McNairy County, was born in 1840, a son of J. G. and Louvinia (Brumblow) Gooch. The father was born in Alabama in 1809, and came to this county with his parents when a child; they were among the earliest settlers. He was a farmer by occupation and a magistrate in the county over fifty years; a great portion of that time was chairman of the county court, holding that office for perhaps a greater length of time than any man in the State of Tennessee. He was twice married, the father of fifteen children. No man was better known or more esteemed. His death occurred August 6, 1885. The mother was born about 1809, and bore six children. She died about 1845. The subject of this sketch spent his boyhood at home, and received a very good education in the district schools. He served about nine months in the Confederate Army, enlisting in the summer of 1861, in Company C, Twenty-first Tennessee Infantry, under command of Col. Pickett, Dr. Whitemore being the captain. He is an ardent Democrat and is a Mason. December 6, 1866, was married to a native of McNairy County, who was born in 1846—Nancy M., daughter of James and Louisa Warren. Their union resulted in the birth of eight children: S. W., J. R., J. C., W. T., Nancy L., D. C., Martha E. and an infant. The most of Mr. Gooch's time has been given to agricultural pursuits, in which he has been unusually successful; has always taken an active part in any enterprise which was for the country's good. August 6, 1886, he was elected magistrate of the Fourth District, and continues to fill the position. As a citizen, officer and neighbor no man is more esteemed. He and his wife are members of the Methodist Episcopal Church.

John M. Hamm, one of the pioneers of the Fourth District, and son of Thomas P. and Tobitha (Huggins) Hamm, was born in Lauderdale County, Ala., in 1822, being the third of thirteen children, two only living. The father, Thomas P., was of Scotch-Dutch ancestry, born in Kentucky in 1778. The grandfather, John Hamm, was a native of South Carolina, born about 1759 and when fourteen or fifteen years of age volunteered his services in the Revolutionary war, served under Gen. Marion; was married in his native State and afterward went to Logan County, Ky., from there to Middle Tennessee, then to Lauderdale County, Ala., finally settling in McNairy County in 1826, where he engaged in farming until his death, October, 1836. He was a magistrate for a number of years. Thomas P. received a common-school education, while residing in Kentucky; married in 1818, and came to McNairy County in 1827, where, with the exception of a few years spent in Hardin County, he remained until his death in 1856. He was a farmer. The mother was born in North Carolina in 1778, and died July, 1886. Our subject, John M., was brought up on his father's place; received such education as the common schools afforded; came to McNairy County with his family, and was married December, 1843, to Elizabeth, daughter of Robert C. and Rebecca Houston. She was born in 1827. Their union was blessed with twelve children, of whom are Archibald B., James R., Rebecca, wife of Wilson A. Smith, of Arkansas; Cynthia Ann, wife of Thomas Ramer; Tobitha, wife of James Prither; Mary E., wife of Dr. J. L. Lawson; Fannie, wife of Jones Reeder; Sallie, wife of Thomas Baker; John H., William and Mac. Mr. Hamm has lived in the vicinity and on his farm since 1865. He at one time owned 800 acres of land, but has divided a portion of it among his children; still has 400 of valuable acres under high cultivation, well improved, three miles east of Ramer. He is a man of great industry, and well informed, possessed of fine business capacity. He takes a deep interest in the advancement of education, has always a helping hand for charitable and religious institutions. At about the time of his majority was elected magistrate, held the office for twenty-five years, was tax collector about twenty-seven years, and in 1880 was census taker. He is a Democrat and has always been. The first presidential vote he cast was for James K. Polk, in 1844. He has been a member of the Masonic fraternity thirty-five years, taking the Royal Arch degree. Both he and his wife are devoted members of the Cumberland Presbyterian Church.

A. B. Hamm, a leading merchant and prominent citizen of Ramer, is a son of John M. and Elizabeth (Houston) Hamm; he was born in McNairy County in 1845, is the eldest of a family of twelve children. He was brought up at his father's home; received such education as the common schools afforded. He enlisted in the Confederate Army January, 1863, in Company B, under command of Capt. W. P. Barnhill, Nineteenth Tennessee, under Col. J. Forrest's command, taking active part in any engagement in which his company participated; surrendered at Gainesville, Ala., May, 1865. He returned home and resumed the agricultural pursuits. After several months of study at a select school he engaged in teaching several years. In December, 1869, he married Miss Nicy J., daughter of J. R. and Martha Hurley. Mrs. Hamm was born in McNairy County, 1849; became the mother of three children, two of whom are still living: John Robert and Flora Lillian. Mr. Hamm gave up farming in 1873 and entered the mercantile business with T. J. Hurley at Chewalla, the firm being known as Hamm & Hurley until 1874, when he bought out his partner's interest, continuing the business alone until 1876, since which time he has been at Ramer, where he met with great success, now carrying a stock of general merchandise valued at $12,000. He is one of the most efficient and flourishing business men of the county; by untiring industry, honesty and good management has accumulated considerable means, and owns 151 acres near Ramer, 175 acres in First District, houses and several lots in Ramer. He is a strong Democrat; his first presidential vote was given H. Greeley. Mr. and Mrs. Hamm are conscientious members of Cumberland Presbyterian Church, well known and greatly respected.

J. M. Hamm, Jr., a well known farmer and saddler of the Fifth District, is a native of McNairy County; was born in August, 1848. His parents were Calvin and Emily Ann (Springer) Hamm. The father was born in Lauderdale County, Ala., in 1822, and came to this county with his parents when about eight years of age, making him one of the old settlers. He is a respected farmer of the Fifth District. The mother was born in Giles County, Tenn., in 1826. Of a family of eight children born to her, five are still living. Our subject was raised at home and received the educational advantages of the district schools. In 1867 he married Miss Laura J. Robertson, who was born in McNairy County in 1847, a daughter of Pleas. and Margaret Robertson, who came to the county at an early day. By their union they have three children living: Minnie, Myrtle and John Calvin. After his marriage Mr. Hamm began farming, which occupation he carried on for some time, when he learned the saddler's trade, in which business he has been engaged since 1873, and has found it very profitable, for by his energy, attention to business and courtesy to patrons, he has succeeded in building up an extensive trade. His work is in great demand. In March, 1886, he was elected magistrate of the district. He is a stanch Democrat. Mr. and Mrs. Hamm are both members of the Primitive Baptist Church, and esteemed by the community in which they live.

B. S. McIntire, a well known citizen and merchant of Purdy, Tenn., was born in McNairy County, November 9, 1835; was one of a family of five boys, two of whom are living. His parents were John and Margaret (Day) McIntire. The father was born in Lincoln County, N. C., in 1797, and located in McNairy County in 1833. He was a farmer, married twice and raised seven children. His death occurred in 1852. The mother was born in Gibson County, Ind., in 1799, and died in 1844. Our subject was brought up on his father's farm and attended the schools near his home, receiving a fair education. During the war he enlisted in an independent company under command of Capt. Algee, and was with them about four months. In the spring of 1862 he enlisted in the Confederate Army from Carroll County, was in Company K, Tenth Tennessee Cavalry, first under Col. N. N. Cox; afterward William De Moss was colonel and Thomas Hutchison captain. Mr. McIntire took an active part in the battle of Chickamauga, and in several other engagements. January 28, 1864, he was so severely wounded at Dibrell's Hill, Sevier County, that it was necessary to amputate his leg the next day. He returned home in the fall of the year. After the restoration of peace he was salesman for T. K. Hall at Paris, Tenn., in the mercantile business, and later with his brother, R. W., who now resides at Jackson. In 1871 he left Paris and located in Purdy, where he has since carried on an extensive dry goods and grocery business, having by his energy, good management and integrity, built up a large trade. In 1875 he married a native of Purdy, who was born in 1852, Miss Maud, daughter of Dr. W. C. and Martha Kindel. By their union there is one daughter, Ophelia V. Mr. McIntire is a warm Democrat and man whom all respect.

Josiah Jeans, one of the best known men of McNairy County, is one of the six children born to James and Tabitha (Prither) Jeans. The father was born in Virginia and went to South Carolina when a young man, and there married a native of the State. He came to McNairy County at an early day and engaged in farming until the time of his death. The mother's death occurred at the same place; she was a sincere Christian and member of the Methodist Episcopal Church. Our subject was born in South Carolina in 1804, was raised on his father's farm, receiving his education in the common country schools. In 1836 he immigrated to McNairy County, located near Falcon on the farm upon which he has since resided. By labor, energy and careful management, he has risen from poverty to one of the most substantial men of the county. He owns 500 acres of land, making him one of the most extensive farmers in the section. In 1828 he married Miss Elizabeth Prither, who became the mother of six children, three of whom are living: James Newton, Josiah T., of Arkansas, and Laura Jane, wife of John Carter, of Falcon. Mrs. Jeans died in the spring of 1880, and in April, 1881, Mr. Jeans married Miss Susan Norman, of Mississippi, who was born in East Tennessee in 1824; she is a consistent and earnest member of the Cumberland Presbyterian Church. Mr. Jeans is an old and stanch Democrat; his first presidential vote was cast for Gen. Jackson in 1828. No man is better known or more generally esteemed.

Robert E. McKinney, clerk and master of the chancery court, of McNairy County, Tenn., was born June 18, 1857, and received his early education at Purdy, but subsequently attended the Mars Hill Academy, in Alabama. At the age of fifteen he was appointed deputy circuit clerk, and afterward held the position as deputy in the register's office for some time. In the winter of 1878-79 he took a course of lectures at the Louisville University, having previously studied medicine at Purdy. In the spring of 1879 he began the practice of his chosen profession, and in April of the same year he received the appointment of the office of clerk and master of the chancery court, was reappointed and continued to hold that position. January, 1881, he married Miss Mollie Stubbs, a native of Baldwin, Miss., born August, 1860, and a daughter of Thomas B. and Virginia Stubbs. August, 1884, our subject was elected chairman of the Democratic Executive Committee of the county and was also congressional committeeman for the county for the same term. He has been a public officer of the county most of the time since he was fifteen years of age; he is a man well known and much esteemed by all his acquaintances as an excellent officer and an obliging neighbor. He is an ardent Democrat in politics. He is one of a family of seven children born to Judge J. F. and Julia A. (Adams) McKinney. The father was born at Fayetteville, Tenn., in 1823. He read law at his native town and was admitted to the bar at that place, after which he came to McNairy County and located at Purdy and began the practice of his chosen profession. He was twenty-four years of age at that time, and practiced in this and adjoining counties for many years. He held the honorable position of both circuit and chancellor judge by commission from the governor, and was one of the leading lawyers of West Tennessee. He died May, 1880. The mother of our subject was born at Purdy, November, 1833, and is the daughter of B. B. and Amanda F. Adams, native Virginians, who came to this place at a very early day.

Gen. John H. Meeks, one of the most influential citizens and leading farmers of McNairy County, was born in Lincoln County, Tenn., in 1814, was the youngest of three sons and the only one now living. His parents were John and Elizabeth (Henderson) Meeks, both natives of Pendleton District, S. C. The father was born in 1783, was well educated, married the first time in 1810 to the mother of John H., and after her death made a second marriage in 1819 with Elizabeth Lane, by whom he had six children. In 1811 he moved to Lincoln County, and engaged in farming until 1844, when he located in McNairy Co., and there resided up to the time of his death, which occurred in 1877. The mother was a daughter of Capt. John Henderson, a gallant and noted man of Revolutionary fame. Mrs. Meeks died in October, 1814, when the subject of this sketch was but an infant; he was taken by his grandfather, Capt. Henderson, with whom he remained until manhood. He received liberal literary and business education, and spent the time from 1835 to 1838 as a teacher, in which capacity he proved most efficient. Since the latter date he has been tilling the soil, either carrying it on himself or having it done by others. In 1830 he was sent by Capt. Henderson to McNairy County, to take charge of a number of men and raise a crop, after which he returned to Alabama, his grandparents having moved there in his childhood. In 1832 they settled in McNairy County. January, 1841, John H. was married to Ellen, daughter of George and Martha Atkins; she was born in Rockingham County, N. C., and came to McNairy County with her parents in 1832. To them were born eight children, only two sons and two daughters are living: Martha E., wife of F. A. Johnson, of Dyer County; Elder Rufus P., an earnest and influential minister of the Christian Church, residing at Jackson, Tenn.; Marcus Henry, a leading attorney at law of Jackson, Tenn., and Zilpah, wife of W. D. Erwin, a prominent merchant of Falcon. Gen. Meeks has been living on his present farm since 1851; it is twelve miles east from Falcon, extends over 600 acres of the county's most productive soil, which is highly cultivated and improved; the dwelling-house is one of the most elegant and well arranged in the country. He also owns about 800 acres of Tennessee River bottom land in Hardin County, which is very valuable. The General is a half-brother to Orvil L. Meeks, of same county. He is a man of unusual strength of mind, a keen financier, and of indisputable integrity; is an ardent advocate of universal education, and gives liberally to all charitable and religious institutions. He has always been a stanch Democrat—the recognized leader of that party in McNairy County, having held various responsible and prominent positions. His public career began in 1849, when he represented his county in the Lower House of the State Legislature, being the first Democrat representative from McNairy County; he was re-elected in 1851; was nominated several times afterward, but declined further election. In 1855 he was offered the nomination for congressman in his congressional district, but positively declined. He was a member of the constitutional convention of 1870. His first presidential vote was cast for Hugh L. White in 1836. He has been a Mason of good standing and prominence since 1848. The entire family are members of the Christian Church. He received the title of general from the militia votes of both Hardeman and McNairy Counties; was not a soldier in the late war, but had two sons who fought bravely in defense of the lost cause. The elder of these, under the command of Gen. Forrest, fell, mortally wounded, in 1864. Gen. Meeks earnestly opposed the first action of the South in bringing about secession, but, finally, when the war was forced on the Southern people, he was afterward an ardent supporter of the lost cause.

Hon. Orvil L. Meeks, farmer and miller, and one of the leading citizens of District No. 14, is a son of John and Elizabeth (Lane) Meeks. He was born in Lincoln County, Tenn., in 1822, and is the eldest child born to his parents. The father was born in South Carolina in 1788, and was of Welsh-English descent. He was reared in Georgia and received his education in the common schools, was a farmer and mechanic, and was twice married, his first wife being Miss Elizabeth Henderson. His second marriage occurred in 1819 in Franklin County, Tenn. He removed to Lincoln County at a very early day, and from there to McNairy County in 1844. He died about 1877. His father, Littleton Meeks, was also a native of South Carolina, but afterward located in Georgia. He was for many years engaged as a missionary among the Indians. The mother of our subject was born about 1806 and died at the age of seventy. She was a woman of rare intelligence, fine culture and high moral attainments. Both parents were members of the Primitive Baptist Church, and much esteemed by their many friends. Our subject was reared at home and received a common-school education. In 1841 he came to McNairy County, and in December, 1845, he married Miss Cynthia L., daughter of John and Rebecca Chambers. In 1854 Mrs. Meeks died; she was the mother of the following children: John C., a wholesale merchant at St. Louis, Mo.; Marcus W., merchant at Corinth, Miss., and Orvil L. (deceased). October 11, 1859, Mr. Meeks married Miss Martha Michie, a native of McNairy County, born in 1839, the daughter of G. G. Michie, and a member of the Christian Church. This union resulted in the birth of eleven children—three sons and eight daughters: George T., Lovinia, James L., Henry, Zilpha (Mrs. David Sharp), Ellen, Josie, Kate, Lillie, Flora and Lucretia. Mr. Meeks has been a resident of his present home since 1845, and is the owner of about 1,500 acres of productive land, four miles southeast from Ramer, nearly all of which he has acquired by his own industry. He is well known throughout the county as one of its best and most successful citizens. He served for some time as colonel of the militia. In 1855 he was elected by the Democratic party to represent Hardeman, McNairy and Hardin Counties in the upper branch of the State Legislature, where he served one term. During the latter part of the late civil war he served for several months in Forrest's cavalry. In politics he is a stanch and active Democrat, and cast his first presidential vote for James K. Polk in 1844. He has been a Master Mason for over thirty years, and is one of the county's most respected citizens.

S. M. Perkins, a prominent citizen and merchant of Adamsville, Tenn., is one of twelve children, ten now living, born to S. M. and C. Perkins, both natives of Middle Tennessee. The father was born in 1814, came to McNairy County about 1834, and now resides in the Tenth District. He is a farmer. The mother was born in 1817 and died 1850. Her maiden name was Houston. Our subject was born in McNairy County in 1840, and received his education in the schools near home. In 1865 he began merchandising at Stantonville and remained in the business at that place for three years. He then engaged in tilling the soil and continued at this until 1883 when he came to Adamsville and engaged extensively in the sale of dry goods and general merchandise. In 1867 he married Miss Mary A. Howell, who was born in Hardin County in 1847, and who is the daughter of Benjamin and Nancy Howell. By this connection our subject became the father of five children: Josie, Samuel, Ida, Estella and Bennie. Mr. Perkins is thrifty, wide-awake and is one of the town's most substantial business men. He is a Democrat in politics and he and wife are worthy members of the Christian Church. In 1861 he enlisted in Company G, Thirteenth Tennessee Infantry (Confederate Army) under Col. Williams, and served with his company two years, after which he joined Forrest's cavalry. He took an active part in the battles of Shiloh, Harrisburg, Ky., and Cross Roads. He was with Hood and was in many minor engagements and cavalry skirmishes. He was slightly wounded four times and was a brave and fearless soldier. He then returned home in the spring of 1865.

J. P. Prince, a prominent citizen and merchant of Purdy, Tenn., was born in Pendleton District, South Carolina, June 29, 1817; was one of a family of nine children born to James and Mary Prince. The father was born in 1778, and was a farmer by occupation. In 1825 he moved to Georgia and was for many years justice of the peace; his death occurred there in 1863. The mother was Miss Mears, born in Virginia about 1786, departed this life November, 1876. Our subject was raised at home, received his education at Clarksville, Ga., and came to Tennessee in 1843, locating in Hardin County, where he taught school for four years. He was in a warehouse at Camp's Landing for five years, at same time doing a mercantile business for himself, going from there to Adamsville, selling goods until 1863, when he went to Paducah, remaining there until the close of the war. For eight years he was in the commission business in St. Louis, Mo., and in 1873 settled in Purdy, meeting with great success and is considered one of the leading merchants. December of 1859 he was married to Eliza Kerby, who was born in Hardin County in 1832, a daughter of John and Nancy Kerby. Mrs. Prince died in 1858, leaving one son, Dr. J. J. Prince, a physician and merchant at Bethel Springs. Mr. Prince is a Republican, and a member of the Christian Church, a man of good business capacity; a fine manager, who has always been prosperous and respected.

John H. Reeder, a farmer, miller, ginner, and prominent man of McNairy County, is a son of Jacob and Sarah (Wesson) Reeder, was born in Lawrence District, South Carolina, in 1822. His great grandfather was a native of Germany, immigrated to the United States where he raised a family of sixteen children, the grandfather of Jno. H., being the youngest boy—all of whom lived to marry and rear children. The father, Jacob, was born in South Carolina in 1799, was married when about twenty-one years of age to a lady of his native State who was born about 1800 and died about 1856. In 1825 Jacob moved to Lauderdale County, Ala., where he engaged in agriculture up to the time of his death in 1861. He and his wife were devoted and esteemed members of the Methodist Episcopal Church South. John H. was raised and educated in the common schools of his native State. February, 1842, he married Miss Rosana, daughter of Frederick Jones of Lawrence District. She was born in 1820; became the mother of eight children, four sons and two daughters still living: Wm. A.; Sarah, widow of Cicero Jeans; James A.; Lydia, wife of J. S. Ramer; John Henry, Jr., and Jones C. In 1843 Mr. Reeder came to this county, but remained only a year, returning to Alabama in 1844; he came back and located near Gravel Hill in 1848, where he now owns 213 acres of good land, fertile and well improved. In 1886 he moved to Ramer, where he is at present engaged in saw-milling and ginning. He is a man of great energy and untiring industry; has accumulated his possessions by hard labor and good management. He was in the mercantile business from 1865 to 1875, and in all his undertakings has met with success. He is a life-long Democrat; gave his first presidential vote to James K. Polk in 1844. He was elected magistrate in 1870, and held the office six years to the satisfaction of the people. He has been a Mason a number of years. He and his wife are members of the Methodist Episcopal Church South, both held in highest respect by the community.

Dr. W. M. Sanders, physician and surgeon at Adamsville, Tenn., was born in McNairy County, August 9, 1849, and is one of a family of eleven children born to the union of W. C. and Martha Sanders. The father was born in East Tennessee in 1819, and came to McNairy County, with his parents when two years of age. He is an extensive farmer and now resides in the Tenth District. The mother was a native of Lincoln County, born about 1830, and her maiden name was Moore. Our subject received his education at the Adamsville Male and Female Institute, and in 1871 began reading medicine with Dr. L. N. Pettigrew, of Adamsville, with whom he remained until September, 1873, when he entered the medical department of the Louisville University and took a course of lectures. The next year he located at Adamsville and began the practice of his chosen profession. In the fall of 1879 he returned to Louisville and took a course of lectures at the Kentucky School of Medicine where he graduated in the spring of 1880. January 27, 1876, he married Miss Jennie Scott, a native of McNairy County, and the daughter of Frank Scott. By this union they have two children living: Daisy and Alma. Since locating at Adamsville Dr. Sanders has built up an extensive and lucrative practice and has made many warm friends. Since 1879, he and his brother, Dr. J. L., have been in partnership. The brother studied medicine under our subject and then completed his education at the medical department of the University of Louisville. They have the leading practice at Adamsville. The Doctor is an ardent Democrat in politics and he and wife are members of the Methodist Episcopal Church South.

J. W. Stumph, chairman of the county court of McNairy County, Tenn., was born in Pennsylvania in 1836, son of W. W. and Nancy (Hyatt) Stumph, both natives of Pennsylvania. The father was born in 1816, and was of German lineage. He was a merchant for many years, and then moved to Illinois, where he cultivated the soil. He died in 1879. The mother of our subject was born about the same time as her husband, and is of English descent. She is now living in Illinois. Our subject was one of a family of seven children, five of whom are now living. He was educated at Uniontown College, and in 1858 moved to Savannah, Hardin County, and the next year came to Purdy, where he has since been engaged in the jewelry business. In 1860 he married Miss Margaret Braden, a native of McNairy County, born about 1841, and the daughter of P. H. and Sarah Braden, old and respected citizens of McNairy County. Mrs. Stumph died in 1872, leaving two children: Fred and Sallie. In the fall of 1873 he married Miss L. Huddleston, a native of McNairy County, born about 1846, and the daughter of Calaway Huddleton. The fruits of this union were five children: Lockie, John, Calaway, Wynn and Oliver. In 1870 Mr. Stumph was chosen magistrate of the Seventh District, and has held that position ever since. In 1876 he was made chairman of the county court, and from 1870 to the spring of 1886 was postmaster at Purdy. He has always been an active, energetic man, and has accomplished much toward the general improvement of the place. He is a stanch Republican in politics. In 1881 he was appointed United States commissioner of McNairy County by Judge Hammond.

R. P. Swain, a well known farmer of the Fourth District, son of William and Rebecca (Williamson) Swain, was born in Lincoln County, Tenn., in 1820. The father was of

Irish descent, born in South Carolina in 1783; when about thirteen years of age he went to Georgia, where he married at the age of twenty-six. He moved to Lincoln County in 1812, and in 1828 went to Henderson, Chester County, and remained until 1840, when he settled in McNairy County, resuming his farming and so continuing up to a year previous to his death, which occurred in 1871. The mother was born in Georgia about 1788; died in 1861; she and her husband were both faithful members of the Primitive Baptist Church. Our subject spent his early life at home, receiving his education from the common country schools. April, 1846, he married Miss Melissia Merrell, of McNairy County. They became the parents of six children, all living but one: Aurelius; Martha, wife of John McCoy; William; Mary, wife of Elihu Blasingain, and Elma. Mr. Swain first located in McNairy County, in 1848 moved to Mississippi, in 1861 returned to the county and in 1874 settled on the farm which he now occupies and owns, a place of seventy acres, one and a half miles east from Ramer. He is a life-long Democrat, having cast his first presidential vote for Jas. K. Polk. Mr. and Mrs. Swain are interested and active members of the Missionary Baptist Church and are esteemed by the community.

Hon. James Warren, a farmer and pioneer of McNairy County, was born in Claiborne County, Tenn., in 1810. He is the only surviving one of a family of eight children born to James and Nancy (Murphy) Warren. The father was a native of Virginia, and moved to Caswell County, N. C., with his father, James Warren. While a resident of the State, he married, it is thought, about 1798. A few years later he located in Claiborne County and resumed his farming, which occupation he continued until his death about 1813. The mother is supposed to have been a native of North Carolina; after Mr. Warren's death she again married and raised another family of children; moved to Arkansas about 1847, where she died. Our subject, bereft of a father's care at three years of age, served as a bound boy until he attained his majority. His educational advantages were of course very meager, having attended school but a few months, but possessing a bright, quick mind; a close observer and lover of literature, by study and application he obtained fair learning. He came to McNairy County with his master when sixteen years of age. At his majority he began life on his own responsibility as a tiller of the soil. March 30, 1836, he married Miss Louisa, daughter of John and Ann Rains, of this county, but a native of Warren County, born in 1815. To this union nine children were born, of whom five are living: Hugh A.; John T.; Nancy, the wife of Wm. A. Gooch; Lucinda K., wife of Dr. L. H. C. Prather, and Martha E., wife of J. T. Jeans, of Arkansas. The first year of Mr. Warren's married life he was a tenant, but soon accumulated sufficient to purchase a home. He has continued to reside in this county, and has been in the Sixth Precinct since 1860. He has always been an industrious, active man, and by his own efforts, became an extensive land holder, owning nearly 1,500 acres. He has risen from poverty and obscurity to be recognized as one of the most prominent and successful men in McNairy County. That he has the confidence and respect of the people, is demonstrated by the fact that he has filled various responsible offices for a number of years. He was first elected constable, then became sheriff of the county in 1838, serving six years; he was a member of the Legislature during 1845 and 1847; was internal revenue assessor a short length of time, and in 1880 was again elected representative. He was formerly a Whig, casting his first vote for Hugh L. White; was a firm Union man during the war; after that event he affiliated with the Republican party until the organization of the Greenback party and the adoption of their platform, which he accepted as the true principles of government. He is deeply interested in the public schools believing in universal education, and a liberal supporter of all laudable public enterprises. He has been a member of the Masonic fraternity since 1845. The entire family are consistent and devoted members of the Missionary Baptist Church.

Hugh A. Warren, one of the prominent farmers and residents of the Fourth District, is a son of James and Louisa (Rains) Warren; he was born in McNairy County, in 1839, and is one of a family of four sons and five daughters, of whom but five are living. Hugh A. spent his boyhood under the paternal roof, receiving his education in the common schools. He was married February 22, 1861, to Julia, daughter of Thomas and

Elizabeth Knight, who was born in North Carolina, in 1837, and came with her parents to McNairy County when she was quite young. She became the mother of seven children; two sons and two daughters still survive: Frances, wife of J. W. Gooch; James A., Martha E., and John T. Mr. Warren has occupied the farm upon which he now lives for several years, owning 270 acres of fertile land under fine cultivation, and upon which are the best of buildings; is situated four miles southeast of Falcon. Mr. Warren has always been an energetic, prosperous farmer; is a strong advocate of general education, a generous contributor to charitable and religious institutions. Politically he is strictly independent, adhering rigidly to principle and not to party ties. His first presidential vote was for John Bell in 1860. He is a sincere member of the Missionary Baptist Church.

John T. Warren, a merchant of Adamsville, Tenn., was born in McNairy County, April 17, 1841; was one of a family of nine children, five of whom are still living. His father is James Warren, a native of East Tennessee, born in 1810 and came to McNairy County at an early day, being one of the oldest settlers. He is a farmer and lives near Falcon. The mother was Miss Louisa Rains, born in East Tennessee in 1815. Our subject was at home during boyhood, and educated at the schools in the vicinity. After the war he located at Purdy, entering into the mercantile business; from there he went to McNairy Station; afterward was in business at Bethel Springs. In 1877 he came to Adamsville where he has since resided and carried on an extensive and profitable dry goods and grocery trade. He has always been an industrious, upright man, successful in all his undertakings. He is a Mason in good standing, an Independent in politics, voting for principle rather than party. In 1869 he married Miss Jennie, a daughter of Dr. J. S. Rogers, a prominent physician of the county. Mrs. Warren was born in this county in 1848, and is the mother of seven children, two of whom are living: Sousan Violer and Virginia Dee. Mr. and Mrs. Warren are esteemed members of the Missionary Baptist Church.

DECATUR COUNTY.

Robert J. Akin, of the Eleventh District, was born in Decatur County, March 9, 1828. Wm. V. Akin, his father, was a native of South Carolina, came to Maury County, Tenn., about 1801, was married first to Miss Edna, about 1816. Our subject is the eighth of eleven children; received his education in the country schools, by careful and constant reading of books and papers of the day, has a well stored mind. His principal occupation since boyhood has been farming, but from 1856 to 1860 was engaged in boating staves to New Orleans; is a blacksmith by trade. He was married March 28, 1860, to Susan T. Hancock, of Decatur County. When war was declared Mr. Akin enlisted in the Tenth Tennessee Cavalry, under command of Col. Cox; served gallantly in the battles of Chickamauga and Morristown, Philadelphia Tennessee and Brentwood. In the winter Mr. Akin on account of sickness was on furlough; at the termination of the war he returned to the farm upon which he has since and is now living. He is a devoted member of the Methodist Church, a Mason and sincere Democrat, a man well known and respected.

E. E. Arnold, a well known resident of Decaturville, and sheriff of the county, is a member of one of the oldest families in the section. His grandfather, Ephraim Arnold, located in the county at a very early day; the exact date is not known, but is thought to have been no later than 1814, as James E. was born in 1824, and was the youngest of six children, born to them after coming to the county. Uncle James Harris was the only other settler at that time. They were subjected to all the privations and hardships of pioneer life, and were greatly troubled with panthers, they being so bold and vicious as to make it necessary to fasten the doors and windows with iron bars. James E., the father, was a farmer; he died in 1866; the mother is still living, they were the parents of eleven children, ten of whom still live. Our subject worked on a farm until he was sixteen years of age, when he became a pilot on a raft, which occupation he continued until 1882; was then elected sheriff of the county, holding that office up to the present time. April 2, 1874, he married Miss Mary E. Crowder, who died March 22, 1883, leaving a family of five children: Melissa A., Ida M., James E., Mary G. and William G. Mr. Arnold married again to Miss Medora Crowder, January 7, 1885; to this union one child has been born, Carry F. Mr. Arnold is prominently connected with the Masons, has been a member since 1872, also belongs to the I. O. O. F. He was one of the Grangers; was master of the county when that organization went down. He is a Democrat and a man who has a large circle of friends and acquaintances, esteemed by all.

Dr. J. F. Aydelott, a successful practitioner of Decaturville, was born April 28, 1835, son of Andrew E. and Sarah E. (Smith) Aydelott, both natives of Tennessee and both of Irish descent. They removed to Henderson County in 1836, where the father followed agricultural pursuits for some time, after which he engaged in mercantile pursuits. He was a very popular man and one of much influence. Politically he was a Democrat but at the same time he was supported by all 'parties when] he chose to become a candidate for any office. He was sheriff for six years and deputy sheriff for four years. He died October 5, 1882, in Texas, where he had recently removed. The mother preceded him to the grave about three years, dying July 3, 1879. Their family consisted of ten children, only .two of whom are living: Dr. J. F. and Sarah E. (Mrs. B. W. Clenny). Our subject's paternal grandfather was a native of Ireland, who immigrated to America shortly after the Revolutionary war. His maternal ancestors were descendants of the old Atlantic coast settlers, and several of them were soldiers in the Revolutionary war. Dr. J. F. was brought up on the farm and received the elements of a common-school education supplemented by considerable training at high schools at Saltillo, Decaturville and other places. He began the study of medicine at Decaturville and afterward took a thorough and comprehensive course of instruction at the Louisville Medical University in 1878 from which he graduated with honor, securing the third prize. He has since resided at Decaturville, where he has a successful and prosperous practice. He is treasurer of the Board of Health of Decatur County. In 1879 he married Miss Anna C. Jones, daughter of Dr. T. W. Jones of Decaturville, and to them were born four children, three now living: Otto H. (deceased), Arbon Y., Floyd C. and Frank Cleveland. The Doctor is politically a Democrat, a man of wide acquaintance and much influence in Decatur and adjoining counties.

B. G. Baker was born in Hickman County, Tenn., January 11, 1818. His father, Dr. Benj. Baker, was of German descent, born in New York City, where he received his medical education, and practiced until about 1812; he then went to New Orleans, and after several years came to Tenn., locating in Hickman, where he continued the practice of his profession. About 1815 he married Mrs. Rachel (Petty) Fields, who was born in Chatham County, N. C., in 1782; her parents were Virginians, but of Scotch-Irish descent. To Dr. and Mrs. Baker two sons and two daughters were born: Winnie, the widow of Lot Akin, of Decatur County; Elizabeth, widow of Wm. Livingstone, of Maury County; Wm. H., married to Miss Arethie Nickols, and farming in Decatur County, our subject being the fourth child. Dr. Benj. Baker died in 1822, and his wife in 1858; she was a faithful member of the Free-Will Baptist Church, a true Christian woman. B. G. Baker received but a limited education in the country schools of Perry (now Decatur) County, but acquired considerable knowledge from the Bible and other books; has read from the best medical authorities until he is competent to practice in his family; was married in 1837 to Emily Hendrick of Decatur County, with whom he had two children; only one survives, and is Mrs. Tennessee Baker (Prim) McClure who is farming in Dyer County, Tenn. Horton Howard Baker, the son was lieutenant in the Confederate Army; after a gallant leadership in the battle of Shiloh he was taken sick and returned home, living but two days after his arrival there. Mrs. Baker died in 1843. In August, 1845, Mr. Baker married Caroline Bassel, of Humphreys County, Tenn., who became the mother of ten children; of those living are James K., a blacksmith by trade, a farmer in Decatur County, married to Elizabeth Harris; Wm. E., a farmer in same county, wife was Theodosia Besley; G. W., farmer in Decatur County, married Georgie D. Hendrick; Mary E., wife of J. A. Haynes, magistrate and farmer of Decatur County; Martha E., wife of John H. Pratt, farmer in Decatur County; Sarah J., widow of Wm. H. Churry, a farmer in Benton County, died in 1886; Winnie M., wife of L. L. Wood, farmer in Decatur County; Rachel C., married Robert Clift, is farming in Decatur County; Ellen, married John Clift, is merchandising and farming in Decatur County. Benjamin and Dora died in infancy. Mr. Baker is an elder in the Cumberland Church, and a firm Democrat, a man well known and highly respected.

William Bolin, a well known and respected resident of the Third District, was born in Chatham County, N. C., August 28, 1823. He is the sixth child of a family of fourteen. His father, Joseph, was a native of Guilford County, N. C., and was married in 1811 to Miss Sophia Cooper. He came to Tennessee but remained only a year to two; returned to his native State and died there in 1844. Our subject has been engaged in farming from early boyhood, receiving his education in the common schools of North Carolina. He was married February 28, 1844, to a lady of his native State; to them were born three children; one died in infancy; the two living are Mary (Bolin) Moore, and Martin, who is engaged in agricultural pursuits on a farm adjoining his father's. Martin was married February 2, 1873, to Miss Elizabeth Ivey, of Decatur County, and by whom he has three children: Mary M., John W. and Martin C. Mr. William Bolin came to Tennessee in 1870, and one year later located in Decatur County, where he is greatly respected and widely known. He is a stanch Democrat, taking considerable interest in the movements and welfare of that party.

John M. Countess, a well known resident of the Third District, was born August 11, 1841, in Warren County, Tenn. His father, Asa Countess, was a native of Tennessee, a brick-mason by trade. He married about 1833 a daughter of John Martin, of North Carolina, who came to Tennessee. To that union seven children were born, J. M. being the fourth and only surviving one. Asa Countess enlisted in the Fifth Confederate Regiment, under command of B. J. Hill. He died in Mississippi after twelve months of gallant and faithful service. Our subject received a fair education in the common schools of Warren County. He enlisted in the Sixteenth Tennessee, Confederate Army, under command of John H. Savage. He remained in the service about one year; took part in the battles of Huttonville and Chute Mountains, Va. He became dissatisfied with the cause he was aiding, and on the morning of May 15, 1862, received a pass at Corinth, Miss., to be good until 10 o'clock. When about eleven miles south of Corinth he met a detachment who claimed his time had expired. He said that his brother was sick in a house at a short distance, and by this means succeeded in passing. Shortly afterward he entered a swamp, and remained there through the day, traveling by night until he reached a point about one hundred miles south. The man whom he hired for a guide had a horse upon which they took turns in riding, in that way resting themselves. While attempting to cross a river with several other fugitives from Tennessee companies, he was arrested by the town authorities, tried, condemned and sent back. Two officers started back to the army with the prisoners, four in number. While at supper, where they were camped for the night, Mr. Countess and his mate finished eating before the others. They stepped back, and covered by the darkness, slipped away unnoticed. They waded a small stream and spent the night about half a mile from the camp, continuing their journey the next morning. When they reached the river they secured a broad plank, and with one on each end crossed in safety and got home without being again molested. About four months later he enlisted in the Fifth Tennessee Cavalry of the Union Army, under command of Col. W. B. Stokes, taking part in the terrific battle of Stone's River. At the close of the war Mr. Countess returned home and resumed his farming. In 1866 he went to Illinois; spent three years there, going to Missouri, and later to Middle Tennessee, finally settling in Decatur County, where he has since resided. April 20, 1866, he was married to Minnie Blackwell, whose parents were natives of Warren County. To their union six children were born. Those living are Mary, wife of Dr. E. G. Howell, a practicing physician of Decatur County; Margaret, John, George W. William B.'s death occurred September 6, 1879, when two years of age. Mr. Countess is an earnest and active Republican, a member of the Masonic fraternity and K. of H.

Nathan C. Davis, a well known resident of Decatur County, was born July 14, 1843, in Hardin County. His father, Joseph Davis, was a native of Wake County, N. C., born February 7, 1805; he came to Maury County, Tenn., in 1829, where he carried on the blacksmith business; from there he went to Hardin County; was married to Harriet Perry, a native of Williamson County, Tenn., but a descendant of North Carolinians. The subject of this sketch is the eighth of fourteen children; received such education as the country schools of that day afforded, at Clifton, Tenn. When war was declared he enlisted in the Ninth Tennessee Cavalry, under command of J. B. Biffle, took part in the Parkers Cross Roads fight, Trenton, Humboldt, also in the engagements at Franklin and Thompson's Station: he followed Straight and participated in combats at Town Creek, Days Gap, Sand Mountain and Gadsden, capturing the enemy at Pine Bluff; Mr. Davis was taken at Clifton by Murphy, but released by Capt. Sam Martin. When peace was declared, he returned home and resumed farming; was married November 12, 1868, to Miss M. A. Johnson, of Hardin County, whose father was a native of that county; her mother was born in Alabama. To Nathan C. and M. A. (Johnson) Davis seven children were born; those living are Thomas J., William N., Benjamin F., Edgar H. and Mary E. James S. and an infant are both dead. November 24, 1882, Mrs. Davis died. Mr. Davis married the second time in January, 1883, to Mrs. Mary R. (Stephens) Harrell, of Savannah, Tenn., a daughter of Col. H. H. Stephens, who was born in Boone, Bourbon Co., Ky.; her mother, Elizabeth (Tharp) Stephens, was the first white child born in Florence, Ala. She was educated at Louisville, Ky. To Mr. Davis' second marriage one child has been born, Perry, a son. Mr. and Mrs. Davis are earnest members of the Methodist Church. Mr. Davis is a steadfast Democrat and a courteous gentleman.

James E. Dees, county court clerk, of Decaturville, was born in Shelby County, Tenn., April 6, 1852. His parents, Green and Martha C. (Lockhart) Dees, were both natives of Anson County, N. C., from which State he moved to Tennessee, Shelby County, near the line of Marshall County, Miss., where our subject was born, and finally settled in Decatur County, in 1852, where he now resides, is by occupation a farmer and planter. Of a family of nine children, four sons and two daughters are living. The mother departed this life in January, 1874. James E. Dees was brought up on a farm, therefore accustomed to an active life. He received an excellent, practical education at Decaturville, and a year's instruction at the Tennessee University at Knoxville. November 20, 1884, he married Miss Mary A. Yarbro, daughter of John T. Yarbro, of Decatur County. Mr. Dees is a strong Democrat of good standing with his party, was elected clerk of the county court, in August, 1882, and has remained in the office since that time. He is a worthy and affable gentleman, enjoying the esteem of an extensive circle of friends and acquaintances.

Curry P. Denison, proprietor of the Denison House, Decaturville, Tenn., is a native of Decatur County, born November 11, 1839, a son of Stephen and Elizabeth (Ingram) Denison, both natives of Pittsylvania County, Va., and descendants of the early English settlers of the Atlantic coast. Of their family of fourteen children all are living but three: Robert, born September 16, 1814, is a farmer of Henderson County; Alfred, born in 1817, died in 1821; Bird, born July 30, 1818, is also a farmer of Henderson County; Eliza, born August 12, 1820, is now Mrs. Jno. McCall, of Chester County; Mrs. Anna (Denison) Newton, born December 12, 1822, lives in Denton County, Tex.; Sanford, born December 14, 1824, home in Red River County, Tex.; Wm. H., born January 24, 1826, lives in Red River County, Tex.; Jackson, born June 10, 1829, died July 26, 1859; Benjamin, born May 18, 1831, lives in Red River County, Tex.; Nancy J., born May 22, 1833, is married to Andrew McCall, of Henderson County; Mrs. Minerva (Denison) Priddy, of Henderson County, was born September 22, 1835; David G., born September 1, 1837, died in 1863; Curry P., the subject of this sketch, and Mrs. Mary Elizabeth (Denison) Brewer, of Henderson County, born May 15, 1844. Stephen Denison took an active part in many of the sieges and battles of the war of 1812. He was a life-long Whig and worthy citizen, leaving to his posterity an honored name; his death occurred in August, 1865, his wife having died in September, 1860. The grandfather was one of the gallant Virginians who served under Gen. Geo. Washington. Curry P. Denison was raised on a farm; accustomed to labor from boyhood, his educational advantages were limited; being a man of no ordinary ability he has by observation and application become well informed. For a number of years he was a merchant of Henderson County, afterward a farmer; but for the past six years has been proprietor of the Denison House. Politically he is a Republican; was an unswerving supporter of the Union during the late war, which, of course, cost him many dangers and hardships, but escaped uninjured. He is one of the strongest advocates of public schools, is a man well known throughout the country and recognized as one of the best citizens. November 4, 1860, he was married to Miss Nancy J. Bray, born November 2, 1845, a daughter of John and Manerva (Walker) Bray, of Henderson County. This union resulted in the following births: Fredonia A., born March 14, 1863, married February 28, 1879, to J. T. Rogers, merchant of Decaturville; Kittie A., born October 17, 1864, married Dr. John McMillan, of Decaturville; Wm. R., born April 13, 1866, resides at Perryville, Tenn.; Mary A., born January 25, 1868, married, January 14, 1883, to Wm. Barry, editor of *Progress*, Lexington, Tenn.; Granville L., born February 18, 1870; Harriet Rosetta, born February 3, 1873; Bertha L., born February 13, 1880, and Allia J., born March 13, 1884. John Bray, father of Mrs. Denison, was born February 10, 1828, and married Manerva Walker November 24, 1842. She was born March 26, 1827.

Wallace Dixon, farmer and owner of the celebrated Oakland Spring farm, was born December 22, 1836, at Cedar Creek Furnace and educated at Masonic College, Clarksville, Tenn. At the age of twenty he became manager of the iron works known as the Antonio Iron Works, of Montgomery County. Five years later he came to Decatur County and engaged in farming. He was married to Miss Elizabeth Finch, who bore him three children: Emily A., William T. (deceased), and Wallace, who is living with his father. The mother of these children died and Mr. Wallace was married the second time to Lucretia E. Finch, who presented him with five children: Sallie B., Thomas Y., William H., Chambers F., all living, and Elinora, who died September 5, 1878. Mr. Dixon is one of the leading members of the Methodist Episcopal Church, and is one of the prominent Democrats of Decatur County. He is universally respected and is one of the most popular men in this county. Mr. Dixon's great-grandfather, Obadiah Dixon, came with Lord Baltimore to America, and brought his family with him. His son, Benjamin Dixon, was a great stock-dealer and engaged largely in importing horses to America. He enlisted and served gallantly in the war of 1812. Wallace Dixon, Sr., son of Benjamin and father of our subject, was born in Maryland, and was married to Miss Eliza Brady, who was a cousin of Gen. Sam Brady, the celebrated Indian fighter. She carried water, when a girl, to the soldiers while they were fighting the Indians. Wallace Dixon, Sr., came to Nashville when that city was but a village. From there he moved to Dixon County and engaged in the manufacture of iron as one of the firm of Valner & Dixon, owning and managing the furnace known as the Cumberland Furnace. After a number of years Mr. Dixon sold his interest in the enterprise to his partner. He then moved to Perry County and built the Cedar Creek Furnace and after several years' successful management, sold the furnace and purchased the farm now owned by Wallace Dixon, Jr. He also purchased other valuable land in Decatur County. To Wallace and Eliza (Brady) Dixon were born five children of whom our subject is the youngest.

James A. England, clerk and master of chancery court, is a native of Henderson County, Tenn., born February 6, 1851, son of John M. and Rebecca (Hanna) England, of the same county. The father was a practicing physician of Henderson County, until 1862 when he moved to Williamson County, Ill., where he died in 1863. The mother was of Irish descent, and lives in Texas. A. R. England, the grandfather, was born in North Carolina; his father was a native of Ireland. In 1866 the family returned to Henderson County, from Illinois, but went to Hunt County, Tex., in 1873, where our subject had gone three years previous to that time. In 1875 James A. came back to Tennessee; he began teaching and studying law in 1876, was admitted to the bar, March, 1877, and has since that time been engaged in the practice of his profession in Decatur County. May 8, 1879, he was married to Mary A., daughter of William Stout one of the oldest and best citizens of the county. To the marriage two children have been born: Nellie J. K. and James S. Mr. England is a Democrat of considerable prominence, was appointed clerk and master of the chancery court, September, 1879, and still fills the position, having the confidence and esteem of the people. He is a genial and courteous gentleman and fine conversationalist.

Tate Family. Elon H. Tate (deceased) was born in Grundy County, Tenn., October, 15, 1817, and was engaged in cultivating the soil in Warren and Grundy Counties, until his removal to Decatur County, August 12, 1870. He located at Decaturville where he remained until his death December 19, 1879. Mr. Tate was a life-long Democrat and a most worthy citizen. His wife, Jane (Turner) Tate, died May 8, 1865. Their family consisted of five children, two of whom died in infancy, and George was killed at Decaturville November 30, 1877. John L. and James H., the two remaining children, were brought up on a farm and accustomed to hard manual labor from boyhood. John L. secured a good common-school education at Philadelphia, Warren County, and James H. at Decaturville. John L. was born December 7, 1849, in Warren County, Tenn., and enlisted in Forrest's Confederate cavalry in 1864. He participated in several skirmishes and was on duty until the close of the war. He returned to Warren County, and followed farming until 1869, when he came to Oak Grove, Decatur County, and the following year came to Decaturville, where he followed merchandising. September 20, 1871, Miss Martha J. Welch, daughter of Henry Welch, became his wife. To them have been born seven children: Mary and Maggie the two oldest, and John Elmer and Grover Cleveland, the two youngest, are deceased. These three are at home: William H., Carrie B. and Anna Jane. Mr. Tate commenced his mercantile business at Decaturville in 1870, and by liberality and close application to business has succeeded in building up a large trade. He is prominently connected with the Masonic order, Lodge No. 218, and is also connected with the K. of H. James H. engaged in the mercantile business, in partnership with John L. In 1884 he went to Perryville and engaged in business there until May 6, 1885, when he lost a large part of his property by fire. He then returned to Decaturville and has been dealing extensively in cotton. He was born in DeKalb County, September 30, 1855, and married December 21, 1875, to Miss Emma Jones, daughter of Dr. T. W. Jones of Decaturville. She has borne him five children, one of whom, Emma Myrtle, is deceased. The others are Jesse, Allie, Lewis L. and James F. John L. and James H. are known throughout the county as good substantial business men, who have made their own way in life. James H. is also a member of the Masonic order and K. of H.

Isham G. Hearn (deceased). Among the leading men who have assisted to a great extent in the welfare and improvement of Decatur County is the honored name of Isham G. Hearn. He was born in Madison County, Tenn., and was a descendant of an old English family that settled in North Carolina at an early day. Isham G. was a man of good attainments, and almost altogether a self-made man. He early developed strong religious sentiments, and when a young man, began a close and thorough study of the Scriptures. He became a minister of the Methodist Episcopal Church South, and was first placed on the circuit in Henderson County. He was afterward transferred to Decatur County, where he became one of the most influential ministers of his time, and was known throughout West Tennessee as a man of much ability and influence. When the clouds of war began to gather over the country, he united his interest with those of the Southern States, and was one among the first to don the uniform and go to the field. He was made captain of Company G, Twentieth Regiment Mounted Infantry. This company received the sobriquet of the "Decatur County Tigers." Capt. Hearn was a man of undaunted courage, was highly esteemed by his men, and in every battle was found in the front, cheering his men to victory or death. On every field of victory or defeat he was the same earnest, faithful Christian which marked his early days. His death occurred at Shiloh, April 6, 1862, while leading his men in that dangerous conflict. He was married in 1852, to

Anna K. Dixon, daughter of Wallace Dixon, whose sketch appears elsewhere in these pages. Since the death of Mr. Hearn his widow married Paul H. Fisher, who has since died. To her union with Mr. Hearn were born four children, one of whom—Isham G., the youngest child—died when just merging into manhood. Flora married Fayette Fisher, a farmer of Decatur County. Wallace D. is a farmer of Decatur County. He was married to Laura A. Fisher, daughter of A. A. Fisher, of Decatur County. Thomas Y. was born February 17, 1857; was reared on the farm, and received such educational advantages as the common schools afforded. In 1880 he married Nancy A. Fisher, daughter of Jonathan Fisher. She died in 1883, about two years after marriage. He was again married to Dixon Smith, daughter of G. W. Smith, of Decatur County. Politically, Mr. Hearn is a Democrat. In 1885 he began a general merchandise business at Decaturville, and by his liberality and fair dealing is building up a large trade.

Dr. J. N. Houston, a son of John L. and Jane (Graham) Houston, was born in Decatur County January 22, 1837. His father came to the county when it was a wilderness. Dr. Houston was educated in the college at Decaturville, and attended lectures in Nashville in 1856-57. In the summer of 1857 he began the practice of medicine in Perry County, at Brown's Mills. In the course of four or five months he returned to Decatur County, where he has since successfully continued the exercise of his noble profession. At the outbreak of the war he enlisted with the Fifty-second Tennessee Regiment of the Confederate Army under command of Col. B. J. Lee; was assistant surgeon of the regiment, at the hospital, and the battle of Shiloh. After twelve months' service he returned to Decatur County. October 30, 1863, he was married to Miss Sarah E. Chaney, who was born near Cincinnati, Ohio. Of eleven children born to them, ten are living: John F., born August 21, 1864; Thadeus E., born March 26, 1866; Laura B., born November 21, 1867; Charles H., born February 20, 1869; Jefferson P., born January 13, 1871; Cora E., born November 17, 1872; Albert L., born September 23, 1874; Sidney C., born November 23, 1877; Mary M., born March 6, 1879; Claudia M., born October 10, 1880; Eliza Jane, born September 23, 1883, and died October 6, 1884. To all of his children Dr. Houston has given the best educational advantages. He is a member of the Republican party, and a Mason. He has almost retired from active practice, and devotes a great deal of his time to farming, in which he is interested. He has a large circle of friends, and is respected by all.

John G. Houston, a well known farmer of the Seventh District, was born March 11, 1824, in Warren County, Tenn. His father was a native of Indiana, went to Kentucky, and in 1818 came to Tennessee, and about that time was married to Miss Jane Graham. This union resulted in the birth of nine children, our subject being one of that number. Since childhood Mr. Houston has made his home in Decatur County. He has a good education. At the age of eighteen he became a surveyor, and was in that business for about thirty years. November 2, 1847, he was married to Martha Ann Arnold, and to them nine children have been born: Mary Jane, Eliza Ann, John L., James C., Martha U., Jefferson P., Ezra J., William F. and another who died in infancy. In 1868 he was elected sheriff of Decatur County, and served a term of two years, discharging the duties of the office in a most creditable manner. He has been a member of the Masonic order for twenty-four years; was a Whig, but has been a strong and able supporter of the Republican party since its organization. He does all in his power to promote school interests; devotes a great deal of his time to farming, and is regarded as one of the most prosperous agriculturists in the county, in which he is well known and esteemed.

Dr. Troy W. Jones, a successful practitioner at Decaturville, is a native of Henderson County, born September 14, 1832, son of Matthew and Anna (Pinnion) Jones, both natives of North Carolina. He came to Henderson County at a very early day, and resided there at the time of his death, which occurred in 1863. He was a life-long Democrat and a consistent Christian. The mother still lives. Of their family of ten children all are living but two. Our subject was the fifth child, and being reared on the farm was accustomed to hard labor from boyhood. He commenced the study of medicine under the preceptorship of Dr. G. H. Derryberry, and afterward studied under Dr. Tryar. He has been engaged in the practice of his profession since 1856, and is considered one of the ablest physicians of Decatur County. In 1859 he married Mrs. Sarah Yarbro, who died in 1875, leaving five children, four of whom yet live: Emma and Ada were twins. Emma married James H. Tate, a prominent merchant at Decaturville. Ada married George W. Bogan, now deputy sheriff of Decatur County. Anna married Dr. J. F. Aydelott, a successful physician of Decaturville, and Flora M. married Reuben Smith, one of the leading merchants of Decaturville. Thomas, the youngest child, was unfortunately burned to death when only seven years of age by the explosion of an oil can. Politically Dr. Jones is a strong Democrat, and he is a member of the Methodist Episcopal Church South. John Jones, grandfather of our subject, served through the Revolutionary war, and never received a wound.

H. M. Jordan, a well known farmer of the Fifth District, was born in Benton County, Tenn., October 30, 1843. His father, Edmund Jordan, was a native of North Carolina, born October 12, 1812, and came to Tennessee when there were comparatively few whites. He was first married to Nancy Haynes, of Tennessee, who was born September, 1812. She became the mother of seven children, of which H. M. Jordan is the fourth. At the time of her death she was a devout member of the Presbyterian Church, a good Christian woman. Edmund Jordan was married the second time to Elizabeth Moore, of Benton County; this union resulted in the birth of two children, only one survives. Elizabeth (Moore) Jordan died in Arkansas, after which Mr. Jordan returned to Tennessee and was married the third time to Mrs. Elizabeth (Maxwell) Howell, who survives him. Our subject was thrown upon his own resources at an early age, therefore, received but a limited education; has been farming since boyhood. When the late war began he enlisted in the Confederate Army, under command of Col. B. J. Lee, and took part in the desperate battle of Shiloh. After one year's faithful service, he returned home, remaining about six months, then enlisted in the Federal service in Second Tennessee Regiment, under command of Col. Murphy, participated in the battle of Nashville, which continued for three days, and in the Centerville raid. They endured many hardships, and had a number of narrow escapes from death, many men in close proximity to him being killed. Twelve months after he entered the Federal Army, was discharged at Nashville; he went to Illinois and farmed for one year, after which time he came to Decatur and resumed his agricultural pursuits on the place upon which he is now living. August 27, 1865, was married to Miss Martha N. Jennings, born in Decatur County, December 3, 1844, a daughter of Hiram and Eliza (Arnold) Jennings, both of Perry County, now called Decatur. Hiram Jennings was born August 23, 1811. December 2, 1863, a party of men calling themselves ———— Texas Rangers, hanged Mr. Jennings, stating that their reasons for so doing, was that they had been captured by Federal troops, two months previous, while taking breakfast at Mr. Jenning's house, and accused him of having reported them, as in many other instances their intention was to plunder and destroy, for after hanging Mr. Jennings, they burned the house. Mrs. Jennings, who was born September 9, 1817, is still living and in the enjoyment of good health. A family of eleven children have been born to H. M. and Martha (Jennings) Jordan: Lucy B. was born September 7, 1866, is the wife of Benj. Moore, a farmer of Decatur County; Ephriam E., born November 15, 1867; Wm. E., born October 20, 1869; Rhoda A., born April 30, 1871; Ara E., born December 21, 1872; John H., born August 29, 1874; Albert L., born June 26, 1876; Charley P., born February 11, 1878; Harvey, born January 2, 1880; Mary Zora, born July 25, 1881; Josiah, born July 16, 1883; with exception of Mrs. Moore, all are living at home, each receiving a thorough education. Mr. and Mrs. Jordan are sincere members of the Baptist Church. He is a stanch Republican, adheres closely to the party principles, is also an affable gentleman, well and favorably known.

Albert F. Keeton was born in Perry County (now called Decatur), August 6, 1835. His father, Robert Keeton, was a native of Lexington, Ky.; was one of the first settlers of Decatur County, locating at Shannonville; was by profession a physician, and practiced for forty years in Tennessee; he married a cousin, Miss Catherine Keeton, of Franklin County, Tenn.; they became parents of eleven children. Albert F. being the seventh; only five are living: Julia M., the widow of Thos. Garrett, who is farming in the country; Adaline A., the widow of Dr. Clardy, is living in Shelby County, Tex.; Marquis D. Lafayette is farming near Brownsport Landing, Decatur County; Sophronia, the widow of F. N. Jobe, is living at Saltillo, Hardin County. Our subject received a liberal education at Center, this county; he was for many years engaged in farming near his birthplace; October 5, 1858, he married Miss Paralee White, of Mississippi, who was raised in Decatur County. Their union was blessed with three children: Wm. R., Lucy A. and Ella U.—all living at home. In January, 1886, he rented his farm and went into hotel-keeping at Center. Wm. R., his son, is farming on his father's place. Mr. and Mrs. Keeton and two daughters, Lucy A. and Ella H. are members of the Methodist Church. Mr. Keeton is a Mason, and one of the leading Republicans of that section; he is also deeply interested in educational matters. He is a man of large circle of friends; has few, if any enemies; is warm hearted—in fact, all that a gentleman should be.

Capt. John McMillan, attorney at law, of Decaturville, is a native of Decatur County, was born April 4, 1823. His father, Gilbert McMillan, came from Stewart to Decatur County in 1822, living until April 4, 1858. The mother, Sarah (Nichols) McMillan, who died August, 1845, bore nine children, six of whom are living. Our subject worked on a farm until 1848, when he became deputy sheriff, holding the position until 1852; he was then elected sheriff of the county, discharging his duties in a creditable manner for six years; was the second man called to that office. He next engaged in merchandising. The first year of the war he organized a company and was elected captain. He served actively and gallantly in the well-remembered battle of Shiloh; also in a number of skirmishes. When the army was reorganized at Corinth, and officers discharged, he returned home. In 1870 he became clerk of the county court, performing his business in such a satisfactory way that he retained the position twelve years, since which time he has managed his agricultural and cotton interests. He is a strong Democrat, a Mason and consistent member of the Southern Methodist Church, a well known and worthy citizen. He was married March 30, 1851, to Mary A., daughter of Thomas Hay, a respected inhabitant of Decatur County. The union resulted in the birth of four children: Leora married J. T. Rogers; John G. is a physician; Wm. I., an Indian agent, located in Arizona Territory, and Ella, who is at home. Mrs. McMillan died October 6, 1888.

James R. McMurry, of the Third District, was born in Decatur County, December 10, 1853. His father, James T. McMurry, was born in Montgomery County March 12, 1827, a mason by trade, also a farmer; was married in 1848 to Katherine Warden; they came to Decatur County in 1850; he enlisted as a volunteer in the Twenty-seventh Regiment of Tennessee, but was discharged on account of sickness after he had served faithfully for two years; he returned home and died December 4, 1880. Our subject is the third of fourteen children; he received such an education as the country schools of the day afforded. He has been engaged in farming from boyhood; was married to Miss B. E. Jones January 29, 1885; she, too, is a native of Decatur County. To them one child was born, but died in its infancy. Mr. McMurry is a Democrat, and a worthy man who has the respect of the community.

Henry W. Myracle, a well known farmer of the Fourth District, was born in Decatur County, in 1838. The father, Lawrence L., was a native of Warren County, but came to Decatur County at an early day, where he married Jane Cox, a native of North Carolina. Lawrence L. was a Baptist minister and farmer, was influential and possessed great nobility of character; he was successful in all his undertakings and managed to accumulate considerable property. He was a strong Union man, and died in March, 1881. The mother bore twelve children; two only are living. She lives near the old home place with her son, J. C. P. Myracle. James K. served in the late war, in the Federal Army; after brave and daring service was captured at Union City, Tenn., confined in the notorious Andersonville prison until the time of his death, five months afterward. J. C. P. is a resident of Decatur County, and chairman of county court. Our subject was raised on a farm, and accustomed to labor. His educational advantages were limited, but by pursuing a course of study, and reading at home, he has become well informed. He enlisted in the Eighty-first Illinois Infantry, Company E, under command of Capt. Dallins, in 1862, serving actively until the close of the war. He participated in the battles of Vicksburg, Jackson, Raymond, Champion Hill and the engagements of the Atlanta campaign, until the capture of Atlanta, from there to the Mississippi River, at Nashville, and during the campaign of General Hood; was afterward sent down the river and took part in the battle at Spanish Fort, Mobile. He returned home at the close of the war without a wound, and located in Decatur, where he has since been engaged in agricultural pursuits, and now owns a valuable farm of about 200 acres, all well improved. He was married in 1868 to Miss Rushing, who died in 1878, leaving two children: James W. and Emma J. His second marriage was with Nancy E. Newsom, in 1879; her death occurred in March, 1880. He married the third time to Catherine Keeton, who has borne him two children: Arthur and Allan. Mr. Myracle has been a devoted member of the Cumberland Presbyterian Church, since 1867. He is a Republican, and a man well known and respected.

Pettigrew family. Among the influential and prominent families that came to Decatur County at an early day was the Pettigrew family. In 1821 or 1822 James M. and Corry Pettigrew, two educated and polished young gentlemen of Armagh County, Ireland, left their native land and immigrated to America. They located in South Carolina, and were engaged in contracting for canals and ditches. After considerable experience there they went to Alabama, and engaged in merchandising until 1825. They then came to Tennessee and located at Perryville. About this time George B. Pettigrew, a half brother, came from Ireland and entered into partnership with them, locating a branch store at Beardstown, Perry County. James M. also located a branch store at Oak Grove, and they operated other stores at Decaturville, Decatur County, and at Spring Creek, Madison County. They were men of superior education and wonderful business ability, accumulated vast possessions and were recognized as the leading business men on the Tennessee River. James M. took charge of the business at Oak Grove, and remained there until his death. He was never married. George, half brother of James M. and Corry, was born June 18, 1807, and August 12, 1830, married Elizabeth Adamson, also a native of Ireland. He died October 29, 1859, and she January 15, 1871. To them were born a family of seven children, five of whom died in infancy. James A. and George B. enlisted as privates in Company G, Twentieth Regiment Mounted Confederate Infantry. George was promoted to second lieutenant before his death, which occurred at the battle of Fishing Creek, Ky. James A. became captain of his company, and was a brave and fearless soldier. He was wounded at Shiloh, April 6, 1862, and was again wounded at Hoover's Gap, Tenn., and taken prisoner where he remained until January 6, 1864. Corry Pettigrew was born May 30, 1800. He managed the mercantile business at Perryville, and was a man possessed of remarkable business ability and untiring industry. April 2, 1840, he married Mary A. Douglass, daughter of Joseph S. Douglass, of Decatur County. He died but his widow is still living. To them were born two children: Thomas Jackson and James K. Polk, both of whom enlisted in the Confederate Army under Gen. Cheatham, August, 1861, and took an active and gallant lead in the engagements of that division—Shiloh, Perryville, Murfreesboro, Chickamauga, Missionary Ridge, Atlanta, etc. At the latter place Thomas J. was wounded, lost his left arm and was disabled from further activity. He was also wounded at Shiloh and taken prisoner but made his escape three days afterward at Pittsburg Landing. In 1863 he was promoted to the rank of first-lieutenant, and served in that capacity until he was disabled at Atlanta. Since the war he has been engaged in mercantile and agricultural pursuits. He owns one of the finest tracts of land in the county. He was married January 7, 1869, to Cordelia Welch, daughter of Henry Welch. She died in February, 1880, leaving a family of four children: Mary E., Corry H., Martha A., and Elizabeth K. James K. followed the fortunes of war in the same company with his brother Thomas. He enlisted as a private but was, by active and gallant service, promoted until he became captain of his company. He was wounded at Shiloh and disabled from active duty. He was born June 13, 1844, and January 25, 1871, he wedded Miss Maggie A. Sherdon, a daughter of Daniel B. Sherdon, of Pennsylvania. She was born March 12, 1852, and by her marriage became the mother of four children: Carrie

P., Lucy B., Maggie M. and Lena H. Thomas J. and James K. are both Democrats and members of the Methodist Episcopal Church South. They are prosperous and worthy citizens.

James K. Pettigrew, born in Decatur County, June 13, 1844, is a descendant of one of the oldest and most honored families. He is named after his uncle who was well known at Spring Creek, Madison County, at Decaturville, Perryville and Bradstown, Perry County, where he was engaged in business. Our subject was educated at Lexington and Mifflin, Henderson County. He took part in the late war, and received a wound in a skirmish one morning after the battle of Kenesaw Mountain, was convalescent in camp at Macon, Ga., when sufficiently recovered was honorably discharged and returned home resuming his business of general merchandise at Oak Grove, Tenn. A year later he opened a branch house at Sulphur Springs, a place owned by Mr. Pettigrew and famous for the medicinal qualities of its waters. January 25, 1871, he married Miss Maggie A. Sherdon, born March 12, 1852, in Sciota County, Ohio, the father, Daniel B. Sherdon, was a native of Pennsylvania and the mother, Mrs. Jane E. (Reynolds) Sherdon, of Ohio. Mr. and Mrs. Pettigrew have become the parents of four daughters: Carrie P., born at Oak Grove, January 27, 1872; Lucy Bell, born May 12, 1875; Maggie May, born March 24, 1877, and Lena H., born September 29, 1878; these three births occurred at Sulphur Springs. To his children Mr. Pettigrew gives the advantages of a thorough college education. He and his entire family are members of the Southern Methodist Church. Mr. Pettigrew is a stanch Democrat, a pleasant gentleman and universally esteemed.

Balaam Rains (deceased) came to Decaturville in 1838 and was one among the earliest settlers of Decatur County. The old pioneer buildings he erected yet stand. "A fortress formed by freedom's hands," and a relic of the olden times. Mr. Rains was a native of North Carolina and a descendant of an old and honored family who settled on the Atlantic coast at an early day. Anthony Rains, the father of Balaam, took an active and gallant part in the struggle for independence under the undaunted Gen. Marion. Our subject was engaged in agricultural pursuits during the greater portion of his life but was engaged in mercantile pursuits for a number of years. He married Miss Matilda Hudson of North Carolina, who bore him four children: William G., Rosetta V. (Mrs. Wm. Stout), Margaret P., (Mrs. James Coggins) and John H., who died when fourteen years of age. William G., the oldest child, was born in Randolph County, Tenn., October 26, 1837. His education was interrupted by the breaking out of the late war. After that event he began the study of medicine under Drs. J. H. Still and J. H. Leonard of Decaturville and completed a thorough and systematic course of instruction at the Nashville University in 1867. He began practicing at Sulphur Springs but in 1868 removed to Decaturville where he has since resided. He has succeeded in building up a large and lucrative practice and is recognized as one of the leading practitioners of the county. December 3, 1867, he married Miss Joan F. Parker, daughter of Joan F. Parker of Henderson County, and the fruits of this union are four children: Ethel C., William G., Lizzie E. and George H.

Granville M. Raney, a native and farmer of Decatur County, was born August 27, 1848. His father, James H. Ramey, was one of the pioneers of Decatur County, having settled here when it was known as Perry County. He was a native of Steward County, married to Miss Amanda Bryant, who was born in North Carolina, but came to Decatur County when a child of twelve years with her mother, who was a good Christian woman and is now dead. To their union twelve children were born; those living are Nancy (Raney) Harrell, who lives on her farm with her children, her husband having died in 1884; Margurite (Raney), wife of W. D. Lacy, a farmer in Decatur County; Ann E. (Raney), wife of G. W. White, also farmer in the same county; James H., and John David, who married Miss Sallie Luton, are both agriculturists in the county, and Barbara, wife of B. A. Tucker, is teaching school in Decaturville. Several of the children have died, the last being Mrs. Martha (Raney) Wright, whose husband is in the steam mill business; Mrs. Wright died in August, 1886. The subject of this sketch received a very fair education in the common schools, was engaged, up to the time of 1878, in farming with his father; at that date he began merchandising at a place in the county known as

Carsonville, continuing in this business until 1884, when he purchased the place upon which he now lives; it was then covered with timber but at present the greater portion of the land is under cultivation. Mr. Raney was married, February 15, 1876, to Miss Lucy Jackson, a native of Decatur County, whose father was a leading merchant and farmer of that section. The marriage resulted in the birth of five children: Maggie, born November 11, 1876; Willie J., born February 9, 1879; Sallie, born April 29, 1881; James, born May 22, 1883, and Edgar, born in June, 1886. Mr. Raney is an exemplary Christian and a member of the Methodist Church. Politically Mr. Raney is a Democrat, but takes no active part, merely voting; he is a man who has an extensive acquaintance and is favorably known.

Green B. D. Rushing, of Decaturville, was born August 22, 1826, is the eldest of eleven children born to Asa and Nancy G. (Hendrick) Rushing, both natives of North Carolina and descendants of old and honored Virginian families. Asa Rushing was a planter by occupation, a strong Whig and worthy citizen. In 1824 he visited Perry, now Decatur, County and in January, 1827, moved from Anson County, N. C., locating on the south side of Beech River, three miles west of where Decaturville now stands; he died in 1851. Mrs. Nancy Rushing went to Texas with our subject and there resided until her death, which occurred in 1875. Green B. D. Rushing's educational advantages consisted of three months' attendance in the year in the subscription schools of that time; being unusually studious and energetic he was able to begin teaching school in Decatur County, when about twenty-one years of age. He continued to teach until 1853, when he moved to Shelby County, Tex., and taught until 1857, at which time he bought a farm and turned his attention to agricultural pursuits. During the late civil war, in 1862, he enlisted in Company A, Twenty-eighth Dismounted Cavalry. He served gallantly and actively in many of the most terrific battles, receiving a wound at Pleasant Hill, La., which disabled him for many months. At the conclusion of the war he returned to Shelby County, Tex., where, owing to his true worth and popularity, he was elected to the office of collector and assessor of taxes, the duties of which he discharged so faithfully that he was re-elected and served eight years. January 8, 1852, he was first married to Miss Sarah J. Stevens, who died in September, 1877; she was the mother of three children, two of whom are married and live in Shelby County, Tex.; the third one is deceased. In 1879 Mr. Rushing returned to the scenes of his boyhood and soon after married his first love, Elizabeth Shipman. He contemplated going back to Texas, but his old friends and acquaintances were anxious to have him remain among them, and at the August election, 1886, elected him recorder. Mr. Rushing is a progressive, intellectual man, taking deep interest in the school and any enterprise beneficial to his country.

David E. Scott, a prominent attorney at law of Decaturville, was born in Henry County, Tenn., April 9, 1850. Of a family of six children born to David M. and Nancy F. (Hagler) Scott, subject is fourth. His parents were both natives of Tennessee; the father is a farmer, and came to Decatur County in 1860, the mother died in 1857. The grandfather, Samuel Scott, was born in 1771, went to Nashville while the second house was in course of erection, and in that city spent a great portion of his life. David E. was raised on a farm; being an industrious boy, he performed many duties not forced upon him, for his father was well supplied with the world's goods. His education was interrupted by the outbreak of the war, but by persistent application to books he soon acquired a fair knowledge. He began the study of law in the office of J. M. Porterfield of Decaturville, afterward attending a course of lectures at the Cumberland University, at Lebanon, Tenn. He entered into the practice of his profession at Decaturville, where he has since resided; he has succeeded in establishing an extensive business. Mr. Scott is a firm Democrat, a man who is well known, and enjoys the confidence and esteem of the people. November 8, 1876, he married Miss Martha E. Porterfield, an estimable lady of Hardin County, who has borne him three children: Frances U., David E. and Mattie B.

Reuben Smith, merchant, is a native of Decatur County, born February 10, 1847, and the son of George W. and Jane (White) Smith, both natives of Decatur County. The father resided on the old home place settled by his father, until about 1850, when he removed to Lexington and began merchandising. In 1860 he returned to the old farm and lived there three years. He removed to Decaturville in 1865, and entered into a partnership with Young & Storm, in the general merchandise business. He remained with this firm until 1874, when he began business with his son Reuben under the firm name of G. W. Smith & Son. He remained in business until his death in December, 1883. The mother yet resides on the old home place. Her family consisted of twelve children, six of whom are now living. John Smith, our subjects' grandfather, came from South Carolina at an early day, and settled on Panther Creek, six miles southwest of Decaturville, where he reared a large family. Reuben White, the maternal grandfather of our subject, came from North Carolina about the time of the settlement of John Smith, and located on Rushing Creek, four miles south of Decaturville. Our subject is the eldest child born to his parents. He was reared on the farm, and at the time of the breaking out of the war was attending the Decaturville Academy; but at this time all the schools were closed, consequently his education was not completed. Soon after the conclusion of the war he began clerking in the dry goods store of Young, Storm & Smith, and in 1874 became a partner with his father in a general mercantile business, which he has continued up to the present. In 1867 he wedded Miss Penelope Yarbro, daughter of Dr. A. M. Yarbro. She died May 3, 1883, leaving a family of six children: Emma (Mrs. William Brasher), Ernest, May and Charlie; Ella and Reuben are deceased. February, 1884, Mr. Smith married Miss Flora Jones, daughter of Dr. T. W. Jones of Decaturville. For a number of years our subject has been one of the leading merchants of Decaturville. He is a Democrat, and has been a member of the Methodist Episcopal Church South for the past twenty-one years. He is a prominent Mason, Lodge No. 218, and also a K. of H.

William Stout. Among the many well known men who came to Decatur County at an early day and have since united their interests with those of Decatur County is the subject of this sketch. He is a retired merchant of Decaturville and is also one among the few of Scotland's sons who have settled in this county. His birth occurred in Forfar County, Scotland, January 6, 1825, and he came of an old and honored family, whose history can be traced back to the early ages of the British Isles. His father, David Stout, was a man of superior education and of much influence. He was possessed of considerable means and gave to each of his three children excellent educational advantages. William, subject of this sketch, was brought up as a merchant, came to America when twenty-two years of age on a tour of pleasure and travel; but accidentally meeting a Mr. Pettigrew he was induced to come west and locate at Perryville, where he afterward became the partner of Mr. Pettigrew. They continued a successful and prosperous business for several years. In 1878 he sold his goods at Perryville and moved to Decaturville, where he has since resided. In 1850 he married Miss Jane Coats who died in 1876 leaving a family of seven children. He was again married in 1878 to Miss Rosetta V. Rains, daughter of Balaam Rains, an old and honored citizen of Decatur County. Mr. Stout is a Democrat and a man of culture and learning. He spends a considerable portion of his time in reading, and his library is filled with a judicious selection of choice books. He is progressive and enterprising and has given his children superior educational advantages. William T., the eldest son, is a merchant at Decaturville; Mary is Mrs. J. A. England, of Decaturville; John is a druggist and the postmaster at Decaturville; Laura J. is Mrs. L. T. Smith, of Sweetwater, Tex.; Thomas is a merchant at Perryville; Kathleen is Mrs. W. F. Young, and George, the youngest, is attending school.

Andrew J. Strate, of the Third District, was born in Pennsylvania March 23, 1852. His father, Daniel Strate, was born in New Jersey in 1806, and married to Miss Betsey Pelzer, of New York, in 1830; to them nine children were born, our subject being the youngest. In 1856 Daniel Strate moved to Pennsylvania, engaged in manufacturing until 1860 when he went to southern Ohio and resumed his manufacturing near Portsmouth. Mr. Strate after receiving a liberal education in Ohio, entered into the furnace business with his father until 1867. During the next few years he traveled extensively, visiting California, Oregon, Washington Territory, Missouri, Alabama, Kentucky, etc., and finally settled in Decatur County as a farmer. In 1875 he married Miss Ellen Shelton, of Ohio;

to this union one child was born, John. Mr. Strate is a Democrat, a popular and respected gentleman.

W. L. Swafford, a well known resident of the Sixth District, was born on the 27th of December, 1827, in Grainger County, Tenn. John Swafford, his father, was born in North Carolina, March 27, 1795, and came to Tennessee in the year 1805. He was a farmer. In 1818 he was married to Mary Fields, also a native of North Carolina, born March, 1799. Of fourteen children born to this union, our subject is the third. The grandfather, William Swafford, was a native of North Carolina, and married Nancy Craig, a native of the same State. They came to Tennessee in 1805. He was a farmer. His death occurred October 27, 1857, and the wife died in 1873. The great-grandfather, James Swafford, was born in Dublin, Ireland, came to America in 1770. He served for seven years as regimental surgeon in the Revolutionary war. He was married to Rennie Howard, of Dublin. Both lived to an old age. W. L. Swafford, the subject of our sketch, received a liberal education at Georgetown, Meigs Co., Tenn. Soon after his school days he began farming in Hamilton County and so continued for about three years. November 10, 1857, he located in Decatur County on the place he now owns. In 1863 he enlisted in the Third Regiment, West Tennessee Cavalry, Union Army and served from June till October, when the regiment was captured; on his way to prison Mr. Swafford made his escape and returned home, where he remained until February then went to Illinois. One year later he again came home and with his family went to Indiana, returning to Tennessee in about six months. January 22, 1853, he was united in marriage to Margurite Roark, a native of Hamilton County. To them were born fourteen children, of whom are living, Mary Ann (Swafford) Moore, John L., Joseph A., Judy C., James W., Isaac D., Henry J., Thomas A., Maggie J., America A., Louisa A. and Sarah C.; Horace M. and an infant deceased. Mr. Swafford is one of the leading Republicans of Decatur County, where he is well and favorably known. He served as magistrate from 1876 to 1882. He is deeply interested in the public schools and all educational affairs. Mr. and Mrs. Swafford are zealous members of the Missionary Baptist Church.

P. L. Thweatt, of the Third District, was born December 26, 1848, in Montgomery County, Tenn. He is the fifth of a family of nine children. His father, P. L. Thweatt, Sr., was a native of North Carolina; came to Tennessee when ten or, twelve years of age; was married about 1836 to Miss Francis Coleman of Tennessee and was a farmer. Our subject was educated in the common schools of the country and has been farming since boyhood. January 21, 1875, he was married to Miss Harriet Yarbro of Decatur County; they have four children living: Alice, Fannie, Anna, and Ella; two are dead. Mr. Thweatt is a good Christian man, and a member of the Methodist Church. He belongs to the Masonic and Odd Fellow lodges; is a good Democrat. No man is better known or more esteemed.

George H. Vise, of the Third District, was born in Spartaenburg District of South Carolina, December 16, 1827. Eli Vise, his father, was a native of South Carolina; was married about 1816 or 1817, to Rebecca Meadows; was by occupation a farmer. About March, 1835, he moved to Tennessee, and died about July. Mrs. Vise survived him nearly four years. The grandfather, John Vise (father of Eli), is thought to have been a native of England; served gallantly in the Revolutionary war, and when peace was declared, settled in South Carolina. George H., our subject, is the fourth of eight children, and received a good education, such as the common schools of the day afforded, in Wayne County; was married August 22, 1850, to Miss Tennessee Wayne Lafferty, of Wayne County. To this union a large family was born; of those living are William, a farmer, married in 1877 to Elizabeth Crawley of Decatur County; Isabella (Vise) Smith, married in 1870 to Dr. Alex Smith, a practicing physician of Benton County; Minerva C. (Vise) Smith, married, January 13, 1876, to a merchant at Peters Landing, Perry County, who died May 1884; Dora Vise, married, March 17, 1879, John Yarbrough, a farmer; George M., married, February 8, 1886, Tennessee Smith, and Eli (Little Jim). Those dead are Mary, whose demise occurred February 20, 1865; Evangeline, died August 20, 1878, and Virginia, died February 25, 1883. Mr. Vise was a Whig in that party's day. He enlisted in Col. Jack Biffle's regiment, Confederate Army, was in a skirmish at Jackson, Tenn., Gen. Forrest leading the boys. The army advanced to Trenton, capturing all before it, Trenton included; after leaving Trenton, were met at Cross Roads by the enemy, and a fight ensued which lasted about ten hours. The army then moved toward Middle Tennessee, near Franklin, where they again met the Federals, and a terrific encounter took place which lasted two days in which many were killed and wounded, but about 300 of the enemy were taken prisoners. In August, 1864, Mr. Vise left the army on account of his wife's illness. Upon his return home, finding his place devastated, his possessions gone, he resumed farming. He is a Democrat, but takes no active part in politics more than voting. He is a member of the Masonic fraternity, and greatly interested in school matters. He and his estimable wife have been zealous members of the Methodist Episcopal Church for about twenty-five years. Socially, Mr. Vise is a genial, warm-hearted man, full of the hospitality so characteristic of the true Southerner.

S. M. Wallace, a respected farmer of the Third District, was born in Decatur County in 1849. His father, Martin Wallace, was born in North Carolina in 1810. The mother, Harriet (Smith) Wallace, is a native of Tennessee, is still living and enjoys good health Two brothers are also living. Our subject received such education as the country schools afforded, working at the same time. In 1875 he married Miss E. E. Fisher, a native of Decatur County; several children were born to them, of whom only four survive: Ella, Anna, Ada and Ida. Mr. Wallace has not connected himself with any church. He has always been a stanch Democrat, upholding the party with success. He is a member of the Masonic fraternity. He takes a lively interest in educational affairs; has always engaged in farming and with favorable results.

HARDIN COUNTY.

James M. Alexander, of the Thirteenth District, was born in Hardin County, February 8, 1838, a son of John Davidson and Charlotte (Horton) Alexander. The father was a native of North Carolina, of Irish descent; he moved to Williamson County at an early day, engaging in agriculture. In 1828 he located in Hardin County, where he resided until his death in 1875. The mother was born in South Carolina, of English descent; her death occurred in 1864; her marriage was blessed with thirteen children, James M. being the sixth. He studied medicine and began to practice when the war broke out; he never again resumed the exercise of the profession. In 1862 he enlisted in the army, remaining in service until 1863, when he took the oath of allegiance. He taught school one session in Kentucky, going from there to Illinois where he was married, in 1865, to Miss Maggie Dunn, of Metropolis, Ill. He returned to Kentucky, entered into the mercantile business at Farmington; in 1867 formed a partnership with his brother at Saltillo, where they continued until 1886. James M. then purchased his brother's interests, and is still carrying on the business; he is one of the leading merchants, has a fine stock of goods, and an extensive and profitable trade. Mr. Alexander is an earnest Democrat, a Mason of prominence, and a K. of H., one of the most enterprising and worthy citizens in the county.

Samuel R. Allen, one of the best known and most respected residents of the Twelfth District, was born in Kentucky, August 16, 1830. His father was also a native of that State, a stone-mason by trade. Mr. Allen was raised by his grandmother, remaining with her until his sixth year, when he went home with Miss Banks traveling for about one year; met with Mr. Stanton of Tennessee, on the Chattahoochee River in Georgia; the following year went to Kingston, Tenn., from there he went on a flatboat on the Tennessee River to Limestone Creek, Alabama, and there met Shep Thacker with whom he came to Hardin County in 1840 and remained with him for twelve years. He then began renting lands and farming. September, 1855, he was married to Miss Harriet Whitlow, of Hardin County who died January 27, 1884. This union resulted in the birth of eleven children, of whom are living Milton J., Sarah M., Granville S., Grant A., Ettie E., William R. and George H.; two died in infancy. Mr. Allen married the second time to Mrs. Isabella (Falls) McDaniel of Hardin County. Mr. Allen is a zealous member of the Christian Church, belongs to the Agricultural Wheel of Tennessee, and is a stanch Republican. He is one of the most enterprising, cordial and esteemed men in the entire commuity.

W. R. Allen, M. D., is the son of Columbus P. Allen, a native of Alabama, though for a number of years an honored citizen of Hardin County. The father is a physician and came to Hardin County, in 1874. He practiced his profession at and near Saltillo until he removed to Weakley County, where he now resides. He married Sarah A. Wroten, a native of Tennessee, though living at that time in Mississippi. Our subject was born in Mississippi, Prentice County, April 27, 1859, and is the eldest of eight children. He was reared in Mississippi and his youth was spent as that of other children of his time. He received an extra education and studied medicine in his father's office after which he attended the medical school at Nashville during the winter of 1880–81 (Vanderbilt University). He returned home and has since been engaged in practicing near Saltillo. J. P., a younger brother, is a successful practitioner in Chester County. November 30, 1881, our subject married Mary A. Moore, daughter of E. N. Moore of Hardin County. She died August 8, 1882, and September 16, 1883, he married Martha C., a sister of his former wife. In connection with his practice the Doctor is engaged in agricultural pursuits and although a young man is doing well in that and in the practice of his profession.

Newton G. Baker, a well known farmer and stock raiser of the Seventeenth District, is a native of Hardin County, was born October 15, 1846. His father, Milton Baker, was a native of North Carolina; he was a farmer, came to Hardin County about 1840 where he resided until his death, which occurred in 1854. His wife was Minerva Hodge, also of North Carolina, who died in 1859; she was the mother of seven children: Richard Haywood was a farmer in Arkansas, died in 1883; Lucinda, died in infancy; James T., a minister of the Christian Church and physician, lives in Texas; Edna, wife of Jackson Thompson of Texas; Mary Jane, widow of James Holmes, who was drowned in the Mississippi River; Lovie Ann, wife of Dennis Caufman of Texas, and Jasper L., who was born January 1, 1850. Newton G. was reared on a farm, and although his educational advantages were limited, by careful reading and close observation he became well informed. In 1862 he enlisted in Crew's regiment, Confederate Infantry, and served about nine months, taking part in the battle of Shiloh. He went to Illinois and enlisted in the Thirteenth Illinois Cavalry, Federal Army, and served with them until close of the war. He participated in the campaigns of Missouri and Arkansas. He was mustered in at Springfield, Ill., sent from there to St. Louis, then to Little Rock, and transferred to Pine Bluff where he remained until the close of the war. He was mustered out at Springfield in the spring of 1865, and returned to Hardin County the following fall, where he has since been engaged in farming, stock raising, and operating saw mills. September 27, 1866, he married Miss Mary P., daughter of Archibald Gammill. Mr. Baker is one of the most extensive and prosperous farmers in the county; he owns about 500 acres of valuable land. He is a Republican, and one of the most worthy and respected men in the community.

Jasper L. Baker, a prominent farmer and resident of Hardin County, is a member of one of the old and honored families; was born in the county January 1, 1850. His father, Milton Baker, was a native of South Carolina; from there he moved to Mississippi and afterward to Tennessee. He purchased a farm in Hardin County where he lived until the time of his death in 1854. He married a lady of his native State, Miss Minerva Hodge, who bore him seven children, of whom Jasper L. is the sixth. He was educated in the common schools of the country, after which he began farming. In October, 1869, he went to Arkansas and continued his agricultural pursuits until 1871, when he returned to Hardin County, settling on the farm he now owns. He was married December 18, 1873, to Miss Elizabeth J. Couch, who was born in the county. Their union resulted in the birth of five children, of whom are living Mary O. and Richard B., the others having died in infancy. Mr. Baker is a true stanch Republican, adhering closely to party principles. He is deeply interested in the school question, doing all in his power for the advancement of general education. He is a genial man, a good neighbor and citizen, well and favorably known.

Samuel P. Barlow, a well known farmer and resident of the Eleventh District, was born in Orange County, N. C., April 25, 1847. His father, Joseph Barlow, was also a native of the same State, and came to Hardin County in 1859, settling in the Fifteenth District. He was married to Miss Lucinda Crossett, of Caswell County, N. C. To them were born ten children, of whom the subject of our sketch was the fifth. He received such education as the common schools of Hardin County afforded in its primitive days. Soon after leaving school he began farming with his father, and so continued until the age of twenty-three. He was married to Miss Sarah J. Churchwell, of Hardin County, October 25, 1869. Six children have been born to them; those living are Cally J., George J., Osborne L., Alice I., and E. and Luke E. (deceased). In 1872 Mr. Barlow purchased the farm upon which he now lives, consisting of between 250 and 300 acres, which is valuable and productive. He is a stanch Democrat, was elected magistrate of the Eleventh District in 1882 and served for four years. He is a good neighbor, a worthy citizen and an esteemed man.

John H. Benton, merchant at Savannah, Tenn., is one of the firm known as Benton Bros., consisting of himself and brother, George F. Mr. Benton is from one of the oldest and best families in Hardin County. His father, George F., was a native of Connecticut. He came to Maury County, Tenn., when but sixteen years of age, and in 1832 located in Hardin County. He was clerk of the chancery court for a number of years, and was married in 1835 to Miss Minerva Kendal, a native of Tennessee. In 1847 he formed a partnership with W. H. Cherry and engaged in mercantile business at Savannah, in which they were very prosperous; the firm was popular and well known throughout the entire country, and continued until Mr. Benton's death, in 1854. He was the father of five children, three of whom are living: John H., Jerusha M., wife of Dr. W. H. Seaman, of Savannah, and George F. The subject of this sketch was educated in the schools of Savannah. After his school days he gave his attention to agriculture for a number of years. In 1873 he entered into a partnership with Dr. W. H. Seaman and his brother, George F. The firm was known as W. H. Seaman & Co. They continued in this business until 1883, when the two brothers sold their interest to the third partner and began the dry goods business, and by their courtesy and integrity have built up an extensive and profitable trade. John H. Benton was married March 7, 1876, to Miss Sallie Cherry, a native of Texas, who came to Tennessee in 1871. To their union two children have been born, both living at home: George H. and Cherry L. Mr. and Mrs. Benton are affable and refined people, held in great respect by all who know them.

Abner W. Blevins, a prosperous farmer of the Seventeenth District, was born in Anderson County, Tenn., March 23, 1816, a son of Richard and Mrs. (Maddox) Blevins, both natives of Tennessee, of English and Scotch descent. The mother removed with our subject, in 1836, to Savannah, where she died about 1856. Abner W. Blevins was left at an early age without a father's care and protection; without means he was thrown upon his own resources. His boyhood was spent as a laborer on various farms. He had no educational advantages whatever, but despite that fact, he can make all his calculations to an astonishing degree of accuracy, without the use of figures. He engaged in farming and stock raising. May 23, 1837, he was married to Miss Margaret Maddox. To them twelve children were born, six of whom are dead, five having died with the measles within ten days. Matilda, whose death occurred in 1883, was the wife of Samuel M. Barnett; Mary A. is the wife of Ben De Berry; Wilson is one of the eminent physicians of the county; Sarah E., wife of John Hetton, of Wayne County; Martha was married to David Allison, of Hardin County; James is a prominent agriculturalist of the county, and Lucinda, wife of Frank Parker, also of Hardin County. Mr. Blevins has given to all of his children the best of advantages. He is an honest, industrious, enterprising man, who by his own energy has accumulated quite a valuable lot of property, owning more than 400 acres of productive soil. No one in the entire county is better known or more respected.

Dr. Wilson Blevins, a practicing and leading physician of Hardin County, was born December 15, 1840. His father, A. W. Blevins, was a native of East Tennessee. He moved to Hardin County when about a man grown and is one of the best known farmers in that portion of the State. He married a Miss Maddox, also a Tennessean. Dr. Blevins was the third child born to his parents. He received his education in the common schools of the country, and gave his attention to farming until the fall and winter of 1878 or 1879, when he took a medical course and attended the lectures at the medical college in Nashville. After his return home he began the exercise of his profession and succeeded in establishing an extensive practice. March 1, 1864, he was married to Miss Margurite S. Falls, a native of Hardin County. Their union resulted in the birth of seven children. Those living are Andrew W., Isabella A., James D. and William A.; those deceased are John M., Jessie A. and an infant. Dr. Blevins and his estimable wife are zealous members of the Cumberland Presbyterian Church. The Doctor is a stanch Republican, strongly upholding the party principles. He takes a profound interest in school affairs, giving his children the best educational advantages. He is an affable, genial gentlemen, and enjoys the confidence and esteem of all who know him.

Thomas M. Brown, a well known farmer and stock raiser of the Fourth District, was born in Giles County, Tenn., January 17, 1826, a son of Thomas Brown; the mother died while the child was an infant, and he was put in charge of Thomas Collins, of Giles County. At the age of eleven years he was apprenticed to Thomas Riddle, of Pulaski, to learn the tailor's trade; in his nineteenth year he went to Somerville, Fayette County, and worked in the shop with the distinguished Andrew Johnson for two years; for S. S. Bobo. In 1851 he went into business for himself at Decaturville, remaining there about four years; he next moved to Mifflin, Henderson County; from there two years later to Corinth, then several other places, still working at his trade. He received an extensive patronage from the Confederate officers; accumulated a large amount of money which he invested in slaves, and of course lost them all. After the war he began the livery business in Corinth, continuing for nine years, at same time farming to some extent. In 1880 he located in Hardin County, where he now resides; the same year he married Mrs. A. Spencer, of Hardin County. They had one child who died. He is one of the leading and most prosperous farmers in the county. Owns 800 acres of land, on which he lives, and 500 in Decatur County. He is enterprising and industrious.

W. H. Carrington, merchant of Savannah, is a native of Piqua, Miami Co., Ohio, and is a son of Ephriam and Christian (Foreman) Carrington, natives of Connecticut and Maryland respectively. In 1840 the father moved with his family to Ohio and engaged in the carpenter trade. His wife was born in Baltimore and became the mother of five children, of whom our subject is the third. He was educated in Ohio and soon after the completion of his education he went to Cincinnati and engaged as clerk in the Odd Fellow and Masonic furnishing house, where he remained until the breaking out of the war. He then enlisted in the Sixth Regiment of Ohio Infantry. Just before the battle of Shiloh the company was compelled to wade Duck River at Columbia in order to get the advance at that place. Mr. Carrington was taken sick in consequence of the exposure, and left at Savannah. Upon his recovery he was made orderly sergeant, and when the post was evacuated he went to Shiloh and from there to Hamburg. After the war Mr. Carrington engaged in merchandising at Savannah, where he has remained ever since. He has been quite successful and is doing well at his business. April 5, 1865, he married Miss Julia Russell, a native of Savannah and a descendant of one of the earliest settlers of Hardin County. To them were born ten children; those living are Fannie, Robert, Ida, Levinia, Nellie, William, Charles, Ethel and Lewis. They have one, Emma, deceased. Mrs. Carrington was born September 28, 1842, and is an estimable lady. Our subject has given his children good educational advantages, and is a man well known and respected throughout the county. He is a Democrat and a member of the H. of K.

Joseph W. Cavender, a leading grocer of Savannah, was born in Maury County, Tenn., May 24, 1846. His father, Joseph W., Sr., was a native of Williamson County, was engaged in agricultural pursuits in Maury County. His marriage was with Miss

Sarah Pierce, of Hardin County. They were the parents of ten children, of whom our subject is the fifth; he has a liberal education; his early days were spent in the common schools of Maury and Davidson Counties; in 1859 he took a two years' course in Nashville, after which he obtained a position in the ordinance department at that place, which he filled for three years. In 1865 he came to Savannah and entered into the ferry business, in 1867 went to Johnson County, Ill., and attended school for nearly two years; in the spring of 1868 he began farming in Laclede County, Mo. In 1872 he married Miss Alice E. Johnston, a native of Dearborn County, Ind., with whom he has had eight children, all living at home: Susan E., Sarah A., Joseph W., Mary A., Delah C., Silas H., Emma M. and Victor T. From Missouri Mr. Cavender returned to Savannah and began the grocery business, in which he still continues. By his fair dealing and courtesy to patrons he has met with great success, having one of the most extensive trades in the county. Mr. Cavender is giving each of his children a thorough education at the college in Savannah; he is a member of the Masonic fraternity, K. of H., an earnest member of the Baptist Church; he is one of the best informed and most respected residents of the county. Mrs. Cavender with her two oldest daughters, Misses Sarah and Susan, are members of the Methodist Church.

John A. Counce, the popular sheriff, of Hardin County, is a native of Hardin County and was born September 27, 1854, a son of James C. and Mary (Hoover) Counce, both descendants of old English families, who settled on the Atlantic coast at an early day, and whose sons were gallant followers of Gen. Marion in the Revolutionary war. Wm. Counce, the grandfather, came to Hardin County many years ago, and located in the Tenth District, where James C. now resides, a respected farmer and stanch Republican; Jacob Hoover, the maternal grandfather, was also an old settler of Hardin County. Mrs. Mary (Hoover) Counce died March 27, 1862; she was the mother of ten children, five of whom are dead. Wm. K. is a farmer in the Ninth District; Fayette is farming in the same locality; George resides in Lincoln County, Ark., where he is engaged in agricultural pursuits; Charles B. is teaching school in Hardin County. James C. Counce married a second time to Miss Elizabeth Spencer, who has borne him two children: Theodosia and Tony. The subject of this sketch was raised on a farm; his educational advantages were very meager on account of the interruption caused by the late war. In 1877 he was married to Judah F., daughter of Joseph Leeth (deceased). December 28, 1872, Mr. Counce was elected sheriff of Hardin County, having previously served as deputy sheriff and constable. He is a Republican, an industrious, enterprising citizen well and favorably known.

Dr. James B. Covey, physician, was born August 29, 1847, in Hardin County, Tenn., and is the son of Noble W. and Martha Ann (Brown) Covey, natives of North Carolina and Virginia respectively and both of English descent. They removed to Hardin County in 1834, and located on Turkey Creek where they yet reside. Of their family of nine children five are yet living: Levin E., the eldest child, is one of the leading physicians of the county, and a graduate of the Louisville Medical University. Our subject was reared on the farm and on account of the war received but a limited education. October, 1867, he wedded Miss Jennie Gillis, daughter of Jefferson Gillis, of Hardin County. In 1872 he went to Nashville and attended Vanderbilt University four years, obtaining a good literary education and a thorough medical course. In 1879 he returned to Vanderbilt and graduated the following spring; the next year he graduated at the old Nashville Medical School. He then returned and resumed his practice in partnership with his brother. He has a large practice and is uniformly successful in diseases of all kinds, especially obstetrics, and has the largest practice of that kind of any man in the county. He is also engaged in farming and stock raising in which he is quite successful. He is United States surgeon for pensioners of the middle division of Tennessee, is a Republican and is prominently connected with the Masonic order.

Eli T. Craven, merchant, is the son of Alex. McNeal and Bethena E. (Emerson) Craven, both natives of North Carolina. They came from North Carolina to Marshall county in 1846, and in 1848 removed to Texas, but not being favorably impressed with the country returned the following year and settled in Wayne County, where they remained until 1855. They then removed to Hardin County and located on White Oak Creek and engaged in agricultural pursuits until 1861. He then removed to Craven's Landing, Tenn., and became connected with the United States gunboat service. In 1864, he, in partnership with two others, purchased the steamer "Llewellyn" and made the Tennessee River from Paducah to Florence. In 1866 his health failed, he abandoned the river and died soon after. He was a strong Union man. The mother is still living at Saltillo. To them were born eight children—five sons and three daughters. Our subject s the sixth child and was born in Marshall County, Tenn., January 7, 1847. He was reared like the average country boy, and in 1877 was united in marriage to Miss Malissa M. Alexander, daughter of John D. Alexander of Hardin County. He first engaged in general mercantile pursuits at Saltillo under the firm title of E. T. & J. H. Craven. In 1876 he moved to Craven's Landing and cultivated the soil until 1882, when he returned to Saltillo and clerked for Alexander & Bro. In 1884 he formed a partnership with W. T. Williamson in the mercantile business, but from October 2, 1883, to January 18, 1884, he ran the business alone. At the latter date he took in Mr. Wilkenson as partner. By their fair dealing they have obtained a good and substantial trade. Mr. Craven is a Democrat and is prominently connected with the I. O. O. F. at Saltillo.

James H. Craven, dealer in general merchandise at Saltillo, is a native of Lamar County, Tex., born April 6, 1849, and the son of Alex. M. and Bethena E. (Emerson) Craven. (For further particulars of parents see sketch of E. T. Craven.) Our subject was the seventh of eight children. He was reared on the farm and went through the usual hardships incident to farm life. The breaking out of the war destroyed his educational advantages, though by personal application he has succeeded in becoming well informed on the current topics of the day. In 1876 he began merchandising at Saltillo, and by his pleasant and agreeable manners to his patrons has succeeded in building up a good trade. June, 1878, he led to the hymeneal altar Miss Anna E. White, daughter of M. White of Saltillo. He is a member of the I. O. O. F. of Saltillo Lodge, No. 180.

Mc. W. Davis, a farmer of the Second District, was born in Maury County, Tenn., November 1, 1833. The father, Joseph Davis, was a native of North Carolina and came to Maury County about 1820, where he married Miss Harriet Perry, by whom he had thirteen children, Mc. W. being the second. In 1844 Joseph Davis came to Hardin County and settled on Hardin Creek, and farmed there until time of his death, which occurred in 1883. The subject of our sketch received his education in Hardin County, and October 28, 1858, was married to Miss Sarah Baker, who died July 22, 1886, at Savannah, Tenn., a member of the Methodist Church, a Christian woman, esteemed by all. She was the mother of eight children, of whom but two are living: Harriet I. and Sarah J.; those deceased were Robert M., William N., Mary E., James, Ann and Cora. During the late civil war Mr. Davis enlisted in the First Tennessee, Confederate Army, in Forrest's brigade, under command of Col. Biffle. He took active part in the engagement at Thompson's Station, Chickamauga and other battles, and served as corporal guard. After nine months of gallant and faithful service he returned home, physically disabled. Mr. Davis has always been a strong Democrat; votes with the party, but takes no active part. He is an earnest member of the Methodist Church, and a Mason; he takes great interest in the advancement of educational affairs, giving his children a thorough collegiate course. He has many friends and acquaintances in the county, and is esteemed by all.

David I. Dickerson, a farmer and resident of the Fourth District, was born in Blount County, Ala., August 8, 1824. His father, Moses Dickerson, was a native of North Carolina. He first moved to Alabama, being one of the earliest settlers of that State. In 1825 he located in Wayne County, Tenn. His wife was Miss Phœbe Parsons, a lady of his native State, who bore him three children, David I. being the eldest. He received his education in Wayne County, and has been engaged in farming since boyhood. November 26, 1846, he married Miss Martha, daughter of George W. Seaton, of East Tennessee, who moved to Madison County, Ala., then returned to his native State. To their union nine children were born, of whom are living Phœbe J., G. C., Pricy D., Emaline and George H.; those dead are Bicca E., Mary E., Sarah C. and William S. When the late war was declared Mr. Dickerson enlisted in Company F, Sixth Tennessee Cavalry, in Federal service, under command of Col. Hurst; took active and gallant part in the battle of Vicksburg; was engaged in a fight in Gen. Hatches' command at Tallahatchie River, also at Nashville, doing faithful service until the close of the war, after which he returned to his family in Wayne County and resumed his farming, which he continued in that locality until 1881, when he came to Hardin County and purchased the farm upon which he now lives. Mr. Dickerson has an extensive acquaintance in the two counties where he has lived; no man is better or more favorably known.

Arch Gammill, a well known farmer of the Sixth District, was born March 25, 1825, in Marshall County, Tenn., and came to Hardin County in 1838 with his father, James Gammill, who was a native of North Carolina, a farmer by occupation; he married Miss Hester Bedell, by whom he had eighteen children, of whom subject of this sketch is the thirteenth. Arch Gammill, received such education as the common schools of Marshall County afforded; has been a farmer since his boyhood. He was married August 13, 1846, to Miss Elizabeth Long a native of South Carolina; but a resident of Hardin County since childhood. To their union twelve children have been born, of whom there are living Franklyn; Miles C.; Moses; Joseph; Columbus; Paralee, the wife of N. G. Baker (a farmer of Hardin County); Samantha, wife of Preston Phillips (farmer of same county); Sallie, wife of J. Couch, also a farmer in Hardin County. The children deceased are James, Pinkney, Alford and Samuel. Franklyn married Miss Mary Shell, a native of the county, and Miles C. was united to Miss Alice Smoot. Mr. Gammill is a stanch Republican, a man of good moral habits and worthy citizen who is esteemed by all who know him.

Hon. James Anthony Hanna, representative of Hardin County, was born July 31, 1848, in Henderson County, Tenn., and is the son of James and E. (Courtney) Hanna, natives respectively of Virginia and Tennessee. They came to Henderson County in 1823 and were among the first settlers. The father was captain of the militia for a number of years and was a worthy citizen. He died in 1867 and his wife in 1873. Their family consisted of fifteen children, our subject being the fourteenth child. He was eighteen years old when his father died and at the age of twenty he left home with 15 cents in his pocket and reached Carbondale, Ill., where he soon entered the Southern Illinois Normal. He attended three years and then returned home and taught at Saltillo, after which he returned to Illinois and finished a scientific course and nearly completed a classical course. He again returned to Saltillo and established a good school at that place which he kept up until December, 1879, when he engaged in mercantile pursuits. The firm was styled Terry, Hanna & Co. October 30, 1879, he led to the altar Miss Alice E. Davy, daughter of Thomas Davy, one of the pioneer merchants of Hardin County, and a good citizen. In 1884 Mr. Hanna was brought forward as the Republican candidate for representative and was elected by a large majority. He served his term with distinction and credit to himself and party. In August, 1886, he was again elected and served another term.

Jesse Hatley, a well known farmer and miller of the Sixth District, was born in Hardin County September 8, 1822. His father, Mark Hatley, was a native of Chatham County, N. C., born in 1790. In 1819 he married Miss Delilah Strann, of same nativity as his own; to them eleven children were born, Jesse being the seventh. Our subject was deprived of educational advantages, for at that early day there were but few white settlers and consequently no schools. He was married in 1851 to Miss Elizabeth Barnham, of Hardin County, who bore him two children: William and an infant, both deceased; his wife died in 1855. In March, 1856, Mr. Hatley was married the second time to Miss Charity Haynes, of Lauderdale County, Ala. To them were born a family of six; those living are Elizabeth Delilah, Nancy Francis, Sarah Ann and George W.; those dead are Jessie J., died in Tennessee, and Belle, died in Texas. Mr. Hatley is an earnest and consistent member of the Primitive Baptist Church and a stanch Republican. He is well known throughout the county and greatly respected.

Henry Reyburn Hinkle, the well known farmer and stock dealer of the Seventeenth District, was born in Hardin County September 24, 1844. His father, Jonathan Hinkle, was a native of North Carolina and of German descent. He was a farmer and blacksmith and came to Tennessee, locating on a farm on the lines of Hardin and Wayne Counties. About 1822 he was married to Miss Elizabeth Paine, a native of Virginia and of English extraction. To them were born fourteen children, of whom our subject was the thirteenth. Henry R. was educated at the academy in Savannah. When the late war was declared Mr. Hinkle's sympathies were with the Union; in 1862 he went to Illinois, soon afterward enlisting in the United States Navy on the steamer "Robb." He served for twelve months, and four months later enlisted in the One Hundred and Fifty-second Illinois Infantry, Company C, under command of Col. F. D. Stevenson, and was color-sergeant of the regiment, with which he remained until the close of the war, and was discharged in September, 1865. He then went to St. Louis, Mo., and attended the Commercial College of Bryant & Stratton, graduating with honors. He returned home and was appointed deputy county court clerk under his brother, B. Hinkle; this position he held until September, 1867, when he was elected county court clerk and retained the office until September, 1882, with the exception of two years. Since that time he has given his attention to farming and stock raising, principally horses and mules. He is at the present time United States Commissioner of the United States Court of West Tennessee. He was married, October 30, 1867, to Miss Amanda Franks, a native of Hardin County. To them six children were born; those living are Horace H., Henry O., Charles C., Harvey and Lula B.; Roscoe is deceased. Mr. Hinkle has given his children the best educational advantages that the county affords; they attend the Ross Academy. Mr. Hinkle is a steadfast member of the Cumberland Presbyterian Church, and an elder in the Ross congregation; is a Past Master of the Savannah Lodge, No. 102, of Masons; an Odd Fellow (as there is no lodge at Savannah of this order, is member of Saltillo Lodge), he is Past Dictator of Hardin Lodge, No. 174, K. of H., and is Post Commander of Farragut Post, No. 6, G. A. R., Department of Tennessee. He is a stanch Republican, does all in his power to promote the school interests, and is a warm-hearted, pleasant gentleman, esteemed by all who know him.

Hon. William F. Hinkle, ex-representative of Hardin County, and dealer in general merchandise at Saltillo, was born in Carrollton, Carroll Co., Ky., October, 14, 1844, son of George D. and Lucy S. (Hawkins) Hinkle, natives of Kentucky and Tennessee, respectively. The father was of English descent and the mother of an old established American family. George D. was a lawyer by profession, and practiced at Carrollton. When a young man he was elected district attorney of his district. He afterward removed to Louisville, where he remained a number of years. About 1876 he removed to Atlanta and was editor of a journal at that place, but afterward removed to Grenada, Miss., where he died in 1881. He was a man of marked ability and was prominently connected with the Masonic and I. O. O. F. orders. Our subject is the eldest of three children. His sister Mary is a lady of education and is the Mother Superior of St. Mary's College, near Terre Haute. She has among her pupils some of the daughters of the most eminent men of the State. His other sister, Bettie H., is Mrs. Samuel H. Howard of Lexington, Tenn. Our subject lost his mother when only seven years of age, after which he went to Louisville and attended the high school of that city. He afterward came to Point Pleasant and clerked for his uncle, P. S. Hawkins, but soon went to Gettysburg, Penn., and attended college for more than two years. The breaking out of the war interrupted his studies, for he left college, and in 1861 enlisted as a private in the Forty-fourth Indiana. For gallantry at the battle of Shiloh, he was promoted to the rank of second lieutenant. He was at Donelson, etc. He afterward returned to Gettysburg with the expectation of completing his studies, but about this time Gen. Lee made his raid, and our subject raised a company from the college and theological seminary and was made first lieutenant of the same. He served in this capacity until the close of the war. He then came to Tennessee and married Miss Mattie J. White, and was one of the prominent teachers of Hardin and adjoining counties for a number of years. He was elected to the

State Legislature in 1869 and served two terms. He is one among the most popular men of the county and was elector on the Seymour-Blair ticket, etc.

Joshua T. Martin, one of the most prominent residents of the Sixth District, was born in Hardin County, December 16, 1844. His father, John Martin, was a native of Coffee County, Tenn. At an early day, when there were but few white settlers, he located on Horse Creek, Hardin County, where, for a small sum of money, he purchased a large tract of land. He was a mechanic by trade, and employed a man to manage his farm. He was married to Miss Nancy McLean, who became the mother of six children, of whom three are living: Margurite, James C. and Jane K.; the deceased were Elizabeth, William and an infant. Mrs. (McLean) Martin died about 1840, and Mr. Martin married Miss Annie Palmer, a daughter of Martin and Hester Palmer, of Hardin County, but at time of marriage were living in Wayne County. To this second union six children were born, of whom the subject of this sketch is the second; the others living are Mary S., wife of Shep Bivens, a mechanic of Hardin County; Joshua T.; Samuel P., married in Texas; Joseph H., married Miss Mollie Barnhill, and moved to Texas; Martha A., wife of H. B. Smith, who is engaged in farming and tanning in Arkansas; Hettie M. is dead. Mrs. (Palmer) Martin died in 1852, an earnest Christian woman and member of the Methodist Church South. Mr. Martin, in 1853, was united to Miss Arminda A. Vermillian; a native of North Carolina, who bore him seven children: John W., married in Texas; Katie, the wife of R. K. McLean, a farmer of Hardin County; Andrew J.; Robert P., married Miss Clemmie Shull, and is farming in Hardin County; Francis; Alice; Sallie, deceased. Our subject, Joshua T., received but a limited education, as the war interrupted the school in that and many other vicinities. When war was declared he volunteered before the age of seventeen, in 1861, and enlisted in the Fifty-first Tennessee, Confederate, in Gen. Cheatham's brigade; he took part in the battle of Shiloh. In going from Cupola, Miss., to Knoxville, in July of 1862, he fell off the train and broke his arm; he was in the hospital at Lauderdale Springs for two months, and then reported for duty. He went to Knoxville and remained in waiting until the command returned from Perryville, Ky. With the command he went to Tullahoma, then marched to Murfreesboro, where he was honorably discharged. On July 1, 1873, Mr. Martin married Miss Mahala J. McLean, of Hardin County, and these children have been born to them: Samuel A., Hester L., Maggie M. and Alma C., Mattie B. and an infant, deceased. The children are all receiving the advantages of a thorough collegiate education. Mr. Martin is one of the prime movers in the establishing of a college in the Sixth District of his county. He has been for many years one of the most successful farmers in the section, and owns a very valuable farm. He served as constable from 1868 to 1874. He is a stanch Democrat, and member of the Methodist Church. He is one of the most influetial residents of Hardin County, where he is well known and respected.

Hon. Archibald G. McDougal, attorney at law at Savannah, is a native of Cumberland County, N. C., and the son of Alex. and Eleanor (Garrick) McDougal, both of Scotch descent and connected with some of the leading families of Scotland, viz.: the Fergusons, the Garricks, the Campbells and the McDougals, all noted clans in days of feudalism, and all Highland Scotch except the Garricks. The father of our subject was a farmer and blacksmith. He removed from North Carolina to Lauderdale County, Ala., in 1817, and remained there until December 24, 1833, when he removed to Lawrence County, and here died in 1843. The mother died in 1854. To them were born a family of eight children, all of whom lived to maturity: John, Daniel, Alex., Archibald G., Mary, Nancy, Eleanor and James F. Of these, Dr. James F., Mary (the eldest sister) and our subject are the only ones living. The latter was reared on a farm and received his education in the common schools and from several months training at an academy. He began reading law at home in 1837, and also clerked in a dry goods store. The following year he studied law under the guidance of Judge Valentine D. Barry, of Hardeman County. Edwin Polk, Henry Barry and our subject were pupils at the same time. In 1839 and 1840 he practiced law in Hardeman County, and in the latter year went to Waynesboro, Wayne County, and practiced in that and adjoining counties. In September, 1845, he married Miss Elizabeth Ann East, daughter of Joseph East, of Hardin County. She died May 31, 1855, leaving two children: Eleanor (Mrs. Judge E. D. Patterson) and Anna (Mrs. Henry E. Williams). The latter died several years since. Mr. McDougal has been a lifelong Democrat, and is a citizen of undoubtable worth and much influence in the State. In 1845 he represented Hardin, Wayne, Lawrence and Hickman Counties in the State Senate, and in 1852 he came to Savannah, where he has since resided. In 1857–58 Mr. McDougal represented Hardin, McNairy and Hardeman Counties in the State Senate. He was also prominently connected with the forming of the new constitution of 1858, and was a delegate to that convention.

Dr. James F. McDougal, physician and farmer, is a native of Lauderdale County, Ala., born July 16, 1820, son of Alexander and Eleanor (Garrick) McDougal, both of Scotch descent. The mother of Alexander was a Campbell, a very prominent family in Scotland. Our subject's mother was a descendant, on her mother's side, of the ancient and honored family of Fergusons. It will thus be seen that our subject is a lineal descendant of the most noted families of Scotland: The McDougals, Garricks, Fergusons and Campbells. The grandfather of our subject, Duncan McDougal, came to America and brought his family during the Revolutionary war. John McDougal was the only one old enough to take part in that struggle. He enlisted in the American Army and took an active part until the close of the war. John died in North Carolina and the other five removed West and settled first (1817) in Lauderdale County, Ala. Here Duncan died. The four brothers then removed to Lawrence County, where they lived and died. They all lie buried in the same cemetery, about three miles from Wayland Springs. Alexander (father of our subject), Samuel, Archibald and James, like their illustrious ancestors of the feudal times, delighted to clan together, and after their pilgrimage of earth was completed they were interred in the same church yard. Our subject grew to manhood on the farm, and when about twenty-two years of age began the study of medicine under the preceptorship of Dr. Edward Bumpus, of Lauderdale County, Ala. He first practiced in Mississippi, but soon removed to Lawrence County, where he successfully practiced his profession. In 1871 he removed to Hardin County, and here he now resides. Dr. McDougal was married, January, 1844, to Mary D. Carmack, of Mississippi, who died September 6, 1879. She was the mother of thirteen children, eight of whom are living: Alexander C. (a physician of Hardin County), Eleanor, Agnes (Mrs. Thomas E. Harrey), M. F. (Mrs. R. D. DeFord), John E., Patience A. C. (Mrs. D. W. Broyles), Capitola A., James T. and Daniel A. October 26, 1881, our subject married Martha A. Powers. He is one among the leading and prominent men of Hardin County, and is respected by all his acquaintances.

Dr. A. C. McDougal, a successful practitioner in the Twelfth Civil District, of Hardin County, Tenn., was born in Tishomingo County, Miss., December 1, 1845, and is the son of J. F. and Mary (Carmack) McDougal. To this union were born thirteen children of whom our subject is the eldest. He was educated in Lawrence and Lauderdale Counties, Ala., and attended the medical college of Nashville, Tenn., where he graduated in 1867 or 1868. He then went to Waterloo and practiced one season. In 1870 he moved to Savannah, where he practiced his profession and taught school until 1874, and then moved to Perry County, Tenn., and practiced there until 1878. He then moved to his present residence, where he has continued ever since, engaged in a successful practice. February 26, 1884, he married Miss Mattie A. White, a native of Hardin County. To them was born one child, Leroy C. Dr. McDougal is a stanch Democrat and is much esteemed in Hardin County. His grandfather was one of the earliest settlers of Lawrence County.

W. C. Meeks, a leading merchant of Pittsburg Landing, Tenn., was born in Lincoln County, Tenn., August 4, 1834. A predominant passion in Mr. Meeks, even from his tender years, is ambition, and the perfect success that has so vividly characterized the many varied enterprises in which he has engaged, should, in a great measure, be attributed to this ruling inclination, as well as to his superior financiering and sound judgment. It has been often and truly said by those who are familiar with his character, that there are united in him some of the most commendable attributes that ever belonged to man; while he is decisive and determined, he is ever ready to hear the advice and solicitations of friends; impregnable in a position assumed from a sense of right and principle, he is pliable to every touch of reason; unfaltering and uncompromising in opposing an imposition perpetrated upon him, he was never known to refuse to pardon an evil with the proper amends, and many instances may be recalled when copious tears fell from his manly cheeks for no other reason than a sympathetic tenderness with a cause entirely free and distinct from the entanglement of preconceived ideas, and personal or selfish interests; thus it will be seen that a true, emotional, tender heart is a marked attribute of his character. W. C. Meeks is a son of John Meeks, who was born in Penilton County, S. C., in 1783. When war was declared against the Creek Indians in 1812, Mr. Meeks volunteered his services. He was nominated for the office of adjutant-general, his opponent being an exceedingly popular gentleman. Mr. Meeks was unanimously elected and served gallantly in this capacity until the restoration of peace. He was married in 1810, to Miss Elizabeth Henderson, daughter of Capt. John Henderson, of Revolutionary fame. To this union three children were born, of whom but one is living—Gen. John H. Meeks, of McNairy County, Tenn.; the other two died in infancy. Mrs. Meeks died October 12, 1814. Mr. Meeks was married the second time to Miss Elisabeth Byrnes Lane, of Mount Sterling, Ky., daughter of Hon. Hiram Lane, who was the father of six children, constituting one of the most distinguished families in the State of Kentucky, and occupied some of the most important official positions in the gift of the people, some of them having been United States Senators. Mrs. Elisabeth Byrnes (Lane) Meeks was very beautiful in form and feature, and possessed superior mental talents. This marriage resulted in the birth of six children, two only are living: Col. O. L. Meeks, of McNairy County, Tenn., who was State Senator from his district in 1855, and the subject of this sketch. The children dead were Margaret A., Edwin T., Mary A. and Martha C. On the 10th of March, 1852, W. C. Meeks was married to Miss Luverna E., daughter of John Chambers, who moved from South Carolina to Middle Tennessee at an early day, and from thence to McNairy County, Tenn., in 1820. Mr. Chambers dealt largely in land and was a merchant in both of which he was very successful. He is said to have originally entered the land on which Purdy, the county seat of McNairy County is situated, and the first merchant that owned and operated a store in that county. He was the father of three children—one son and two daughters—only one now living, Lafayette Chambers, who resides in Corinth, Miss. The two daughters, Lucretia and Luverna E., possessed great personal attractions and were exemplary in their decorum. To this marriage resulted the birth of three children: Rebecca E., wife of J. T. Andrews, a merchant at Whitt, Tex.; Orval C., who is postmaster at Pittsburg Landing, Tenn., and a partner of his father in the mercantile business, and Cynthia L., wife of J. T. Gipson, who is engaged in the milling business at Whitt, Tex. Mr. Meeks located on his farm at his marriage, where he resided peacefully and happily until the late civil war was declared, when he received an order from the Secretary of the Confederate Army to assist in supplying Gen. Forrest's command, which he did until 1862, when he left Corinth as guide for Gen. Breckinridge to Shiloh, where the struggle lasted two days. He also engaged in the battle of Harrisburg, and was honorably discharged at Corinth, Miss., in 1865. He returned to his home in McNairy County, resumed farming, and owing to the destruction caused by the war was greatly discouraged, but after a few years of hard work was again in a prosperous condition. On November 7, 1865, his wife died, the effect of which, together with the destruction and trying ordeals of the war from which he was just emerging, made him very sorrowful indeed. About that time he entered into the mercantile business at Corinth and Marietta, Miss., when he met with unusual success. He married the second time Miss Rebecca J. Chambers, the eldest daughter of C. L. Chambers. Mrs. Meeks is an exemplary member of the Missionary Baptist Church, to which she has belonged many years. In 1870 Mr. Meeks visited northwestern Texas prospecting; came back and made two more trips in 1871 and 1872, each time with droves of horses, traveling by land, which was very tiresome, requiring two months to make the journey. For twelve years he traded between Tennessee and Texas, at the same time keeping up his agricultural interests in McNairy County, Tenn. In 1879-80 he was engaged in the mercantile business at Whitt, Tex., and in 1881-82 in the same business at Dublin, Tex., from whence he returned to the place of his nativity. Mr. Meeks is a sterling Democrat; an enterprising, courageous man who has met with success in all his undertakings, and who has the respect of the entire community in which he lives and is well known.

M. F. Parker, a well known farmer and resident of the Third District, was born in Wayne County. Tenn., on Second Creek, November 5, 1855. His father, W. L. Parker, is a native of York District, South Carolina, a farmer from boyhood. He married Miss Fannie Hipp in North Carolina, and moved to Mississippi. Mrs. Parker was the mother of two children: John A. and Sylvia E.; she died six years after her marriage. Mr. Parker united the second time to Miss Adeline Collier, a native of Lincoln County, S. C., and moved to Tennessee with her brothers Matthew and Brown Lee. Mrs. Adeline (C.) Parker bore six children: Alexander, James Monroe, Nancy E., M. F., Mary E. and Alonzo S. After Mr. Parker's second marriage he lived three years in Lafayette County, Miss.; he returned to Wayne County and purchased a farm on Second Creek, six years later went to Chalk Creek, near Waynesboro, and remained until 1867, and again changed, going to Horse Creek, Wayne County. From 1840 to 1881 he taught school and managed his farm. The subject of our sketch was educated in his native county; has always been engaged in agriculture. He farmed three years in Lafayette County, Miss., from 1874 to 1877; came back to Wayne County, and December 19, 1880, was married to Miss Lucinda R., daughter of A. Blevins, one of Hardin County's most respected residents and settlers. To this union two children were born: C. B. and Ora M. Mr. Parker the first two years after marriage farmed with his father-in-law, and in 1882 purchased the farm upon which he has since lived, situated on Turkey Creek, a fertile and valuable piece of land. Mr. Parker is a Democrat and one of the most enterprising men in the section. Mrs. Parker is a devoted member of the Cumberland Presbyterian Church.

Hon. Alfred Pitts, a farmer and magistrate of the Thirteenth District, was born in Henderson County July 28, 1826; he is a son of Barbee and Melissia (Wilson) Pitts, both natives of Tennessee and members of some of the old families who emigrated from North Carolina. The father moved to Henderson County at an early day, locating about ten miles north of Lexington, where he engaged in farming until his removal to McNairy County, and afterward to Hardin County, where he died January, 1857. He was a strong Democrat, a man of considerable influence, and highly esteemed. He was colonel commandant of the McNairy company, receiving his commission from Gov. Carroll. He served actively and gallantly in the Florida war of 1836. The mother's death occurred in December, 1856. They had a family of seven sons, three of whom are dead: Wm. W. was in Johnson's home guard in Federal service; John was in Company B, Forty-sixth Ohio, Federal Army, and Nicholas was lieutenant in Company H, under Gen. Hurst; Burrell was conscripted and forced into the Confederate Army, where he died after about two years' service; Theo died in 1854; Barbee lives in Hardin County; the other child died in infancy. Alfred was the first born; was raised on a farm, and has been connected with the political affairs of the county for years. In 1851 he began public service as a constable; then deputy sheriff and as justice of the peace in 1860; in 1867 was elected to represent Hardin County in the State Legislature; for past four years has been chairman of the county court. He was married in 1856 to Mary A. Sumner, who died August, 1855, leaving him three children: John A., who is farming near his father's place; William P., a leading merchant of Milledgeville, McNairy County, and Sarah, wife of John Short, a farmer of McNairy County. Mr. Pitts in December, 1862, united in marriage with Elizabeth Rice, who has borne him four children: Nicholas, Alfred Thomas, James Irwin and Mary Louisa. Mr. Pitts is a stanch Republican, a Mason of prominence, one of the most respected residents of the Thirteenth District, where he owns a fine and valuable farm.

Henry M. Porterfield, a prosperous farmer of the Sixth District, was born in Hardin County, November 19, 1857. His father, William C., is a native of Rutherford County, Tenn., came to Hardin County at an early day, when there were but few white settlers; purchased a large tract of land on Horse Creek. His marriage was with Miss Ursula

Graham of Giles County, Tenn. To them were born thirteen children, Henry M. being the youngest. He was educated in the Hardin and Decatur County schools. He has been farming ever since his boyhood, and now owns the place upon which he lives. In 1880 he married Miss Maggie, daughter of W. G. Thomas, one of the most influential residents of Hardin County. Mrs. Porterfield was a true Christian woman, beloved by all who knew her; was a consistent member of the Methodist Church, and her death occurred November 1, 1885. She was the mother of four children; those living are Cora and Oscar; the two dead are Effie and Willie T. Mr. Porterfield has been for many years a devoted member of the Methodist Church. He is a stanch Democrat and an affable, respected man, well and favorably known throughout the county.

R. W. Reynolds, a well-to-do farmer of the Third District, was born in Hardin County December 25, 1839. His father, Henry Reynolds, was a native of Virginia and came to Williamson County at an early day, and after residing there a year or two went to Alabama; one year later came to Hardin County, settled on Turkey Creek and there lived until his death. His wife was Miss Matilda Smith, a native of Hardin County, who bore him four children, of whom our subject was the youngest. He received a fair education in the common schools of his native county, after which he began farming until war was declared. He enlisted in First Confederate under command of Col. Cox, and took part in the ever-to-be-remembered battles of Shiloh, Perryville, Ky., Murfreesboro and Chickamauga. Mr. Reynolds was made, by his gallantry, first lieutenant of Robinson's company, and served bravely in that capacity until close of the war in 1865, when he returned home and resumed his farming pursuits. He was first married to Miss Sarah B. McCown of Hardin County, who died in 1865. She bore him five children, of whom only one survives, William J., who is a practicing physician in this county; those who died were Andrew J., Henry H., Pleasant M., and Sarah B. (who died in infancy). Mr. Reynolds was married the second time to Miss Nancy E. Kiser of Hardin County, who became the mother of six children: Jacob W., Fannie B., Sarah J., Minnie E., A. L. and Elzey. Mr. Reynolds is an earnest Democrat, adhering to party principles, has met with unusual success in business life, is an affable and highly esteemed man.

Benjamin F. Shelby, farmer of the Eighth District, was born in Hardin County, June 21, 1831. His father, Levi Shelby, was a native of Mecklenburg County, North Carolina, and located in Hardin County in 1819, at which time there were but few white settlers; he located on the place where Benjamin now lives. He married Margurite, daughter of John White, of North Carolina, who took an active and gallant part in the Revolutionary war. To the union of Levi and Margurite Shelby five children were born, the subject of this sketch being the fourth. He received his education in his native county, and in 1850 obtained a position as bookkeeper in a mercantile house at Savannah, and later on at Eastport, Miss., in 1854. He was married, December 9, 1856, to Miss Letitia A. Johnson of Lauderdale County, Ala., who died December 28, 1881; to them nine children were born, of those living are Laura V., Margurite A., Mattie L., Julia E., Minnie G., Benjamin F., and William W.; those dead were Levi and Jeremiah E. At the outbreak of the late war Mr. Shelby enlisted in the First Confederate, under command of Col. Cox. He remained in service but a short time when he returned home and resumed his farming. Although his sympathies were with the South he was not a secessionist. He is a stanch Democrat and does all he can for the advancement of his party's interests. He is one of the best and most respected men in Hardin County.

David T. Street, P. M. and merchant of Savannah, was born in Lunenburg, Va., October 16, 1830. His father, David A. Street, was a lawyer, and a graduate of Washington College, Lexington, Va. He practiced law at Lunenburg C. H., Va., and in 1837 came to Jackson, Tenn. He edited a paper in that city for a number of years and then resumed the practice of his profession. In 1846 he moved to Savannah to practice law in the courts of Hardin and adjoining counties. In 1828 he married Miss Mary D. Woodson who bore him seven children, of these the subject of this sketch is the eldest and the only one living. He was educated in the common schools of Lunenburg County, Va., and at Jackson, Tenn. After finishing his education he engaged as clerk for James Irwin in Savannah. He soon engaged in the mercantile business with Edgar Cherry, and styled the firm Cherry & Street; this they continued successfully until 1874 when the firm sold out their business. Mr. Street was appointed county clerk and served two years. He also served as county treasurer several terms. November 23, 1863, he married Miss Sarah P. Marrow, a native of Savannah, whose father came to Hardin County at a very early day. This union resulted in the birth of these children: David M., William T., Mary W., Nannie, Inez, John R., George M., Charles, Maggie O. and Blanch. In 1879 Mr. Street engaged in the drug business with Mr. Franks, the firm being styled Franks & Street. This they continued five years. Mr. Street then sold out and was appointed postmaster in 1884. He has held the office ever since greatly to the satisfaction of the public. He has given his children the advantage of a thorough education in the college of Savannah. Mr. Street is a stanch Democrat, and he and wife are members of the Methodist Episcopal Church.

W. G. Thomas, a prosperous farmer of the Fourth District, was born in Franklin County, Tenn., October 15, 1824. His father, William Thomas, was a native of North Carolina and settled in Franklin County at an early day, when there were but few whites in that section. He was a farmer by occupation; was married to Miss Hannah Young, a lady of his native State; to them eleven children were born, W. G. being the second. Our subject had very limited educational advantages, but had a bright, keen intellect, and acquired a great deal of knowledge by careful reading. He began farming when quite young. April 16, 1848, he was married to Elizabeth B. Howard, a native of Hardin County. To their union twelve children were born: Mary J., Martha E., Willis L., Salina E., I. F., Henry M.; deceased are William, Benjamin W., Eliza N., Margurite P. (was married to H. M. Porterfield, at her death left two children, George and John, who are living with Mr. Thomas). When the late war was declared Mr. Thomas volunteered and enlisted in the First Confederate under command of Gen. Cleburne, he served only a short time and returned to his farm. He is a Mason and member of the Methodist Church, and one of the most popular men in the county. He has several times been solicited to announce himself as candidate for office, but has invariably declined, believing his interests better guarded at home.

William J. Watson, clerk of the county court, was born in Lincoln County October 30, 1851, and is the son of Nimrod W. and Mary B. (Randolph) Watson. The father is a native of Davidson County, and descendant of an old English family who came to America before the Revolutionary war. When a young man he accompanied his uncle, James Williams, on a surveying tour through Arkansas in 1835-36. After spending some time first in Lincoln County, then in Madison and Marshall Counties, Ala., he settled in Hardin County, Tenn., where he now resides, engaged in farming; a great portion of his life has been spent in overseeing; he is a most worthy and respected man. The mother was born in Lincoln County, Tenn., was a daughter of James Randolph, one of the earliest settlers of the county and descendant of the honorable Randolph family of Virginia. Mrs. Watson was the mother of nine children, all of whom lived to reach maturity, the eldest two brothers died in 1886. The subject of this sketch was the fourth child; was reared on a farm and received the most limited educational advantages, and when at the age of twenty-one had about only six months' schooling. He first attended the Saltillo Academy, taught by J. A. Hanna of the Southern Illinois Normal University. Mr. Watson taught school and thus paid his expenses. He afterward attended six months in the Southern Illinois Normal at Carbondale in 1878; during 1879-81 he again taught in Marshall County, Ala., two years of which he was instructor in a high school. He returned to Hardin County, Tenn., and began the study of law, and was elected school superintendent for 1885-86. In August of 1886 was elected clerk of the county court, which position he now fills in a manner satisfactory to all. He was married October 30, 1879, to Letitia, daughter of Thomas W. and Martha T. Ice of Marshall County, Ala. Mr. Watson is a Republican and a young man who has by his industry, intellect and moral courage, made himself one of the most respected and honored citizens of Savannah.

John J. Williams, a member of the firm of J. J. Williams & Bro. of Savannah, was born November 10, 1846. His father, John J. Williams, Sr., was born in North Carolina in 1800, and came to Hardin County about 1823-24, located on Horse Creek, and taught school there for some time; about 1830 he came to Savannah and engaged in the liquor business, receiving permission from the Legislature to sell without license. In 1838 he began selling dry goods, which he continued until 1861, and was very successful. He was three times married. The first wife, Susan Wagenor, he united with September 7, 1826; she died July 21, 1827, the infant which she bore also passing away. His second marriage occurred December, 1827, with the deceased wife's sister, Martha Wagenor, who became the mother of three children; she died November 17, 1833. He was married the third time to Catherine Graham September 15, 1841, her birth occurred in Giles County, Tenn., from which section her father, James Graham, moved to Hardin County in her childhood. By the third marriage Mr. Williams became the father of ten children, John J. being third. The death of John J., Sr., occurred in 1863. Our subject had but limited educational advantages, his knowledge having been mostly gained by reading of choice literature. In 1865 he began the dry goods business at Savannah, where he has built up an extensive and lucrative trade, having the confidence and respect of the people. He is a Mason of good standing. January 14, 1874, he married Miss Lizzie Ricketts, of Wayne County, Tenn., to their union six children have been born: Mamie, John, Nellie, Sallie, Samuel, and Ansel (deceased.)

Index Prepared By:
Karon Mac Smith
Rt. 1 Box 190, Nixon, Texas

Note: Pages 821-822 and 877-878 are not included in this index as they had been torn from the original book.

Abernathy, A. J. (Chancellor)
  816, 838
  Bessie L. 870
  Florence W. 870
  George M. 870
  J. R. 840
  Mary 870
  M. R. 826, 827
  M. R., Prof. 870+
  Orpheus 870
  Pearl 870
  Smith, Dr. 870
  Terry W. 870
  William K. 870
Adams 827
Adams, Amanda F. (___) 875
  B. B. 875
  George M. 828
  James 828
  J. R. 823, 825
  Julia A. 875
  L. F. 828
  Susan 847
Adamson, Elizabeth 889
Akin, Capt. 802
  H. E., Mrs. 840
  J. W. 840
  Lot 881
  Robert J. 880+
  Samuel 816
  William V. 880
  W. R. 817
Aldredge, John 838
Alexander, James M. 894+
  J. M. 839, 841
  John 894
  John D. 899
  J. R., Rev. 838
  Malissa M. 899
  W. P. 839
Alexander & Bro. 899
Allen 801
Allen, Charles J. 807
  Columbus P. 895
  Ettie E. 895
  George H. 895
  Grant A. 895
  Granville S. 895
  J. P., Dr. 895
  J. S. 818
  Milton J. 895
  Samuel R. 894+
  Sarah M. 895
  William R. 895
  W. R., M.D. 895+
Allison, David 896
Anderson 802
Anderson, A. A. 811
  Allen 831
  Catherine (___) 846
  Emily Melvina 841
  Henry 846
  Jackson 841+
  James Y. 841
  John 841
  John Slater 841
  J. W. 805
  L. J. 812
  Mary E. 846
  Mary Jane 870
  R. 810
  R. D. 870+
  Sam N. 801
  S. E., Rev. 812
  Stephen 831

Anderson, Cont.
  Susan 868
  Thomas 870
  William H. 841
  William R. 870
  William T. 822
Andrews, J. T. (Tx.) 904
Anthony, Clarissa 862
  Philip 862
Antry, William & Bro. 805
Argo, Easter 856, 857
Arnis, James 871
  Mary (___) 871
Arnold, Carry F. 881
  E. E. 816, 880+
  Eliza 887
  Ephraim 815, 880
  Ida M. 881
  James E. 880, 881
  Martha Ann 886
  Mary G. 881
  Melissa A. 881
  William 807
  William G. 881
Ashcraft, H. C. 812
  Henry C. 813
  Mattie M. 813
Ashcraft & Co. 809(2)
Ashley, ___ (Elliot) 210
Ashrott, James 833
Atkins, Adolphus S. (Ar.) 871
  Artimesia 871
  Ellen 876
  George 871(2), 876
  James E. 871
  John Peyton 871
  Joseph 871
  J. P. & _ro. 841
  Martha 871
  Martha (___) 876
  Nancy 871
  Peyton 871+
  Pickney C. (Ar.) 871
  Robert Tolbert 871
Atkinson, Dr. 828
Atwood & Murray 827
Austin, H. W. 805
  P. M., Dr. 805
  Woodward E. C. 805
Aydelott, A. E. 800(2)
  Andrew E. 881
  Arbon Y. 881
  Floyd C. 881
  Frank Cleveland 881
  J. F., Dr. 881+, 887
  Otto H. 881
  Sarah E. 881
Babb, D. W., (Ms.) 871
Baird & Bro. 809
Baker, Benjamin 881, 882
  B. G. 881+
  D. M. 824
  Dora 882
  Edna 895
  Elizabeth 881
  Ellen 882
  G. W. 882
  Horton Howard 881
  James 798, 799(2)
  James K. 881
  James T., Dr. (a minister) 895
  Jasper L. 895+
  Lovie Ann 895
  Lucinda 895

Baker, Cont.
  Martha E. 882
  Mary E. 882
  Mary Jane 895
  Mary O. 895
  Milton 895(2)
  Newton G. 895+
  N. G. 900
  Rachel C. 882
  Richard B. 895
  Richard Haywood (Ar.) 895
  Robert 799
  Sarah 899
  Sarah J. 882
  Tennessee 881
  Thomas 873
  William E. 882
  Winnie 881
  Winnie M. 882
  W. Y., Capt. 823
Baker & Bro. 840
Ball, R. C. 810
Ballard, F. M. 810
Balright, William F. (2d Lieut)
  817, 823
Baltimore, Lord 884
Bank, James 809
Banks, Miss 894
Barbam, John 863
  Mary H. 863
Barbee, Hattie 826
Barbrough, J. C. 815
  (Yarbrough?)
Barcroft, Daniel 798
Barger, E. M. 861
Barham, E. A. 841
  John 813, 831
  J. W., Lieut. 835
  Richard 801, 810
  R. J. 813(3)
  Robert 831
Barlow, Dr. 839
  Alice I. 896
  Cally J. 896
  E. 896
  George J. 896
  J. K. 837, 840
  Joseph 896
  Luke E. 896
  Osborne L. 896
  Samuel P. 896+
Barlow & Cooper 840
Barlow & Hughes 840
Barnes 827
Barnes, Mr. 831
  James 831, 833(2), 834,
    836(2), 837, 838, 839
Barnett, A. D. 810
  Calvin 801
  George W. 827(2)
  J. C. 816
  John 801
  John O. 838
  Joseph 820
  Samuel M. 896
  William, Dr. 820
Barnett & Bro. 806
Barnham, Elizabeth 900
Barnhill, J. N. 826
  John N. 871
  J. T. 871+
  Mollie 902
  T. J. 825
  William 827
  William (Tx.) 871

Barnhill, Cont.
  W. P., Capt. 873
Barr, T. 801
Barrand, Dr. 860
Barrett 807
Barrett, John, Rev. 803
  Joseph 825
  J. S. 811
  Sallie 811
Barry, Dr. 828
  C. D. 842
  Charles L. 842
  Daniel, Dr. 842
  Henry 902
  Henry D. 842
  Valentine D., Judge 902
  William 884
  William V. 842+
Barry Son 828
Bartholomew, Helen M. 848
  Jacob 798
  Mary Ann 855
Bassel, Caroline 881
Bateman, Thomas P., Judge 800, 810, 816, 835
Basye, E. T. 838
Beacham, Daniel S. 842
  George H. 842
  G. W. 842+
  John W. 842
  Josephene 842
  Levina Jane 842
  Lucinda 842
  Mahala 842
  Mary Ellen 842
  Nancy Ann 842
  Sallie 842
  William E. 842
Bean, A. L. 810
Beard 820
Beard, Franklin, Rev. 825
  George W. 818
Beatty, J. W., Capt. 802
  William 820
Beaty 827
Beaver, Carroll 811
  Nancy 811
  Stephen 807, 808
Beaver & Carver 809
Beaver, Carver & Co. 809
Beaver & Son 810
Beaves, William H. 824
Beck, T. R. 825
Bedell, Hester 900
Bell 827
Bell, Dr. 828
  Asa 825, 827
  Bettie 802
  F. M. 825
  I. T. 800
  J. H. 828
  Job 825(2)
  John 846, 880
  John M. 825
  R. D. 810
  Thomas H. 825
  W. Y. 828
Bell & Bros. 810
Bell & Wisdom 827
Beloate, W. 801
Bemis, Dr. (La.) 844
Bennet, W. H. 818
Bennett, John W. 817
  R. E. 838
Bentley, Lee M. 816
Benton, Cherry L. 896
  George F. 838(2), 840, 896
  George F. (Sr.) 896
  George H. 897
  J. H. 840
  John H. 896+
  Jerusha M. 896
Benton & Bro. 840

Benton Bros. 896
Berry, J. G., Capt. 835
  Michael 832, 833
  W. V. 805
Besley, Theodosia 882
Beuler & Webb 840
Bevel, Dr. 805
Biffle, Col. 899
  Jack, Col. 893/4
  J. B. 883
Billingsly, William 807
Bird, N. L. 859
  W. R. 859
Bishop, S. J. 810(2)
Bivens, Shep 902
Black, John H. 825
  T. N. 801
Blackard, ___ Rev. 813
Blackburn, John 819(2)
Blackman, B. F., Rev. 813
Blacksheer, Jacob 831
Blackwell, ___ 832
  John 833
  Minnie 882
Blaine, James G. 851
Blaine and Logan 852
Blair, R. C. 803
Bland, J. R. 810
  Mary C. 813
Blasingain, Elihu 879
Blevins, A. 905
  Abner W. 896_, 897
  A. W. 837, 897
  Isabella A. 897
  James 896
  James D. 897
  Jessie A. 897
  John M. 897
  Lucinda 896
  Lucinda R. 905
  Martha 896
  Mary A. 896
  Matilda 896
  Richard 896
  Sarah E. 896
  William A. 897
  Wilson, Dr. 896, 897+
Blount, E. P. 837, 840
Blunt, Elias ("Gov.") 818
Blythe & Boundurant 818
Boatman, James L. W. (Capt.) 823(2)
Boatmore(?), J. L. W. (1st Lieut.) 817, 825
Bobo, S. S. 897
Bogan, George W. 887
Bolin, John W. 882
  Joseph 882
  Martin 882
  Martin C. 882
  Mary 882
  Mary M. 882
  William 882+
Bomar, Maria 826
Bond, F. P. 800
Boone, Daniel 861
  Hiram 831, 836(2)
Boothe, Mattie 812
Boren, Elijah 868
  Eliza E. 868
  Mary (___) 868
Boswell, Thomas H., Capt. 835
Boswell, Fielder & Co. 804
Bowlin, Frances 852
Boyd, James 825, 827, 833
  James Sr. 833
  John 833(2)
  William 934
Braden, P. H. 827
  W. H. 827
Bradford, Col. 863
  A. H., Col. 802, 817, 823
  R. H. 866

Bradford & Cobb 854
Bradley, Capt. 835
  Mr. 849
  Hezekiah 838
Bradley, William 831
  William, Col. 837
Bradley & Co. 841
Brady, Eliza 884
Brady, Sam. Gen. 884
Bragg, Gen. 835
Brandon, C. S. 816
Brashears, A. 813
Brasher 801
Brasher, Mr. 814
  P. R. (2d Lieut.) 816, 817
  Robert S. 815
  Samuel 815, 818
  William 892
  W. T. 817
Bray, Alice 843
  Artie 843
  Askew 843
  Demonia 843
  Eleanor 843
  Felix R. 842+, 843
  F. R. 806
  F. R. & Co. 806
  James H. 843
  John 842, 884
  John R. 862+
  J. R. 810(2)
  Katie 843
  Lizzie 843
  Mary (___) 862
  Mary C. 862
  Matthew 862
  Millie 843
  Nancy J. 843, 884
  Polk, 809
  Samuel 812, 862
  Samuel, Rev. 812
  Sidney M. 843
  William M. 842
  W. M. & Co. 809
Bray and Co. 842
Brazelton 838, 839
Brazelton, Mrs. 831
  Benjamin 830
  B. G. 838
  Elizabeth 831
  Hannah 830
  John 830(2), 831
  Nancy 831
  Sally 830
  Sarah 831
  Simon 830
  William 831
Breckinridge, Gen. 904
  John C. 849, 857, 872
  W. K. M. (Lieut. Col.) 823, 835
Brewer, Elizabeth (Denison) 883
  Sterling 799
Brigance 798
Brigance, William 816
  William, Dr. 805
Brigham, John 798
  William 798
Bright, W. B. 816
Britt, W. R. 800
  W. S. 818
Brooks 827
Brooks, J. J., Rev. 802
  John 798, 803, 804(2), 826, 827
  Marion 834
  W. F. 801, 803, 843+
  William 798, 799, 803, 804, 843
Browder, Sarah B. 864
  W. F. P. 828
Brown, Alex M. 825

Brown, Cont.
  A. M. 825
  Andrew E. 863
  B. H. (Lieut. Col.) 801(2), 808, 817
  B. H., Dr. 862+
  Cornelia S. 862
  David W. E. 862
  George 810
  G. W. 828
  H. H. 838
  James 807
  Jessie E. 863
  J. D. 808
  John 808
  Joseph 818
  Martha Ann 898
  Milton (Chancellor) 801, 838
  Nancy 825
  Thomas 897
  Thomas M. 897+
  T. M. 837
  William F. 825
  Willis C., Dr. 863
  W. M. 825
Brown & Parrish 801
Brown & Co. 805
Browning, W. H., Rev. 839
Brownlow, Gov. 848
Broyles, ___ 834
  C. 838
  D. W. 835, 903
  J. L. & Co. 841
  L. H. 840(3)
Broyles & Irvin 840
Bruler, Samuel 832
Brumblow, Louvinia 872
Brummer, John 807
  W. A. 813
Bruton, Samuel 833
Bryan, A. D., Rev. 802
Bryant, A. D. 838
  Amanda 890
  Asa 831, 833
  Elisha 841
Buchanon, James 848
Buck, G. H. 800
  J. L. (1st Lieut.) 817
Buckley, C. A. 863
  John 863
  John H. 869
  Lucy D. 869
  Mary C. (___) 869
  N. T. 801, 809, 810
Buell 836
Bullock 801
Bullock, Micajah 801, 804
Bumpus, Edward, Dr. 903
Burk, S. B. 841
Burkhead 813
Burkhead, Nehemiah 807
  Wesley 807
Burnet, ___ 831
Burns, Jerry, Rev. 826
Burtwell, John T. 827
  J. T. 827
Busick, Jane A. 869
Butler, Callie 863
  David R. 863
  G. C. 810
  Hattie P. 863
  John W. 863
  L. H. 863
  Mary E. 863
  Obadiah 863
  Thomas O. 863
  T. J. 863+
Cahal, Terry H. 834
Cain, Andrew 869
  Rittie 869
  Sarah (___) 869
  William 798

Calhoun, J. H. 834
Campbell 902, 903
Campbell, A. B. 838
  Mary I. 856
  May J. 813
  Robert 817
Cantrell, J. W. 834
Caraway & Stegall 845
Carender, J. W. 840(2)
Carmack, J. R. 816
  Mary 903
  Mary D. 903
Carrington, Charles 897
  Emma 897
  Ephriam 897
  Ethel 897
  Fannie 897
  Ida 897
  Levinia 897
  Lewis 897
  Nellie 897
  Robert 897
  W. H. 840, 897+
  William897
Carroll, Gov. 905
  William 819
Carroll & McLeod 809
Carson, S. M. 800, 803
Carter 827
Carter, John 875
  J. T. 838
  Robert 798
Case, W. 827
Casey, Albert (1st Lieut.) 823
  Joel 834, 839
  Joseph 833
Cash, William 810
Cason 813
Cason, Col. 807
  B. P. 863
  Caleb M. 813
  C. H. (Lieut. Col.) 823
  Charles M. 813
  C. M., Col. 802, 808, 813, 817, 863+
  D. K. 863
  J. E. 863
  John B. 863
  J. R. 863
  Mary 813
  Mary H. 813
  R. E. 863
  Sue 812
  Susie 863
  William 807, 813(2), 822, 863
  William T. 813
  W. T. 812, 863
Cason, Estes & Co. 809
Cass, Gen. 867
Cathel, Judge 861
Caufman, Dennis (Tx.) 895
Cauthorn, Alice C. 813
Cavender, Delah C. 898
  Emma M. 898
  Joseph W. 897+, 898
  Joseph W., Dr. 897
  Mary A. 898
  Sarah A. 898
  Silas H. 898
  Susan E. 898
  Victor T. 898
Cawthorn, John L. 868
  Lessie 868
  Martha (___) 868
Caygle, N. C. 810
  W. C. 810
Chambers, C. L. 904
  Cynthia L. 876
  Elizabeth 871
  Elizabeth (___) 871
  John 820(2), 827, 829, 831, 876, 904

Chambers, Cont.
  John & Nathaniel Griffith 827
  Lafayette (Ms.) 904
  Lucretia 904
  Luverna E. 904(2)
  Polly 798
  Rebecca (___) 876
  Rebecca J. 904
  Samuel 820(2), 871(2)
Chamles, John 827
Chandler, William, Capt. 817, 823
Chaness, W. C. 827
Chaney, M. B., Mrs. 826
  Sarah E. 886
Cheatham, Gen. 889, 902
  T. N. 828
Cheney, S. J. 825
Cherry, Edgar 907
  F. M. 810(2)
  Isham 831, 833(3)
  Jesse 831
  Sallie 896
  W. H. 838, 839, 896
  W. L. 808
Cherry & Benton 840
Cherry & Street 907
Chester, John, Col. 817
  R. I., Col. 808, 809
  R. L. & W. S. Wisdom 827
Chissum, James 837
Choat, Mrs. 837
Christopher, ___ 837
  J. 811
  J. D. 828
  J. E. 868
  W. C. 810
Churchwell, Sarah J. 896
  William, Col. 835
Churry, William H. 882
Clardy, Dr. (Tx.) 888
Clark, R. L. 840
Clay, Henry 848, 865
Clayton, T. M. 823
  W. B., Capt. 823
Cleary, William, Lieut. 835
Cleburne, Gen. 907
Clenny, B. W. 881
Cleveland, (Grover) 853
Clifford, James 807
Clift, John 882
  Robert 882
Clifton, Henry 831
Cloftin, Henry 833
Cloud, J. F.827
Coats, Mrs. 834
  Jane 892
  Pleasant 826
Cobb, D. W. 827
Cochran, Dr. 869
  Amy Bemis 844
  J. L., Prof. 843+
  S. M. 843
  Thomas A. 844
Coffey, Sallie 861
Coffman, Isaac 820
Coggins, James 890
Coghill 802
Coleman, Francis 893
Collier, Adeline 905
  Brown Lee 905
  James 831
  Matthew 905
Collins, Henry 805
  Peter 807
  Thomas 897
  William 804, 809
Combs, Archibald 871
  Frank 811
  Guy 872
  Henry 871
  James 871

Combs, Cont.
  John 871
  John G. 871+
  J. W. 833
  Lee 871
  Maggie 871
  Peter 871
  Thomas 827, 871
  Willie 871
Comer, James 826
Conner, C. G., Rev. 826
  Harriet A. 813
Conyers, Mary 848
Cook, Abel 811
  Albert, Capt. 835
  Isaac S. W. 833
  M. B. 803
  Nancy 811
Cooper, John 802
  R. C. 810, 863
  Sarah B., Mrs. 863
  Sophia 882
Corbet 802
Corey, Wesley 838
Couch, Elizabeth J. 895
  J. 900
Counce, Charles B. 898
  Fayette 898
  George (Ar.) 898
  J. A. 838
  James C. 898
  John A. 898+
  Theodosia 898
  Tony 898
  William 898
  William 898
  William K. 898
Council, George W. 851
Countess, Asa 882
  George W. 883
  John 883
  John M. 882+
  Mary 882
  William B. 883
Courtney, Benjamin 831
  E. 900
  James 831
  John 831
  Jonathan 831
  Melvinie 831
  Nelly 831
  Ona 831
  Stephen 831
Covey, A. K. 843
  James B., Dr. 898+
  Levin E., Dr. 898
  M. E. 843
  Noble W. 898
  N. W. 837
Cox, Col. 880, 906(2)
  Anderson 870
  Betsy 855
  H. J., Prof. 839
  Jane 888
  Javan 820
  N. N., Col. 874
  Rachel M. 870
  Rebecca (___) 870
Crabb, Susan P. 856
Craig, A. B. 849
  Nancy 893
Craugh, Thomas 823(2)
Craven, Alex. McNeal 898, 899
  Eli T. 898+
  E. T. & J. H. 899
  James H. 899+
Craven & Wilkinson 841
Crew 895
Crews, Col. 835
Criner, H. D. 863+
  J. A. 810
  John 810
  John A. 863

Criner, Cont
  Robert 808, 810, 863+
Crittenden, W. C. 809
Crockett, David 819
Crook, Dr. 807
  A. B. 812(4), 813
  Elizabeth 868
  Hattie E. 813
  H. D. 810
  J. A., Dr. 808, 809
  John 807
  Joseph A., Dr. 811
  Mary G. 846
  Mary V. 812
  Mattie, Mrs. 869
Crook & Keeland 810
Crook & Thomas 810
Cross, Albert, Capt. 823
  Alphonso 825
  J. P. 801
  Maclin 820, 824, 825, 826, 827(2)
Cross & Cates 827
Cross & Moore 827
Crossett, Lucinda 896
Crow, J. G. 828
  M. L. 841
Crowder, J. W. 818
  Mary E. 881
  Medora 881
Crump 827
Crump, Richard, Dr. 831
Cunningham, A. B. 844+
  J. A. 835
  J. G. 838
  J. M. 812
  John 844
  Josella 844
  Martha 844
  Ransom (Ramson?) 802, 844(2)
  Walter 844
Curry, James H. 825
  J. T., Rev. 839
  T. H. 827
Curtis, Aaron 801
Dalbey, T. F. 825, 827
Dallins, Capt. 889
Dalton, W. M. 818
Dameron, Robert, Capt. 823
Darden, Elizabeth 850
  Miles (Durdin?) 805, 850
Darnett, John, Rev. 798
Davey, Sarah 851
Davidson, John D. 844
  John D., Sr. 844
  R. A., Dr. 844+
Davis, Ann 899
  Benjamin F. 883
  Cora 899
  Edgar H. 883
  G. B. 805
  Harriet L. 899
  James 899
  James S. 883
  Jefferson 864, 865
  Joseph 883, 899
  L. E. 817
  Mc. W. 899+
  Mary E. 883, 899
  M. D. 810
  Nathan C. 883+
  Perry 883
  Robert M. 899
  Sarah J. 899
  Sophia V. 813
  T. 801
  Thomas J. 883
  W. G., Rev. 839
  William 838
  William M. 883, 899
Davison, M. V. 813
Davy, Alice E. 900
  B. 834

Davy, Cont.
  Jehu 831
  Thomas 900
Day, Margaret 874
  Reuben, Rev. 826
Dean, H. J. 810
  H. T. 810
  Job 807
Deaton, Elias 818
DeBerry, Ben 896
  J. H. (Deberry?) 810
  Lemuel 807
Decatur, Stephen, Capt. 814
Dees, Green 883
  James E. 883+
  J. E. 816
DeFord, C. H. (1st Lieut) 823
  L. F. 837
  R. D. 903
  R. D., Capt. 835
DeFord & Morris 840
Delaney, Jacob 829, 831
  J. W. 818
DeMoss, William 874
Denison, Alfred 883
  Allia J. 884
  Anna 883
  Benjamin 883
  Bertha L. 884
  Bird 883
  Curry P. 883+
  David G. 883
  Eliza 883
  Elizabeth 883
  Fredonia A. 884
  Granville L. 884
  Harriet Rosetta 884
  Jackson 883
  Kittie A. 884
  Mary A. 884
  Minerva 883
  Nancy J. 883
  Robert 883
  Sanford (Tx.) 883
  Stephen 883
  William H. (Tx.) 883
  William R. 884
Dennison 815
Dennison, Andrew Sr. 852
  C. P. 842, 843
  Jane 852
  Mollie A. 842
  Nancy J. (___) 842
  P. J. 803, 845+
  Robert R. 845
  Stephen 845
Dennison & McCall 845, 852
Dennison & Muse 804
Denny, James 827
Derryberry, Capt. 802
  G. H., Dr. 886
Devault 827
Dickerson, D. J., Capt. 835
  Bicca E. 900
  David I. 899+
  Emaline 900
  G. C. 900
  George H. 900
  Mary E. 900
  Moses 899
  Phoebe J. 900
  Pricy D. 900
  Sarah C. 900
  William S. 900
Dickson, James 819
  John 831
  M. M. 837
  R. M. 831
Diffee, Bettie May 845
  Charles V. 845
  Clark 845+
  Dora B. 845

Diffee, Cont.
  Johnnie 845
  John T. 845
  Moses 845
  Robert L. 845
Dinwiddie, A. G., Rev. 839
  Arantha Jane 861
  Robert, Gov. (Va.) 861
Dismukes, William 798
Dixon, Anna K. 886
  Benjamin 884
  Chambers F. 884
  Elinora 884
  Emily A. 884
  Hannah 860
  Obadiah 884
  Sallie B. 884
  Thomas Y. 884
  Wallace 884+, 886
  Wallace (Jr.) 884
  Wallace Sr. 884
  William H. 884
  William T. 884
Dodd, E. & Co. 841
  J. C. 828
Dodds, Annie L. 846
  Carrie E. 846
  James 846
  James C. 845+
  James W. 846
  John A. 837
  John S. 846
  Lura E. 846
  Maggie May 846
  Mamie C. 846
  Oscar L. 846
  Robert B. 846
  Robert E. 846
  Thomas M. 845/6
Doherty, James W. (Chancellor)
    801, 816(3), 825, 838
  W. F. 801
Dollins, John 833
Donnell, Martha (___) 871
  Nancy 871
  William 871
Doran, Alex. 837
Doren, James G. 831
Dorris, A. S., Rev. 826
Dougal, A. S. 839
Douglass, A. G. 800, 850
  Joseph S. 889
  Mary A. 889
Duckworth, G. A. 839
  Hattie E., Mrs. 808
  T. M. 833
  Wiley J. 833
  W. J. 831, 838(2)
Duke, F. P. 826
  J. K. 827
  J. P. 806
Duke & Sullivan 806
Dunaway, William M., Rev. 825
Duncan 829
Dunn, Maggie 894
Dyer, R. J. 800, 857
  Robert 799
East, Elizabeth Ann 903
  Joseph 903
  Reuben 839
Edna, Miss 880
Edwards, Annettie 864
  Carl 864
  Helen 864
  Hubert 864
  John H., Capt. 835
  John R. 864+
  J. R. 810
  Lizzie 864
  Nancy 867
  T. 804, 805
  Thomas F. 834
  Samuel T. 864

Edwards, Cont.
  William 804
Eldridge, J. W., Col. 835
Elkins, Mr. 799
  Bessie 846
  Scion 846
  William 846+
  Willie 846
  W. R. 804
Elliott, James 834
Ellis, Helen 851
  Jonathan, Dr. 851
Emerson, Bethena E. 898, 899
  Isaac 831, 833
  James 831, 833
England, A. R. 884
  J. A. 816, 892
  James A. 884+
  James S. 885
  J. H., Dr. 805
  John M. 884
  Nellie J. K. 885
English, ___ 833
  J. A. 816
  James 831(2), 833
Epay, N. C. 801
Epps, J. P. 828
Errin 832
Erwin, Mary (___) 873
  Mary D. 872
  N. A. 872+
  N. A. (Sr.) 872
  Nathaniel 873
  Pearl 872
  W. D. 876
Erwin Brothers 872
Eskredge, R. W. 823
Esle, John, Lieut. Col. 817
Essary, G. W. 800
Estes, Capt. 802
  A. E. 811
  E. & Co. 810
  E. A. 810
  Ed 808
  J. W. 825
Estes & Ozier 809
Estes & Randolph 810
Estis, Roxy 853
Etheridge, Dixon 872+
  Jackson 872
  John H. 872
  Julia Ann 873
  Kindred 872
  Mary E. 872
  Nathan Clark 872
  Robert D. 872
  Serena Massingale (___) 872
  Willoughby 872
  Winnie 872
Evans, J. D. 860
  Margaret (___) 860
  Vina 860
Ewing, Elizabeth, Mrs. 802
  Fannie 813
  Rhoda F. 812
Falkner, Lewis 837
  Lewis N. 834
Fall, Isabelle 895
Falls, Margurite S. 897
Farrar, Jeff. 833
Fentress, James 799, 824
Ferguson 902, 903
Fesnure, A. 805
Fielder, Celestia A. 851
  John S. 849, 851
  J. S. 802, 804
  Lyda 849
  Mary P. (___) 851
Fields, Mary 893
  Rachel (Petty) 881
Fields, Moore & Co. 805
Fields, Powell & Co. 805
Fillmore (President) 845, 856

Finch, Elizabeth 884
  Lucretia 884
Fisher, A. A. 886
  E. E. 894
  Fayette 886
  Jonathan 886
  Laura A. 886
  M. J. 816(2)
  Nancy A. 886
  Paul H. 886
  P. H. 818
  W. H. 815
Fitzgerald, B. A. F., Capt.
    835
Flake, Bettie 847
  Dudley L. 846
  E. 799, 850
  Euphrates 846+
  Howard 847
  Samuel 846
  William B. 846
Flatt, Capt. 835
  Sol 835
Florence, G. W. 804, 847+
  J. T. 847
Forbes, Robert 831, 838
Ford, Richard 831, 833
Foreman, Christian 897
Forrest, Gen. 823, 869, 894,
    899, 904
  J., Col. 873
Fortner, Lewis 833
Foster, Fannie W. 847
  George 847
  H. 801
  H. W. 847+
  James H. 847
  Josephine L. 847
  Joshua 847
  Joshua B. 847
  Leora D. 847
  Mollie A. 847
  Nancy S. 847
  Phillip T. 847
  Samuel H. 842
Fraley, M. F. 841
Franklin, David 864
  David J. 812, 864
  David J., Rev. 812
  D. J. 812, 813
  Etna 864
  Evie 864
  H. D. 809, 813, 864+
  Rubie 864
  Sarah B. 812
Franks, Mr. 907
  A. F. 838
  Amanda 901
Franks & Street 907
Freeman, B. R. 837
  C. J. 872
  F. M. 828, 872+
  Hattie 872
  James 872
  Josie 872
  Minnie 872
  Napoleon 872
  R. H. 828
Friedley, L. G. 818
Frizzell, Frances 861
Fry, Catherine (___) 865
  J. A. 865
  James 810
  H. H. 808, 810
  Joseph 865
  W. B. 810
Fryar, H. C. 818(2)
  J. M. 818
  W. C. 815
Fuller, Alice 859
  C. H. 805
  E. B. 812, 813
  Eleanor (___) 843

Fuller, Cont.
  Ephraim B. 848
  Harriet F. 848
  James H. 843+, 848
  J. H. 812
  J. H. (A.M.) 813
  Joseph W. 848
  J. P. 799
  Kittie 843
  Martha J. 848
  Mary I. 848
  Patrick F. 848
  Tallitha C. 848
  William 848
Funderburk, David B. 818(2)
  D. B. 815, 816(2)
Gains, G. N. 818
Galbraith, I. J. 812(2), 813(2)
  I. G. & Co. 809
  J. N. 813
  J. W. 812
Galloway, Amanda W. 848
  J. M. 804
  Mary 846
  M. J. 848
  M. L. 805, 848+
  M. S. 846
Galloway & Elkins 846, 848
Gammill, Alford 900
  Arch 900+
  Archibald 895
  Columbus 900
  Franklyn 900
  James 900(2)
  Joseph 900
  Mary P. 895
  Miles C. 900
  Moses 900
  Paralee 900
  Pinkney 900
  Sallie 900
  Samantha 900
  Samuel 900
Gann, William 831
Gantt, J. B. 834(2)
Gardner, John 844
Garfield, James A. 852, 853
Garland, Jack 809
  Jordan H. 909
  Oliver 811
  Thomas 807
Garner, Henry 810, 832
  James 833
Garret, J. 815
  John 818
  Lewis 817
Garrett, J. H., Rev. 808
  John H., Rev. 813
  Thomas 887
Garrett & Kirkland 827
Garrick 902
Garrick, Eleanor 902, 903
Gates, Jane 870
Gatham, P. 810
Gayle, P. S., Rev. 826
Gee, E. W. 833
Gholston 809
Gibbs, C. C. 838(2)
  John P. (1st Lieut.) 823
Gilbraith, J. H. 800
Gillespie 801
Gillespie B. 803, 810
  John 834
  John, Rev. 825
Gilliam, John 825(2)
  Rosanna 825
Gillis, Jefferson 898
  Jennie 898
Gillum, Calvin 798
Gipson, J. T. (Tx.) 904
Gladden, Gorin & Co. 853
Glass, James 807

Glass, Cont.
  James E. 804
Glover, Joe (Negro) 810
Gooch, D. C. 873
  J. C. 873
  J. G. 872
  J. R. 873
  J. W. 880
  Martha E. 873
  Nancy L. 873
  S. W. 873
  W. A. 872+
  W. T. 873
Gooden 829, 838
Gooden, Hannah 831
  Joseph 830, 831(2)
Goodin, James 831
  Thomas 831
Gordon, B. 838
  Lucinda 860
Gould, Lucy A. 851
Graham 831
Graham, Charles 818
  Isaac 831
  Jane 886(2)
  Rosa F. 812
  Ursula 905/6
Grant, U. S. 836, 843, 851, 855
Gratham, J. M. 813
Graves, Carroll 816
  W. W., Rev. 839
Gray, Thomas 834, 837
Greeley, Horace 847, 869, 870, 871, 874
Green, John A. 804
Greer, George 811
Grice, Elizabeth 855
Grier & Cotter 805
Griffin, Thomas 820
Griffith, A. E. 827
  Nat 827
Grimes, W. E. 828
Grisham, G. W. 841
Grundy, Felix 834
Hagler, Nancy F. 891
Halford, Bradley 838
Haliburton, David, Rev. 826
Hall, A. R. 847
  Isaac 806
  J. N. 803, 804, 848+
  John F. 849
  Joseph 806
  Loraine 826
  Lyda 849
  Robert W. 848, 849
  R. W. 804
  T. K. 874
  W. B. 800
  William 807
Hall & Bro. 827
Halpin, Rachel D. 826
Halton, Ezekiel 809
Halton & Cason 810
Hamilton, G. M. 838, 839
  G. W. 838
  J. G. 838
  Mary H. 813
Hamlet 802
Hamlett, F., Mrs. 867 (nee Trice)
  J. F. 807
Hamm, A. B. 828
  Archibald B. 873+
  Calvin 874
  Cynthia Ann 873
  Fannie 873
  Flora Lillian 874
  James R. 873
  J. M., Jr. 874+
  John 820, 873
  John Calvin 875
  John H. 874

Hamm, Cont.
  John M. 873+
  John Robert 874
  Mac 873
  Mary E. 873
  Minnie 874
  Myrtle 874
  Rebecca 873
  Sallie 873
  Thomas P. 873
  Tobitha 873
  William 873
Hamm & Hurley 874
Hancock 845
Hancock, Susan T. 880
Hanes, G. W. 816
Haney, Owen 801
Hanna, Calvin, Lieut. 835
  David Alexander 831
  Huel 831
  J. A. 838, 907
  James 831, 900
  James, Capt. 849
  James Anthony 900
  J. H. 839
  John 831
  John (Jr.) 831
  Miranda 849
  Rebecca 831, 884
  Samuel D. (2nd Lieut.) 823
  Thomas 831
  William 831
Hannum, Thomas 831, 833
Harbert, G. W. 838
  J. A. 837
Harbet, Hugh 838(2)
Harbour, E. B. 841
  Samuel 833
Hardage, Elizabeth 866
  Margaret (___) 866
  Zachariah 866
Hardeman, Benjamin F. 865
  C. G. 857, 865+
  C. Maude 865
  Cora 865
  Elizabeth 865
  Jasper G. 865
  Sarah Alice 865
  Thomas B. 865
Hardin 838, 839
Hardin, Amos 831
  Arthur (2d Lieut.) 835
  Benjamin 831(2), 838
  E. L., Lieut. 835
  Elender 831
  Gipson 831
  James 830, 831(4), 832, 833(3), 834, 837, 848
  James (Jr.) 831
  James, Col. 831, 836
  Jane Kizzie 831
  J. G. 815
  Joseph 831
  Joseph Jr. 830
  Joseph, Col. 830, 831
  Margaret 831
  Mary Elizabeth 831
  Nelly 831
  Ophelia 844
  Robert 831
  Robert, Rev. (D.D.) 844
Hardwick, James L. (2d Lieut) 823
Hare, M. A. 799
Hargrove, S. M. 838
Harmon, Adaline A. 860
  Adam 805
  John 860
  John T. 803
  John T., Maj. 798, 799, 800
  J. T. 803
Harrell, Mary R. (Stephens) 883

Harrell, Cont.
　Nancy (Raney) 890
Harrey, Thomas E. 903
Harris, Gov. 835
　Alfred M. 837
　B. R. 827
　Charles, Rev. 839
　Elizabeth 882
　Uncle James 880
　J. G., Rev. 802
　Uncle Jimmy 815
　Sallie 857
　Harrison 854
Hart, A. T., Lieut. 802
　James 802, 805
　J. M., Rev. 826
　John M. 807
Harwell 827
Harwell, R. S. 820, 825
Harwell & Shull 827
Haskell, Joshua (Judge) 800, 833, 834(2)
Haskins, W. M. 803
Haslett, James A. 803(2)
Hassell, Isaac W. 805, 849+
　Isaac W. (Jr.) 849
　John W. 849
　Minnie A. 849
　Nathaniel G. 849
　Nellie 849
Hatch, Gen. 900
Hatley, Belle 900
　Elizabeth Delilah 900
　George W. 900
　Jesse 900+
　Jessie J. 900
　Mark 900
　Nancy Francis 900
　Sarah Ann 900
　William 900
Hawkins 801
Hawkins brothers 841
　A. G. 801, 825
　(Chancellor)
　Isaac R., Lieut. 802
　L. L. 800
　Lucy S. 901
　P. S. 901
　S. C. 858
　W. S. 841
　W. T. 805
Hay, Mary 888
　Thomas 888
Haynes, Charity 900
　G. W. 838
　J. A. 882
　Nancy 887
　R. J. (A.M.) 812
Hays, A. N., Capt. 802
　B. A., Rev. 814
　Burt 836
　Thomas 817
　William 798
Hearn, Flora 886
　Isham G., Rev. 885+, 886
　Isham G., Capt. 817
　Thomas Y. 886
　Wallace D. 886
Heaslet, James A. 801
Hefner, C. L. 840
　H. L. 835
Helm, ___ Lieut. 802
Helms, Augustus 857
　Charles A. 857
Henderson, Elizabeth 875, 876, 904
　James, Col. 799
　John, Capt. 875, 876, 904
Hendrick, Emily 881
　Georgie D. 882
　John H. 813
　Nancy G. 891
Hendricks, Jere 807(2)

Hendricks, Cont.
　R. L. 810
Hendrix 7 Bro. 828
Henkle, W. R. 838
Henry, Caroline (__) 854
　Felix 853, 854
　H. C. 805
　J. A. 800, 805
　John 813
　Louise 853
　Louisa (__) 853
　Samantha A. 854
　William 818
Henson, Ursley 849
Herring, D. W. 838
Herrod, Joseph 831
Hetton, John 896
Hewitt, William 806(2)
Hewlett, J. F. 808
Hicks, B. A. 809
Hill 820, 827
Hill, B. J. 882
　Daniel 820
　J. J. 799, 803
　Reuben 825
　Robert A. 816(2)
　W. L. 812
Hinkle, B. 901
　Bettie H. 850, 901
　Charles C. 901
　George D. 901
　Harvey 901
　Henry O. 901
　Henry Reyburn 901+
　Horace H. 901
　Jonathan 901
　Lula B. 901
　Mary 901
　Roscoe 901
　W. F. 838
　William F. 901+
Hipp, Fannie 905
Hippe, T. A. 827
Hite, B. S. 811
Hodge, Minerva 895(2)
Hodges, E. J. 825
　Elijah J., Capt. 823
　Elisha 827
　Harry, Capt. 823
　Josiah 867
　J. N. 813
　Mary J. 867
　W. H., Rev. 826
　William J., Rev. 812
　W. J. 812(2), 813
Hodgin, G. W. & Co. 806
Hodgins, Nancy Jane 842
Hollam, J. C., Dr. 805
Holland 829
Holland, Fred C. 819
　James W. 831
　Jesse W. 832
　J. S. 841
Hollenburg, H. G. 811
Hollis, Skinner & Co. 810
Holloway, J. F. 810
Holmes, James 895
　Jesse 841
　S. H. 801
Holmes & Son 805
Holt, William C. & Co. 835
Holton, John 807
Hood, Gen. 889
Hoover, Jacob 898
　Mary 898
Hopkins, H. H. 798, 801
　William 827
Horn, David 825
Horton, Charlotte 894
　L. D. 857
Houdon, Mary 825
House, James 846
Houston 815

Houston, Albert L. 886
　Archibald 820
　Charles H. 886
　Claudia M. 886
　Cora E. 886
　Eliza Ann 886
　Elizabeth 873
　Eliza Jane 886
　Ezra J. 886
　James C. 886
　Jefferson P. 886(2)
　J. L. 818
　John F. 886
　John G. 886+
　John L. 886(2)
　J. N., Dr. 886+
　Laura B. 886
　Martha U. 886
　Mary Jane 886
　Mary M. 886
　Rebecca (__) 873
　Robert C. 873
　R. S. 825
　Samuel 820
　Sidney C. 886
　Thadeus E. 886
　William F. 886
Howard, Benjamin, Dr. 805
　Bina 847
　Charles F. 850
　C. F. 863
　Elizabeth B. 907
　James N. 850
　John, Dr. 845
　Melvina 850
　Nancy 846
　P. J. 806
　P. J., Jr. 806
　P. J. & Co. 809
　Rennie 893
　R. J. & Co. 810
　Richard W. 850
　Samuel 799, 843, 847, 849+
　Samuel H. 901
　William 849
Howell, E. G., Dr. 882
　Elizabeth (Maxwell) 887
　John 800
Hubbard, John 807
Huddleston, D. N. 825
　I. F. 828
　James 833
　John (Lieut.) 823, 834, 837
Hudson, C. D., Rev. 838
　Eli 830
　Mary E. (__) 863
　Matilda 890
　Richard W. 863
Hudspeth, T. G. 827
Huggins, J. J. 828
　Tobitha 873
Hughes, Mrs. 835
　W. E. 840, 841
Humphreys, Hester 798
Hunt 803
Hunt, E. C. 825
Hunter, R. P. 810(2)
Huntsman, Adam 801
Hurley, J. R. 828, 874
　Martha (__) 874
　Nicy J. 876
　T. J. 841, 874
Hurst, Col. 900
　Gen. 905
　D. L., Capt. 823
　Fielding 800, 816, 823, 825(2), 827, 835
　T. M. 830
Hurt, Patience 853(2)
Hutchison, Thomas 874
Ice, Letitia 907
　Martha T. (__) 907
　Thomas W. 907

Ingram, Elizabeth 883
  N. P. 811
Inman, J. B. 812(2)
  J. B., Prof. 863
  J. B., Rev. 813
  Sue 812
  W. G., Rev. 813
Irvin, Francis, Mrs. 839
  James 837, 839, 840(3)
  J. J. 838
  J. W. (1st Lieut.) 835
  L. B. 835
  James 839, 906
Ivey, Elizabeth 882
  Laura 812
  Phillip 817
Ivy, William 817
Jackson, Gen. 875
  Alva S., Capt. 823
  Andrew 818
  Harriet E. 841
  Henry 817
  Henry A., Rev. 810
  Jacob 820
  K. S. 810
  Lucy 891
  Martha (___) 841
  William P. 841
James, Thomas 832
Harman, William 818
Jeans, James 875
  James Newton 875
  Josiah 874+
  Josiah T. (Ar.) 875
  J. T. (Ar.) 879
  Laura Jane 975
Jennings, Hiram 887
  James 815
  Martha N. 887
Jepling, William D. 835
Jester, J. S. 810
  J. T. 813
Jetton, Robert 824
Jobe, F. N. 888
Johnson, Gen. 823
  A. H. 799
  Alva 826(2)
  Andrew 897
  C. W. 847
  F. A. 876
  Hiram 810, 813(2), 865+
  Hiram H. 865
  Jacob 818
  J. D. 812
  John M. 825(2), 838
  Joseph 807, 865
  Joseph D. 865
  Letitia A. 906
  M. A. 883
  Maggie 865
  Marvin 865
  Milton H. 825
  Samuel 833
  Temple 831
  Thomas 802
  W. C. 810(2)
Johnston, Alice E. 898
  A. S., Gen. 836
  John 819(2)
Jones, A. B. 801
  Ada 887
  Anna 887
  Anna C. 881
  Balaam 815, 818
  B. E. 888
  Benjamin 825
  Calvin 800
  Calvin, Chancellor 838
  C. C. 810
  D. M. 840
  E. E. 818
  Emma 885, 887
  Flora 892

Jones, Cont.
  Flora M. 887
  Henry 833
  Isaac 833
  J. 837
  James 856
  J. C. B., Capt. 870
  Jesse 831(2), 833, 834
  John 855, 887
  J. W. G. 801, 802
  L. 831
  L. M. 861
  Mahan(?) 833
  Matthew 886
  Micajah 807
  Minerva M. 854
  R. B. 800(2), 802, 803
  R. R., Rev. 839
  Thomas 887
  Troy W., Dr. 886+
  T. V., Dr. 892
  T. W., Dr. 881
Jopling 827
Jopling, W. D. 825(3)
  William D. 825
Jordan, Albert L. 887
  Ara E. 887
  Charles P. 887
  Edmund 887
  Ephriam E. 887
  Harvey 887
  H. M. 887+
  James 804
  John H. 887
  Josiah 883
  Lucy B. 887
  Mary Zora 887
  Rhoda A. 887
  W. H. 801
  William E. 887
Judkins, J. W. 833, 834(2), 837, 838
Julin, James N., Lieut. 835
Junell, Robert 807
Kee, C. M. & Co. 810
Keeton, Adaline A. 888
  Albert F. 887+
  Catherine 887, 889
  Ella U. (H.?) 888
  Julia M. 887
  Lucy A. 888
  Marquis D. Lafayette 888
  Robert, Dr. 887
  Sophronia 888
  William R. 888
Kelley, Lawson 818
  R. G. 805
Kelly, Joseph 817
Kelough, James 818
Kelsey, J., Rev. 802
Kemp, Nathan, M. D., Capt. 823
Kendal, Minerva 896
Kendall, E. C. 840
  John 840
  S. J. 841
Kendrick & Roberts 818
Kennedy, D. C. 816
Kerherdon, G. 799
Kernodle, Simpson 825
Kerr, ___ 831
  Eliza A. 870
  H. M., Rev. 825
  Josie 872
  Mary (___) 870
  Mary A. (___) 872
  Samuel 831
  T. A. 837
  Thomas 870, 872
  William 810, 831
Keys, C. M. 846
Kidd, Ann 825
  George 825(2)
Kilber, Mildred H. 869

Kincaid 827
Kincaid, A. J. 825
Kincaid & Harwell 827
Kincannon, David 831, 833(2)
  Francis 833
  James 832
Kindel, Martha (___) 874
  Maud 874
Kindel, W. C., Dr. 874
Kindle, James L. 827
  John 833, 836
  W. A. 826
King, O. H. 800
  Robert 831(2)
Kirby, John 838
  William W. (2d Lieut.) 823
Kirkland, Henry 824
Kiser, Nancy E. 906
Kissee, Rhoda 866
Knight, Elizabeth (___) 880
  Julia 879
  Thomas 879/80
Knowles, Edmond 850
  Hubert F. 850
  James D. 850
  John M. 850
  J. W. H. 850+
  Lura V. 850
  Martha 851
  Mary F. 850
  Robert E. 850
  Susan A. 850
Kootz, John 807
Lacefield, Daniel 831
  James 831
  Jesse 832
  John 831
  Larkin 831
  Robert 831, 833(2)
Lackhead, John C. 851+
  John W. 851
Lacy, Hiram 816(2)
  J. J. 816
  W. D. 890
Lafferty, Tennessee Wayne 893
Lain, S. L., Rev. 839
Lambert, Albert, Rev. 813
Lane, Elisabeth Brynes 904
  Elizabeth 875, 878
  Hiram 904
  James 827
Lawler, C. C. 826
  William T. 853
Lawrence, Jacob 825
Laws, G. L., Dr. 850+
  G. W., Dr. 855
  Hiram 850
  Joseph H. 851
  Martha 856
  William D. 851
Lawson, J. L., Dr. 873
Leas, B. J., Col. 817; 887
Lee, Gen. 901
  B. J., Col. 886
  Simpson 831, 833
  Stanton 810
Leech, L. M. 828
Leeth, Joseph 898
  Judah F. 898
Leonard, J. H., Dr. 890
Lewis, J. C. 805
  Samuel 825
  Samuel, Capt. 823
Lewter, J. T. 841
Liening, M. J., Maj. 823
Lilly, Noah 832, 833, 834, 837
Lincoln, A. 842
Lindsey, H. C. 800
Lipscomb, John 857
  Judith (___) 857
  Sarah 857
Littlefield, J. L. 825

Livingston, H. J., Chancellor 311
Livingstone, William 881
Lock, Barrett 826
  W. T., Rev. 802
Lockey, J. A. 823
Lockhart, Martha C. 883
Lofton, J. H. 804
Logan, John Sr. 851
  John F. 852
  John H., Dr. 851
  W. T. 801, 851+, 853
Lollar, Mary 845
Lollor, Isaac 854
Long, Elizabeth 900
  Jefferson 852
  Robert 808
  W. B. 806(2)
  William B. 852+
Lorance, Abram 820
Love, Samuel Maj. 801, 817
Lovelace, C. T. 812
Lovelady, Thomas 831
Luton, Jo(h?)nathan 817, 818
  Sallie 890
Lyle (Lisle), George 816
McAllister, Wilson, Rev. 839
McAlpin, J. M. 826
  Thomas 827
McBride, A. S., Rev. 839
McCall, Addie 853
  Andrew 848, 852(2), 883
  Andrew Jr. 852
  Caledonia I. 852
  Eleanor 848
  Ella 852
  George T. 852
  G. W. 845, 852+
  Henry, Dr. 850, 852
  James C. R. 852
  Jane (___) 848
  John 810, 883
  John E. 851, 852+, 859
  M, Jennie 852
  Patrick H. 852
McCallum, Annie 853
  Duncan E., Dr. 853+
  Francis P. 853
  John R. 853
  Joseph 853
  Peter 853
  Peter E. 853
McCampbell, Andrew (Chancellor) 800, 838, 868
McCann 820
McCann, Calvin 810
McCauley, Margaret 843
McClanahan, Samuel 801
McClannahan, M., Col. 837
McCleary, Richard 807
McClellan, George B. 843
McCleod, Bettie 865
  Dickson C. 865
  Martha M. (___) 865
McClish, Billy 833
McClover, John 818
McClure 798
McClure, Samuel 818
  Tennessee (Baker) Prim 881
McCollu, Christina 865
McConnell 839
McCorkle, A. C. 810
  J. M., & Co. 810
  Robert, Rev. 807
  T. J. 810(2)
McCorkle & Thompson 810
McCown, Sarah B. 906
McCoy, John 879
McCracken, J. M., Rev. 839
McCrary, E. 872
McCree, R. A. 803
  Richard 803

McCullar 822
McCullar, Alexander 825(2)
  Jane 825
McCulley, J. A. 812
  J. M. & Co. 809
McCullum, Capt. 802
  J. M. 810
  W. C. & Co. 809
McCully, John 813(2)
McDaniel, Isabella (Falls) 895
  Nancy 862
  N. T. 838
  Wesley 828
McDonald, Hiram 831
  Hugh 831
  John 831
McDougal 902
McDougal, ___ 838
  A. C., Dr. 903+
  A. G. 801, 835, 838(2)
  Agnes 903
  Alexander 902, 903
  Alexander, Jr. 902
  Alexander C., Dr. 903
  Anna 903
  Archibald 903
  Archibald G. 902+
  A. 903
  Capitola A. 903
  Daniel 902
  Daniel A. 903
  Duncan 903
  Eleanor 902, 903(2)
  James 903
  James F., Dr. 902, 903+
  James T. 903
  J. F. 903
  John 902, 903
  John E. 903
  Leroy C. 903
  Mary 902
  M. F. 903
  Nancy 902
  Patience A. C. 903
  Samuel 903
McDougal & Braden 828
McEwen, Levi 800
McGee 798
McGee, Absalom 799
  A. P. 866
  Millie 866
  P. (___) 866
  W. J. 815
McGill, T. J. 839
McGinnis, C. H. 838
McGraw, J. S. 813
McHaney, ___ 862
  Amanda 858
  Amanda J. 853
  Bessie May 854
  Caroline 854
  C. D. 854
  Cornelius 853, 854
  Cornelius F. 853
  Elizabeth 853
  F. W. 804
  Guy 854
  Henry A. 854
  Ida 854
  John C. 853
  John E. Co. 804
  La Fayette F. 854+
  Louisa (___) 862
  Mary S. 853
  Nannie L. 853
  Robert 854
  W. C. 853(2), 854(2), 858, 862
  William 854
McHenry, Mary P. 849
McIntire, B. S. 874+
  John 874
  Ophelia V. 874

McIntire, Cont.
  W. S. 827
McKamey, D. A. 801
McKee, A. M. 825
  Andrew 825, 826
McKelvey & Paulk 841
McKelvy, Clemmie 845
McKenzie, David 826
  J. H. 805
  M. E. 873
  William L. 817
McKinney, James F. 827
  J. F., Judge 875
  Robert E. 825, 875+
  W. D. 825(2)
McKinnie, J. F. 826
McKinnon, A. H. 809
McKinzie, A. L. & Son 841
  David 825
McKnight, Caleb 866+
  Hugh 812(2)
  M. 812
  Mary 863
  Melvina 812
  William 807, 866
McLaughlin, A. B. 827
McLean, Mahala J. 902
  Nancy 902
  R. K. 902
McLellan, Charles 811
McLeod, Norman 807
McLoed, Daniel 818(2)
  Samuel 818
McMahan, Joe 833
  Wilson 826
McMahon 839
McMahon, James 831, 833
  James F. 832, 841
  Joseph 833
  T. C., Capt. 835
McMeans, J. R. 833, 834
McMillan 815
McMillan, Capt. 802
  Ella 888
  Gilbert 818, 888
  Isaac 816
  J. B. 816
  John 815, 816(3), 817, 818
  John, Capt. 888+
  John, Dr. 884
  John G., Dr. 888
  Leora 888
  William I. (Az.) 889
McMurray, Harriet 855
McMurry, James R. 888+
  James T. 888
McNair, James E., Lieut. 835
McNairy, John, Judge 824
McNatt, P. 810
  R. 811
  R. M. D. 810(2)
  W. R. 810
McNight, Caleb, Capt. 822
McRhea, Robert 806
McWhirter, J. S. 872
  Mollie 872
Mackey, P. 806
Maddox, Miss 897
  ___ 896
  Margaret 896
Magill 827
Mahan, Henry 831, 833
Mains, M. A. 857
Mainey, George (Gen.) 835
Mangum, Doc 836
  James A., Lieut. 835
Manny, Jordan 833
Marion, Gen. 873, 890, 898
Marrow, Sarah P. 907
Marsh, D. M. 813
  Elizabeth (White) 848
Marshall, R. 804
  Robert 800

Martin, Alice 902
  Alma C. 902
  Andrew J. 902
  Elizabeth 902
  Francis 902
  G. W., Rev. 839
  Hester L. 902
  Hettie M. 902
  James 824
  James C. 902
  Jane K. 902
  J. D. 837, 838
  John 833, 882, 902
  John W. (Tx.) 902
  Joseph H. (Tx.) 902
  Joshua T. 902+
  J. W. 833(3)
  Katie 902
  Maggie M. 903
  Margurite 902
  Martha 871
  Martha A. 902
  Mary S. 902
  Mattie B. 903
  Robert P. 902
  Sallie 902
  Samuel A. 902
  Samuel P. (Tx.) 902
  William 902
Mason, Mary J. 813
Massengill, ___ 831
  H. L. 810
  Stephen 799
Mathews, Lydia 798
  Silas 798
Matthews, Elizabeth 850
Maury, Abram 799
Maxedon, John 820
Maxwell, Elizabeth 887
  Thomas 838
May, J. M. 808
  J. W. 808
  Mary 858
  William 817
Mayo, J. W. 815
Meadows, Rebecca 893
Meeks, Cynthia L. 904
  Edwin T. 904
  Ellen 876
  Flora 876
  G. E. 825
  George T. 876
  Henry 876
  James L. 876
  John 875, 876, 904
  John (1st Lieut.) 823
  John C. (Mo.) 876
  John H. 825
  John H., Gen. 875+, 904
  Josie 876
  Kate 876
  Lillie 876
  Littleton 876
  Lovinia 876
  Lucretia 876
  Marcus Henry 876
  Marcus W. (Ms.) 876
  Margaret A. 904
  Martha C.904
  Martha E. 876
  Mary A. 904
  M. H. 811
  O. L., Col. 904
  Orval C. 904
  Orvil L. 876+
  Orvil L. (Jr.) 876
  Rebecca E. 904
  Rufus P., Elder 876
  W. C. 903+
  W. C. & Co. 841
  Zilpha 876
Merrell, Melissia 879
Messenger, W. L. 809

Michie, G. G. 876
  John, Capt. 823
  Martha 876
  R. W. 825
Middleton, Henry 832
  John 831(2)
Milam, Solomon 802
  W. H. 816
  William 855
Miles, Charles 818, 831
Miller, Austin 826, 827, 834
  C. H. 803
  Eudora, Mrs. 826
  Francis 865
  J. A. 809, 825, 865+, 866
  James M. 826
  P. M., Chancellor 838
  R. D. 826
  R. S. 865
Miller, Moore & Wisdom 827
Milligan, R. L. 841
Mitchell, A. B. 838
  H. B. 827(2)
  James, Dr. 825
  J. C. 838
  J. H. 808, 810, 825
  J. W. 808
  Robert 810
Mitchell & Hinkle 841
Mitchem, Anderson 806
Moffet, S. J. 841
Montgomery, James, Maj. 832
Moody, J. A., Rev. 802
  Nancy 855
Moore, A. Jeff 825
  Alfred 825, 826
  Benjamin 887
  C. H. 825
  Elizabeth 887
  Eliza J. 842
  E. N. 895
  George M. 825
  G. M. 825
  John A. 825
  John W., Capt. 835
  Laney 824, 825(2), 827
  Martha C. 895
  Mary A. 895
  Mary Ann (Swafford) 893
  Mary (Bolin) 882
  Miles 825
  Reuben 827
  S. H. 810
  W. G. 805
Moore & Tally 827
Morgan, George 815
Morphis, J. L. 823, 825
Morris, Elizabeth 861
  W. E. & Co. 841
  W. P. 838
Morrison, Fanny, Mrs. 840
Morrow, G. D. 839, 840
  James 832
Morvin, Joe, Dr. 823
Moss, G. W. 800
Mulry, E. & Co. 841
Murchiser 809
Murphy, Col. 887
  John (Lieut. Col.) 817
  Nancy 879
Murray, Dr. 858
  Abel V. 824
  A. V. 825, 827
  A. W. 825
  William 825
Murrell, John A. 818
Muse, E. E. 848
  T. C. (Chancellor) 799,
    808, 811(2), 862
Mynders, A. 854
  Clarence 854
  Hamon 854
  S. A. (A.B.) 803, 854+

Myracle, Allan 889
  Arthur 889
  Emma J. 889
  Henry W. 888+
  James W. 889
  J. C. P. 888
  Lawrence L., Rev. 888
Nailer, J. C. B. 810(2)
Nance, ___, Rev. 839
Narborough, C. R.
  (Yarborough?) 810
Nash, Isaac W. 825
  I. W. 827
  L. D. 813
Naylor, George 866
  Margaret E. 866
  Martha (___) 866
Neal, Mary 859
Needham, Miles 827
Neel, H. B. 838
Neeley, Maj. 807
  W. M., Rev. 838
Neely, H. L., Lieut. 835
  Margaret 856
Neill, James 807
  Samuel 807
Neislar, A. 842
  David 842
Nelson (Negro) 834
Nelson, Charles B. 832
Nevill, Alexander 838
Newell, J. B. 828
Newson, J. F. 811
  John 810
  Mahala (___) 867
  M. A. 867
  Richard W., Rev. 813
  W. A. 823
  W. V. 867
Newsome, Nancy 889
Newson, W. A., Lieut. 835
Newton, Anna (Dennison) (Tx.)
  883
Nichols, Sarah 888
Nickols, Arethie 881
Nielson, C. B. 833
Nixon, Chancellor 808
  George H. (Chan.) 816
  G. H. 801
  G. H. (Chan.)825, 843
  G. W. (Chan.) (?) 838
  T. J., Rev. 838
Norcott, Zachariah (1st
  Lieut.) 823
Norman, Susan 875
Norris, Martha 848
Norwood, George 831(2)
Nunley, J. W. 819
O'Neal, C. H. 807
  Curtis 819
  J. F. 812
  J. F. O. & Co. 809
  Mary C. 813
  M. F. 868
  M. M. 810
Orman, Mary Ann 843
Orr, George 831
Orton, S. A. 800
  S. B. 803
Outlaw, M. B., Dr. 806
Owen, L. E. 840
  Thomas, Rev. 826
Owens, Robert M. 825
Oxford, Abel 819
Ozier, Bettie 813
  J. W. 810, 812(2), 813
  M. F. 811, 813
Pace, J. W. 811, 828
  Samuel 827
  S. D. 826
  S. O. 826
Page, Ben F. 801
Paine, ___ 833

Paine, Cont.
  Elizabeth 901
Palmer, Annie 902
  Hester (___) 902
  Martin 902
Pare, M. D. 808
Parharm, John 808(4), 812
  R. J. 812
Parker, Alexander 905
  Alonzo F. 905
  C. B. 905
  Eveline 855
  Frank 896
  James Monroe 905
  Joan F. 890
  John F. (Male) 890
  John A. 905
  Mary E. 905
  M. F. 905+
  Nancy E. 905
  Ora M. 905
  P. E. 846
  Sylvia E. 905
  W. L. 905
Parrish, Isaac 808
  John A. 866+
  Thomas A. 828
Parsons, John, Dr. 845
  Mary B. 845
  Phoebe 899
Pate, E. E. 818
Patterson, A. B. 808(2)
  E. D., Judge 835, 903
  E. P. 838
  G. J. 810
  James 872
  Katie (___) 872
  Mary Jane 872
  N. C. 847
  William 818
Patton, R. T. 832
  William 799
Pavatt, S. C. Chancellor 825
  Stephen C. 800
  Stephen C. Chancellor 816, 838
Pearce, Arthur 801
Pearson, Ethel 855
  James N. 855
  Jemima 855
  Jemima M. 851
  John 854, 855+
  L. 855
  Lou Emma 855
  Martha 855
  Mary 851
  Mary Ann (___) 851
  Melvina E. 855
  Nathan 855
  Peter 851, 854+
  Peter S. 855
  Priestly 855
  Shadrack 855
  Sidney A. 855
  Walter C. 855
  William Dudley 855
Peddy, A. J. 810(2)
Pelzer, Betsey 892
Perkins, E. D. M. 838
  J. S. 828
  J. W. 808
  M. A. 810
Perkins & Atkins 828
Perry, Frances, Mrs. 871
  Harriet 883, 889
  James, Rev. 813
  Oliver Hazard, Commodore 814
Peters, George B. 838
Pettigrew 815
Pettigrew Family 889+
  Mr. 892
  Carrie P. 889, 890
  Corry 889

Pettigrew, Cont.
  Corry H. 889
  Elizabeth K. 889
  George B. 889
  James K. 890+
  James K. Polk 889
  James M. 889
  J. M. 818
  Lena H. 890
  Lucy B. 890
  Lucy Bell 890
  Maggie M. 890
  Maggie May 890
  Martha A. 889
  Mary E. 889
  Thomas Jackson 889
Pettigrew & Coats 818(2)
Petty, Rachel 881
  William L. 801
  W. L. 804
Phelps, William 807
Philips, Benjamin 856
Phillips, Columbus 801
  James 798
  John 824
  Joseph 827
  Preston 900
  W. J. & J. S. 841
Philpot, Job 799
  J. W. 803
Philps, J. L. 805
Pickens, Joe 833
  John 831
Pickett, Col. 873
  ___ 834
Pierce, Sarah 898
Pigott & Bro. 828
Piles, Martha 842
Pinnion, Anna 886
Pitts, Alfred 838, 905+
  Alfred Thomas 905
  Barbee 905(2)
  Burrell 905
  James Irwin 905
  John 841, 905
  John A. 905
  Mary Louisa 905
  Nicholas 905
  Nicholas, Lieut. 835
  Sarah 905
  Theo 905
  William P. 905
  William W. 905
  W. P. 828
Polk, E. 838
  Edwin 902
  James K. 818, 834, 879
Pool, W. L. 840
Porter, R. I. 838
Porter & Sheild 840
Porterfield, Cora 906
  Effie 906
  George 907
  Henry M. 905+
  H. M. 907
  John 907
  J. M. 891
  Martha E. 891
  Oscar 906
  William C. 905
  Willie T. 906
Post, Helen 812
Poston, J. D., Capt. 835
Potts, B. F. 828
  William 798
  Z. T. 828
Powell, L., Rev. 839
  George 798
Powers, Capt. 835
  Adore A. 855
  Andrew 855
  Frank W. 855
  Joel W. 855

Powers, Cont.
  John H. 855
  John S. 855
  Martha A. 903
  Nancy L. 855
  Stephen 855
  Stephen L. 855
  Tennessee C. 855
  T. J., Capt. 835
  William P. 855
  W. T. 835, 840
Powers & Haynes 840
Prather, J. W. & J. W. Simper 828
  L. H. C., Dr. 879
Pratt, John H. 882
  M. H. 841
  William 815
Prewitt, M. 811
Price, Thompson 827
Prichard, Hannah (___) 855
  Mary 855
  Scion 855
Priddy, Col. 809
  B. A. 850
  G. L. & Co. 809
  G. W. 847
  James 800
  J. M. 809
  J. S. 799
  Margaret J. 813
  Minerva (Denison) 883
  William 809
Prim, Tennessee (Baker) 881
Prince, F. M. 826
  J. J. 828
  J. P. 826
Prither, Elizabeth 875
  James 873
  Tabitha 875
Province, Andrew 868
  Mary (___) 868
  R. 868
Pryor, S. N. 827
Pugh, Mary 861
Purdy, J., Col. 807
  John 798, 799, 803, 804
  John, Col. 827
  Rebecca 813
  Robert 807, 813
Putnam, F. M. 810
Pyburn 829
Pyburn, Jacob 831(2), 832
Pyle, Addison 800
Raines, J. T., Dr. 854
Rains 815
Rains, Ann (___) 879
  Anthony 890
  Balaam 890+, 892
  Ethel C. 890
  George H. 890
  J. A. 818
  John 879
  John A. 816
  John H. 890
  J. P. 816(2)
  Lizzie E. 890
  Louisa 879, 880
  Margaret P. 890
  Rosetta V. 890, 892
  William G., Dr. 890
  William G., Jr. 890
Ramer 828
Ramer, Thomas 873
Ramey, James H. 890
Ramsey, Elizabeth 870
Randolph, James 907
  Mary B. 907
Raney, Ann E. 890
  Barbara 890
  Edgar 891
  Granville M. 890+
  James 891

Raney, Cont.
  James H. 890
  John David 890
  Maggie 891
  Margurite 890
  Martha 890
  Nancy 890
  Sallie 891
  Willie J. 891
Rankin 820
Rankins, Robert 827
Raphael, Pena A. 849
Rawlings, J. A. 832
Ray, J. R. 823
Rayburn, John 838(2)
Reams, J. M. 808
  Martin 810(2)
Reaser, John 818
Reaves, William H. 825
Redges, Lucy 798
Reed, ___ 834
  Frank, Lieut. 802
  James 827
  James (Uncle Biddle) 824
  J. L. 805
  Joseph 798(2)
  P. A. 848
  R. N. 810
  W. A. 848
Reeder, Jones 873
Reese, John 826
Reeves, Susan 798
Reiley, Milton 801
Renshaw 802
Renshaw, Rev. 802
Resser, J. C. 828
Reynolds, A. L. 906
  Andrew J. 906
  Benjamin 824
  Elzey 906
  Fannie B. 906
  Henry 831, 833, 907
  Henry H. 906
  Jacob W. 906
  James Sr. 833
  Jane E. 890
  Minnie E. 906
  Pleasant M. 906
  R. W. 837(2),906+
  R. W. (3d Lieut.) 835
  Sarah B. 906
  Sarah J. 906
  William J., Dr. 906
Rhodes, A. H. 799, 800(2), 805, 843
  Benjamin 810
  L. C. & Co. 809
  Robert 798
  W. S. 808, 810
Rice, Elizabeth 905
  Sarah 844
Richards, James 827
Richardson, Willis 811
Richerson, Alfred, Capt. 854
  Bettie (___) 854
  Pobrecitta 854
Ricketts, J. G. 805
Riddle, Charles, Rev. 807, 838
  Thomas 897
Rigg, W. C. 825
Riggs, B. J., Capt. 823
  N. C. 825
  S. W. 838
Roach, Stephen 831, 833, 836
Roark, Margurite 893
Roberson, L. H. 828
Roberts, Andrew, Capt. 817
  D. A. 838
  Elijah, Capt. 823
  Elisha, Capt. 817
  Houston 818
  J. C. 816
  P. O. 816

Roberts & Moreland 818
Robertson, B. 810
  Benjamin 810
  C. 857
  Charlotte 864
  H. 812, 813
  Holcombe 813
  Laura J. 874
  Margaret (___) 874
  Mary 857
  Mary Ann 857
  Pleas. 874
Robinson, C. S., Capt. 835
  David 831, 834, 838, 839(2), 840(3)
  James 837
  Thomas 834, 869
Rodgers, Elizabeth 798
  J. P. & E. F. 828
  J. T. 818
Rogers, Jennie 880
  J. S., Dr. 880
  J. T. 884, 888
Rose, R. H. 800
  R. H., Chancellor 816(2), 825, 838
Ross, Bettie 813
  Clarissia 857
  Hugh 807, 813
  I. W. 838
  James 846
  John 832
  Lou 813
  Nannie 846
  Reuben, Elder 826
  S. L. 807, 838
  W. D. 811
  William B. 819
  W. U 838
Rosser, Bros. 853
Rosson, Charlotte (___) 871
  Docia 871
  Joseph T. 871
Roswell, R. O. F., Lieut. 835
Rowsey, Robins & Co. 809
Rudd, James 831, 832, 840
Ruleman, William 827
Rundle, J. G., Maj. 817
Rush, George T. 866
  J. 810
  John A. 866
  Mary E. 866
  M. B. 866
  Sarah F. 866
  William 807, 808(2), 809, 810(2), 866+
  William A. 866(2)
Rushing 815
Rushing, Miss 889
  Asa 891
  Clavin 818
  G. B. D. 816
  Green B. 818
  Green B. D. 891+
  W. W. G. 817
Russell, Capt. 802
  Julia 897
Russells, J. A., Capt. 835
Rutledge, Martha 798
Sanders, A. A. 824, 826
  A. M., Rev. 826
  Ellen 865
  James M. (2d Lieut.) 823
  V. A. (Miss) 871
Sanders & Atkins 841
Sandford, Rachel (Negro) 810
Saunders, A. A. 820, 827
  Lindsey 820, 825(2)
  L. & Bro 827
Savage, Dr. 853
  George, Prof. 812
  John H. 882
  Lewis, Rev. 826

Sawyer, Capt. 835
  C. F. 825
  W. C. 835
Sayle, A. S. 812(3), 813
  S. A. 801
Sayles, A. S. 809
Scarbrorough, C. R. 867+
  Edmund 867
  Fannie L. 867
  Jessie F. 867
  Lorenzo 867
  Mary E. 867
  Samuel A. 866
  W. L. 867
  William H. (Ar.) 867
Scheorer, O. H., Lt. Col. 823
Scott, Gen. 841, 845, 850, 861
  C. R. 800, 803
  David E. 891+
  David E., Jr. 891
  David M. 891
  D. E. 816
  D. M. 815(2), 816
  Frances U. 891
  James 801, 834(3)
  James, Judge 816
  J. D. & Co. 806
  J. W. 852
  Mattie B. 891
  Micajah 805
  Samuel 891
Scott & Stanford 804
Scurlock, T. P. 801
Seaman, W. H. 840
  W. H. & Co. 896
  W. H., Dr. 869
Seaton, George W. 899
  J. H. 841
  Martha 899
Segraves, John H. 856
  Mary H. 856
  Moses 856+
  Nancy C. 856
  Sherrod 856
  Sidney J. 856
Self, Isaac 826
Sellars, David 834
Senter, William 810
  William M. 809
  W. M. 810
Seymour & Blair 844, 847, 861
Shackleford 798
Shackelford, James 807
  Richard 807
Shannon, John 834
  Nathan 841(2)
  Robert 819
  Thomas 815, 831(2), 832, 840, 841
  W. B. & Co. 809
  William 841
Sharp, David 876
  J. J. & Co. 818
Shaw, R. A. 838
Shelby, A. B., Col. 837
  Benjamin F. 906+
  Julia E. 906
  Laura V. 906
  Levi 906(2)
  Margurite A. 906
  Mattie L. 907
  Minnie G. 907
  W. H. 800
  William W. 907
Shell, Mary 900
Shelton, Ellen 892
  J. D. 810
  N. 810
Shepard, Vina 842
Sherdon, Daniel B. 889, 890

Sherdon, Cont.
  Maggie A. 889, 890
Sherrell, J. W. 808(2)
Sherrill, Hugh 813
  Mary C. 813
Sherwood 802
Sherwood, A. B. 864
  Alonzo 864
  Harriet (___) 864
Shipman, C. W. 838
  C. W., Capt. 835
  Elizabeth 891
Shoat, John 833
Short, John 810, 905
Shrewsbury, A. G. 801
  A. G., Maj. 858
Shull, Calvin 825
  Celia (___) 871
  Clemmie 902
  Isaac J. (2d Lieut.) 817, 823
  J. W. 810
  Margaret 871
  P. E. 827
  Peter 871
  Peter E. 825
Siler, O. T. 866
Simmons 809
Simmons, Alvis 847
  J. M. 808
  L. D. 810(2)
  Mary E. 813
  S. M. 854
Simpson, Harrison 833
Sims, G. A. 850
Singleton, Henry 817
  S. 817
Sipes, G. W. 828
Skinner, J. H. 838
  Margaret 865
Sloan, Alex. 831
  John L., Rev. 825
Small, Alex. 859
  J. N. 801
  Louisa H. 859
Smith 815, 829, 838
Smith, Dr. 828
  ___ -01
  Alex, Dr. 893
  Amanda F. 812
  Benjamin 847, 856, 857
  Benjamin O. 857
  Charlie 892
  Chelton 833
  Christopher C. 857
  Daniel 831, 833(3), 834, 837(2), 838(2)
  Dixon 886
  Easter 847
  Ebel 833
  E. E. 802
  Elisha 833
  Elizabeth 856
  Elizabeth E. 813
  Ellen 892
  Emma 892
  Ernest 892
  F. A. 813
  F. A. L. 835+
  George W. 857, 891
  Grant 856
  G. W. 810, 886
  G. W. & Son 892
  Harriet 894
  H. B. (Ar.) 902
  Isaac 831
  Isabella (Vise) 893
  James 856
  James F. 857
  James H. 856
  James L. (1st Lieut.) 823
  J. B. 825
  J. D. 809, 810, 812

Smith, Cont.
  Jennie O. 856
  J. J. 823
  John 800, 809, 892
  John, Maj. 802, 817, 823
  John A. 856+
  John D. 812(2)
  John P. 857
  Joseph 806
  Joseph N. 857
  Lem 856
  Lettie May 856
  L. T. 828
  L. T. (Tx.) 892
  Martha J. 857
  Mary C. 857
  Mary E. 856
  Matilda 806
  May 892
  M. C. 812
  Minerva C. (Vise) 893
  Nancy 847
  Nancy A. 857
  N. G., Rev. 826
  Reuben 818, 887, 891+
  Reuben Jr. 892
  Robert W. 812
  Sarah E. 881
  T. A., Dr. 809
  T. A., Maj. 800, 802(2), 805(2), 812, 813, 856+
  Tennessee 893
  Thomas B. 856
  Warren 838
  W. B. 840
  William 831, 833
  William T. 857
  Wilson A. (Ar.) 873
  W. J. 823
  W. J., Col. 823
  W. T. (1st Lieut.) 823
  Zachariah 857
Smithers, James 809
Smoot, Alice 900
Sneed, Capt. 835
Snell, Elizabeth 798
Southerland, B. H. 818
Sowell, P. A., Rev. 839
Spencer, A., Mrs. 897
  Ann 813
  Elizabeth 898
  William 807
Springer, Emily Ann 874
Stanfield, Patsey Ann 863
  L. B. 817
Stanford, Arcadius 857
  George W. 857
  James 857
  Johnnie 857
  L. A. 799, 803, 857+
  Lemuel 857
  Lizzie 857
  Ruby 857
  Thomas 857(2)
Stansill, J. T. 810
Stanton, Mr. 894
Steed 807
Steele 813, 829
Steele, J. A. 839
  James H. 833
  Ninean 831, 833(2), 836
  Robert 831, 833
Stegall, W. L. 808
Stephens, Col. 840
  H. H., Col. 883
  Mary R. 883
Stevens, Sarah J. 891
Stevenson, F. D., Col. 901
Stewart, Abel 808
  A. M. 805
  G. W. 805
  John 804
  Joseph W. 813

Stewart, Cont.
  Martin 813
  Mary 813
  Mary C. 813
Still, George 807
  J. H., Dr. 890
Stockard, G. C., Rev. 838(2)
  S. J. 839
Stockton, Thomas 839
Stoddert, William 804
Stokes, W. B., Col. 882
Stone, Gov. (Ms.) 810
  Martha 866
  N. T. 805
Storm & Smith 818
Story, W. E. 838, 840
Stout, David 892
  George 892
  John 892
  Kathleen 892
  Laura J. 892
  Mary 892
  Mary A. 885
  Thomas 892
  W. F. 818
  William 885, 890, 892+
  William T. 892
Stout & Scott 818
Stovall, A. W. 811, 825
  J. R. 825, 828
Stow, R. I. 813
Strann, Deliah 900
Strate, Andrew J. 892+
  Daniel 892
  John 893
Straton, Catherine 871
Street, Blanch 907
  Charles 907
  David A. 826, 906
  David M. 907
  David T. 906+
  D. T. 838
  George M. 907
  Inez 907
  J. C. 838
  John R. 907
  Maggie O. 907
  Mary W. 907
  Nannie 907
  William T. 907
Strong 798
Strong, James 804
Stubblefield, Amanda 865
  Amanda C. 857
  Beverly M. 857
  Charles H. 857
  J. M. 801
  Margaret E. 857
  Martha J. 857
  Mary E. 857
  Nancy N. 857
  Peter 857
  Sallie (___) 865
  Sarah E. 857
  Thomas 865
  Thomas F. 857
  T. M. 857+
  William F. 857
Stubbs, Mollie 875
  Thomas B. 875
  Virginia (___) 875
Summers, L. O., Dr. 823
Sumner, Mary A. 905
Suratt 827
Swafford, America A. 893
  Henry J. 893
  Horace M. 893
  Isaac D. 893
  James 893
  James W. 893
  John 893
  John L. 893
  Joseph A. 893

Swafford, Cont.
  Judy C. 893
  Louisa A. 893
  Maggie J. 893
  Mary Ann 893
  Sarah C. 893
  Thomas A. 893
  William 893
  W. L. 893+
Swain, ___ 878+
  (Missing pages here at
    time of indexing)
  Aurelius 879
  Elma 879
  Martha 879
  Mary 879
  Mary 879
  William 879
  William H. (2d Lieut.) 823
Swank, Catharine 863
  Mary C. (___) 863
  Wilburn 863
Swann, Delia 826
Swayne, J. H. 801
Sweat 827
Sweeney, Alex M. 833, 838
  Alex. W. 831, 834, 836
Swift, R. S., Rev. 802(2)
Tabler, Alfred, Dr. 807
  A. N. 810
Talbot, Hugh 834
Talley, Nancy 843
Tarbet, Hugh 838
Tarbutton, W. (___) 867
Tarkington, J. O., Capt. 835
Tarrant, E. H. 799, 800
Tate Family 885+
Tate, Allie 885
  Anna Jane 885
  B. H. 798
  Carrie B. 885
  Elon H. 885
  Emma Myrtle 885
  George W. 816
  Grover Cleveland 885
  James F. 885
  James H. 885, 887
  Jesse 885
  J. L. 818
  John 818
  John Elmer 885
  John L. 885
  Lewis L. 885
  Maggie 885
  Mary 885
  Samuel G. 804
  T. W., Dr.885
  William H. 885
Tatum 827
Tatum, O'Neal & Co. 828
Taylor, A. 862
  Abner 798
  Daisy A. 858
  Elizabeth A. 862
  F. (___) 862
  H. S., Mrs. 812
  H. S., Rev. (A.M.) 812
  James 834
  Jesse 798, 800, 858
  John 816
  John M. 853, 858+
  John M., Capt. 801(3), 805
  Mary Lou 858
  Nancy 841
  Penelope 854
  R. R. 806
  Teressa 861
  William 858
  Zachariah 865
Teague, Arthur 859
  Birdie 859
  Ernest E. 859
  Hattie 859

Teague, Cont.
  Isaac 859
  J. A. 800(2), 805(2), 859+
  James J. 859
  J. R. 799
  J. W. 859
  L. A. 859
  William R. 859
Teas, Charles 827
Tedford, Polly 867
  W. E. 828
Temple, Hattie E. 813
  Joseph W. 813
Terry, C. G. 809
  W. B. 810
  Willey B. 825
Terry, Hannah & Co. 900
Terry & Wisdom 827
Thacker, Elender, Mrs. 831
  Shep 894
  Shepherd 831
  William 831
Tharp, Elizabeth 883
Thomas, Capt. 802
  Benjamin W. 907
  Daniel 804
  Eliza N. 907
  Henry M. 907
  I. F. 907
  James 807
  J. H. 817
  J. P. 810
  L. G. 812
  Maggie 906
  Margurite P. 907
  Martha 848
  Martha E. 907
  Mary J. 907
  N. L. 825
  Salina E. 907
  W. G. 906, 907+
  W. H. 809
  W. J. 838
  William 907(2)
  Willis L. 907
Thomasson, Capt. 802
Thompson, A. M., Capt. 823
  Jackson (Tx.) 895
  R. M. 825, 827
  R. M., Maj. 823
  S. G. 813
  S. J. 810
Thorington, J. H. 823
Thorn, R. H. 801
Thornton, M. V. 841
  "Tobe" 834
Threadgill, H. G. 799
  William H. 806
Thweatt, Alice 893
  Anna 893
  Ella 893
  Fannie 893
  P. L. 893+
  P. L., Sr. 893
Tidwell, E. S., Maj. 823
  J. F. 823
  Mary 866
  Wilson 801
Tilden, J. S. 864
  S. J. 846
Tillman, B. M. 825
  B. M., Capt. 867+
  E. M. 825
  John 867
  John V. 867
  T. R.867
Tilman, P. M. 838
Timberlake, Addie 853
  Charles 859
  Eddie 859
  Edward 859
  Edward L. 853
  E. J. 800, 859+

Timberlake, Cont.
  Jessie 859
  Kate 859
  Louanna 859
  Lula (___) 853
  Mary 850
  Mary (___) 850
  Richard 850, 859(2)
  W. P., Capt. 801
Totten, B. C. 834
  J. C. 801
Travis, Emma 868
  Joseph, Dr. 868
Treadwell, Georgie 842
Tremble, R. B., Rev. 813
Trice 798
Trice, Callie R. 868
  Eva B. 868
  Harrison 868
  H. C. 810
  Job 807
  John C. 868(2)
  John H. 868+
  Lessie 868
  Lora A. 868
  Luke L. 868
  M. A. 825
  Mattie H. 868
  Tabitha 859
  William C. 867+
Troutt, James McCord 868
  J. M. 811, 812, 868+
  J. R., Dr. (Ky.) 868
  William 868
True, Joseph, Dr. 805
Tryar, Dr. 886
Tucker, Alice R. 869
  B. A. 890
  Elender, Mrs. 830
  Francis M. (1st Lieut) 823
  Lucy D. 869
  Mary 869
  Mildred A. 869
  Nathaniel A. 869
  Pitts 831
  W. C. 869
  W. C., M. D. 869+
  William F. 869
Tull, Alice 869
  D. M. 869+
  Ernest 869
  Guy 869
  Inez 869
  John 869
  Nicholas 869
  Thomas 869
Turner, E. R. 825
  E. R. (2d Lieut.) 823
  Jane 885
Tuton, Benjamin F. 816
  W. R. 816
Tyler, Abner 799
Umstead, R. A., Rev. 813
Vance, Catharine 813
Veal, John (2d Lieut.) 823
Vermillian, Arminda A. 902
Vise, Dora 893
  Eli 893
  Eli (Little Jim) 893
  Elizabeth Crawley 893
  Evangeline 893
  George H. 893+
  George M. 893
  Isabella 893
  John 893
  Mary 893
  Minerva C. 893
  Virginia 893
  William 893
Vivian, Catharine 859
Volner, F. M. 805
Wadley, J. M. 800
Waggoner, T. B., Lieut. 835

Walker 827
Walker, Ben (old) 820
  B. S. 823
  Elijah 801
  Elijah, Judge 817, 834, 835
  J. C. 837
  Joel 838(3)
  Joseph 825
  J. S. 815
  Manerva 884
  Minerva Ann 842
  Nancy D. 845
  Reuben 824
  W. C., Rev. 838
Wallace, Ada 894
  Anna 894
  Ella 894
  Ida 894
  J. J., Lieut. 802
  Martin 894
  S. M. 894+
Walsh, Hattie 813
  W. C. 813
  William C. 813
Wamble, E. C. 810
Wambler 813
Wambler, J. R. 810
Wann, G. T., Lieut. 835
Ward, S. 833
Warden, Katherine 888
Ware, W. B. 801
Warnal, William 833
Warner, S. L. 827
  W. H. 803
Warren, Dr. 804
  A. A., Mrs. 802
  Frances 880
  Hugh A. 879+
  James 822, 824, 825(2),
    827, 873, 879+, 880
  James (Sr.) 879
  James A. 880
  John T. 879, 880+
  Louisa (___) 873
  Lucinda K. 879
  Martha E. 879, 880
  Nancy 873, 879
  Robert 859
  S. L. 823, 825(2)
  S. L., Maj. 823
  Sousan Violer 880
  S. C. 838
  Virginia Dee 880
  William A. 879
  William H., Dr. 859+
Warrington, J. S. 841
  Worley 819(2)
Washburn, E., Rev. 826
Washington, George 884
Wasson, Mary 844
Watkins, Isabella 868
  J. 833
  William 809
  W. J. 838
  H. E. 839
Watson, James H. 799
  J. M. 835, 839
  John, Rev. 839
  Nimrod W. 907
  William J. 907+
  W. J. 835
  W. T., Dr. 806
Weathers, J. E. 805
Weaver, John 820
Webb, William 850
  William C., Capt. 817, 823
Weir, F. H. 810, 869+
  Mary (___) 869
  S. L. 869
Welch, Cordelia 889
  D. A. & T. J. 840
  Henry 885, 889
  J. L. & Co. 818
  Martha J. 885

Wells, L. H. 840
  Thomas 834
Wesson, Capt. 802
  N. A. 817
West, Ben (Negro) 811
  John 809(2)
  John, Dr. 804
  R. B. 810
Wharton, 827
Wharton, John 825
Wheatley, James 813
  J. M. 809
  J. N. 810
  Samuel C. 801
Wheeler, Gen. 835
  J. H. 867
Wheeler & Edwards 810
White, Anna E. 899
  Bennett G. 860
  Elizabeth 848
  Ellison 834
  G. W. 890
  Hugh L. 858, 860, 876, 879
  Jackson 819
  Jane 891
  John 831, 833, 841, 856, 906
  John H. 800
  J. S. 810, 811(2)
  Louisa 860
  Lucinda 860
  M. 899
  Margurite 906
  Mattie A. 903
  Mattie J. 901
  O. P. 860+
  Paralee 888
  Reuben 815, 892
  Samuel 833
  Stephen Finney 860
  Thomas 833
White & Craven 841
Whitehead, E. G., Dr. 860+
  Ella E. 860
  Lela 860
  Lula 860
  Richard 860(2)
Whitemore, Dr. 873
Whitlow, Harriet 895
Whitney, Samuel 846
Whitten, T. G., Rev. 802
Whyte, Joseph 857
  Margaret 857
  Mary (___) 857
Wilcox, Reuben 803
Wiley, J. W. 815
Wilkenson, Mr. 899
Wilkerson, Robert 801
  J. R. 800
Willett, Edward 866
  Elizabeth 865
Williams 801
Williams, Capt. 802
  C. H. "Kit", Col. 801, 817
  Charles 861
  Elizabeth 855
  Gecovy 861
  Hardin 837
  Henry E. 903
  James 833
  J. B. 805
  J. G. 833, 837
  J. J. 834, 840
  J. J. & Bro. 840
  John 832
  John G. 832, 834, 839
  J. S. 836
  Kerney C. 861
  L. L. 852
  Lyda 858
  Mahala 872
  Nancy 863
  R. I. 837
  Richard 861+
  Thomas, Dr. 823

Williamson, Thomas 838
  W. T. 899
Willis, William (Bud) 801
Willoughby, Will (Negro) 811
Wilson, Capt. 802
  A. N., Col. 823
  C. 810(2)
  Emma 861
  George W., Rev. 813
  G. W. (A.M.) 812
  G. W., Rev. 812, 813
  Henry Arzo 861
  Henry S. 825
  J. A. 804
  J. B. 861
  John A., Dr. 798, 800, 801
  J. T. 861+
  J. W. 828
  Lizzie 861
  Lular 861
  Lydia 825
  Margaret 861
  Melissia 905
  Samuel 799(2), 800, 803(2),
    804(2)
  Samuel, Col. 810
  Samuel C. 804
  Theodore 861
  W. B. 825(2)
Winborn, J. S. 838
Wingo, J. R. 801
Winningham, Alex (3d Lieut.)
  823
Winston, A. P. 805
Wisdom, William 831
  William S. 824, 826,
    827(2)
  W. S. 830, 827
Wisdom & Dickens 827
Wisdom & Shull 827
Wisdom & Walsh 827
Wolf 829
Wood, H. P., Prof. 839
  Levi, Judge 853
  L. L. 882
  Walter 833
  William 801
Wood(s?), Mary D. 906
Woods, Georgia A. 862
  Levi S. 800, 861
  Levi S., Judge 851, 861+
  L. S., Judge 801
  Myrtle 862
Worley, George 831, 833
  J. A. 813
  Margie 813
Worsham, M. J. 813
  Thomas 813
Worton, M. (1st Lieut.) 823
Wright, Prof. 826
  Benjamin 820, 825(2), 827
  James 804, 819
  Marcus J., Gen. 820
  Martha (Raney) 890
Wroten, Sarah A. 895
Wyly, C. K. 847
Yancy, E. G. 838
Yarbro, A. M. 816
  A. M., Dr. 892
  Harriet 893
  John T. 883
  Mary A. 883
  Penelope 892
  Samuel 816, 818
  Sarah, Mrs. 887
  William (Yarbrough?) 815
Yarbrough, John 893
Young, 802
Young, Belle 864
  B. J. 808(2), 844
  George N., Rev. 826
  Hannah 907
  H. H. 864
  I. P. 827

Young, Cont.
  Jacob 810
  Mary (__) 864
  Mary Elizabeth 844
  W. F. 892
  W. J. 810
Young & Johnson 818
Young, Storm & Smith 892
Youngblood, J. W., Lieut. 835
Yount, John 824, 827
  J. P. 827

___, James 827
___, Will 811

Erratum:
Hodges, Mary (__) 867

www.ingramcontent.com/pod-product-compliance
Lightning Source LLC
Chambersburg PA
CBHW020656300426
44112CB00007B/410